Sovereignty in the Age of Global Terrorism

Library of Congress Cataloging-in-Publication Data

Names: Feinberg, Myriam, author.
Title: Sovereignty in the age of global terrorism : the role of international organisations / by Myriam Feinberg.
Description: Leiden ; Boston : Brill Nijhoff, 2016. | Series: Nijhoff law specials, ISSN 0924-4549 ; volume 89 | Includes bibliographical references and index.
Identifiers: LCCN 2016009007 (print) | LCCN 2016009200 (ebook) | ISBN 9789004299573 (paperback : alk. paper) | ISBN 9789004299580 (E-book)
Subjects: LCSH: Terrorism (International law) | Terrorism--Prevention--Law and legislation. | International agencies--Law and legislation. | Sovereignty.
Classification: LCC KZ7220 .F45 2015 (print) | LCC KZ7220 (ebook) | DDC 341.26--dc23
LC record available at http://lccn.loc.gov/20160090

Typeface for the Latin, Greek, and Cyrillic scripts: 'Brill'. See and download: brill.com/brill-typeface.

ISSN 0924-4549
ISBN 978-90-04-29957-3 (paperback)
ISBN 978-90-04-29958-0 (e-book)

This book is printed on acid-free paper and produced in a sustainable manner.

In Memory of Gernot Biehler and Boris Hoffman, Passionate Mentors

Contents

Acknowledgments

This book is an updated version of my PhD thesis. Like the thesis, its writing was only possible because of the support of many wonderful people.

My PhD supervisor, Professor Robert McCorquodale, offered much advice, support and constructive criticism for my PhD and this book. I am grateful for his continued attention and friendship, which go beyond the usual duty of supervisors. I hope to one day emulate his methods and approach as an educator and researcher.

I also want to thank my PhD examiners, Professor Guglielmo Verdirame and Professor Matthew Happold, for their comments on the thesis and advice for its improvement.

Lindy Melman and Bea Timmer at Brill/Nijhoff have been fantastic publishers and their enthusiasm and patience have been invaluable in this process. I thank them and Kim Fiona Plas for their trust in this project and their work towards its completion.

I am indebted to both the ERC-funded Global Trust Project at Tel Aviv University and the Minerva Center for the Rule of Law under Extreme Conditions at the Faculty of Law and Department of Geography and Environmental Studies, at the University of Haifa for their financial support and strong academic structure. They have ensured that I completed this book to the highest of standards.

My aunt, Risa Vandersluis, has – once again – worked her magic and edited this text with her exceptional professionalism, speed and elegance.

Many friends have made this process more enjoyable and I want to thank, in particular, Anna, Amir, Emilie, Mirjam, Natalie, Natanya, Rebecca, Shifra and Sivan for providing academic and personal advice and for sharing many coffees and work dates with me.

I cannot thank my family enough for their enduring love, encouragement and sense of humour. A special thank you goes to my brother, Michael, for the book's title.

Last, but definitely not least, I am grateful I could share this experience, and many others, with my husband, Michael, who makes everything that much better with his love and many jokes.

MF December 2015

List of Abbreviations

ACHR	American Convention on Human Rights
AU	African Union
CFI	Court of First Instance
CICTE	Inter-American Committee Against Terrorism
CTC	Counter-Terrorism Committee
CTED	Counter-Terrorism Committee Executive Directorate
EAW	European Arrest Warrant
EC	European Community
ECHR	European Convention on Human Rights
ECJ	European Court of Justice
ECtHR	European Court of Human Rights
EU	European Union
FTF	Foreign Terrorist Fighters
GA	United Nations General Assembly
IACHR	Inter-American Commission on Human Rights
IACtHR	Inter-American Court of Human Rights
ICC	International Criminal Court
ICJ	International Court of Justice
NATO	North Atlantic Treaty Organization
OAS	Organisation of American States
OAU	Organisation of African Unity
OMPI	People's Mujahadeen of Iran
PIA	Preliminary Implementation Assessment
PNR	Passenger Name Record
SC	United Nations Security Council
TEU	Treaty of the European Union
TFEU	Treaty on the Functioning of the European Union
UK	United Kingdom
UN	United Nations
UNITA	National Union for the Total Independence of Angola
US	United States of America
WMD	Weapons of Mass Destruction

Introduction

1 Context

Just as the scope and intensity of the terrorist attacks of September 11, 2001 were unprecedented, this was also the first time that an international terrorist group had managed to carry out such an attack on American soil with such devastating results. As a result of this and of many other attacks, countering terrorism has now become one of the highest priorities for many States and international actors alike.[1] The terrorist attacks of September 11, 2001 not only created emotional shock and political consequences, but also raised many important legal issues. Since these attacks, legal scholars have generated a plethora of studies both on terrorism and counterterrorism.[2] In this book, counterterrorism will be analysed through the lens of sovereignty because terrorism 'directly undermines democratic values and institutions'[3] of a State and its prevention is therefore considered a core competence of sovereigns.

More specifically, terrorism challenges the sovereignty of a State because it questions the State's ability to protect its citizens against violence – 'as a guarantor of security, the government needs to respond to acts of terrorism, or at the very least be perceived as responding.'[4] Terrorism used to be largely considered a national phenomenon[5] and although different approaches have been

---

1 Eminent Jurists Panel on Terrorism, Counter-Terrorism and Human Rights, 'Assessing Damages, Urging Action' (International Commission of Jurists, 2008). See also 'The EU as a counter-terrorism actor abroad: finding opportunities, overcoming constraints', EPC Issue Paper No. 60, September 2010 by Peter Wennerholm, Erik Brattberg and Mark Rhinard and 'Integrate to Grow, Innovate to Prosper', Dmitri Medvedev, website of the Kremlin, available at http://eng.kremlin.ru/transcripts/3370 (last accessed 05.12.2015).

2 It would not be possible to include here all the sources that have significantly contributed to this literature. Suffice to say that there is now specialised literature both on terrorism and on counterterrorism, which is becoming more and more specialised. Throughout this book, there will be references made to the sources related to the topic.

3 Ben Saul, 'Reasons for Defining and Criminalizing "Terrorism" in International Law' (2006) 6 *Mexican Yearbook of International Law*, 419.

4 Elena Pokalova, 'Legislative Responses to Terrorism: What Drives States to Adopt New Counterterrorism Legislation?' (2015) 27 *Terrorism and Political Violence*, 474, 480.

5 For historical accounts of terrorism, see, among others, Bruce Hoffman, *Inside Terrorism* (Columbia University Press 2006); Bruce Maxwell, *Terrorism: A Documentary History* (1st Revised edition, CQ Press, 2002); and Walter Laqueur, *A History of Terrorism* (Transaction Publishers, 2011).

 DOI 10.1163/9789004299580_002

used, responses to terrorism were traditionally adopted at the national level and were usually included in the criminal law of a State.[6] However, after the events of September 11, 2001, terrorism became an international phenomenon and a global situation that needs to be addressed, and it now constitutes a challenge to the nature of the State in international law[7] and to the international community as a whole.

In parallel, the attacks of September 11, 2001 questioned the existing counterterrorism regimes of States because they showed that national legislation and jurisdiction were not sufficient to deal with this major issue. In other words, traditional responses appear to have failed and terrorist threats seem to have superseded territorial and nationality concepts. Yet, if terrorism constitutes a challenge to the concept of State sovereignty, any international response will also inherently challenge State sovereignty. Since security is a core component of State sovereignty, the actions of international organisations in counterterrorism means that the State is not the only actor to deal with security threats in its own territory. Instead, international and regional organisations have become fundamental actors in counterterrorism.

This tension between the two challenges to sovereignty is particularly interesting and its study in this book shows the trade-offs that States will face and the compromises they will adopt in order to balance the protection of their citizens and territory with their desire to retain the primary responsibility in national security. This is the kind of sovereignty-bargain that makes States enter into regional or international agreements when it suits them.[8] By necessity, and since September 11, 2001, States have had to engage in a process of internationalisation of counterterrorism. Most international conventions on terrorism have responded to the internationalisation of terrorism action by an internationalisation of the reaction.[9] In other words, judicial and political cooperation have been encouraged and have led to bi-lateral and international

6 A majority of domestic regimes against terrorism are under criminal law and show an increase in the use of force. See Robert Cryer and others, *An Introduction to International Criminal Law and Procedure* (Cambridge University Press, 2007) 284.

7 John Dickey Montgomery and Nathan Glazer, *Sovereignty Under Challenge: How Governments Respond* (Transaction Publishers, 2002) 5.

8 The concept of sovereignty-bargains was developed by Karen Liftin in the context of environmental issues. See Karen Litfin, 'Sovereignty in World Ecopolitics' (1997) 41 *Mershon International Studies Review* 2.

9 See Gilbert Guillaume, 'Terrorism and International Law'(2004) 53 *International & Comparative Law Quarterly* 3, 541.

agreements on extradition and prosecution.[10] Nonetheless, this internationalisation is inherently limited, because there is no general definition of terrorism and no international court or tribunal has been granted jurisdiction to deal specifically with international terrorism.

These responses to terrorism have, in turn, generated case law on the extraterritoriality of national and regional laws[11] and debates on the militarisation of the crime.[12] While it was originally excluded, the protection of human rights is now considered to be an integral part of the international response to terrorism.[13] The language on terrorism itself significantly changed days after the September 11, 2001 attacks when President Bush declared that the United States of America (US) was at war against Al-Qaida.[14] This declaration led the US and other States to an armed conflict in Afghanistan and raised new legal issues concerning the response to terrorism.

Therefore, while sovereignty is often considered to be a dated concept,[15] both the events of September 11, 2001 and the reaction to these events, in particular the increasing role of international organisations, show that the

10 One example is the European arrest warrant that was created by the 2002/584/JHA: Council Framework Decision of 13 June 2002 on the European arrest warrant and the surrender procedures between Member States.

11 *Al-Skeini & Ors v United Kingdom* [2011] ECHR 1093 (7 July 2011); *United States v Ahmed* (SDNY Oct. 21, 2011); *Rasul v Bush,* 215 F. Supp. 2d 55, 56 (D.D.C. 2002); and *United States v Bin Laden,* 92 F. Supp. 2d.

12 Ben Saul, 'Terrorism as Crime or War: Militarising Crime and Disrupting the Constitutional Settlement? Comment on Thomas Vs. Mowbray (2007) 237 ALR 194; 81 ALJR 1414; [2007] HCA 33', (2008) 19 *Public Law Review* 1, 20; Sean D. Murphy, 'Terrorism and the Concept of Armed Attack in Article 51 of the U.N. Charter' (2002) 43 *Harvard International Law Journal* 41; and Thomas M. Franck, 'Terrorism and the Right of Self-Defense' (2001) 95 *American Journal of International Law* 4, 839.

13 UN Security Council Resolution 1963 (2010); Section IV United Nations Global Counter-Terrorism Strategy; creation of UN special Rapporteurs on torture and on human rights while countering terrorism; EU Counter-Terrorism Strategy; and Council of Europe Guidelines on human rights and the fight against terrorism (see Section 4 of Chapter 9 for more details of this evolution).

14 President Bush, 20th September 2001, Address to a Joint Session of Congress and the American People. Transcript available at http://www.washingtonpost.com/wp-srv/nation/specials/attacked/transcripts/bushaddress_092001.html (last accessed 05.12.2015).

15 See for instance, A/47/277 – S/24111, 17 June 1992, 'An Agenda for Peace, Preventive diplomacy, peacemaking and peace-keeping', Report of the Secretary-General pursuant to the Statement adopted by the Summit Meeting of the Security Council on 31 January 1992 and Eric Engle, 'Beyond Sovereignty? The State After the Failure of Sovereignty' (2008) 15 *ILSA Journal of International and Comparative Law* 1.

concept is still very much relevant to the way States act. For Saul Newman, the relationship between terrorism and sovereignty is summarised as follows:

> It would seem that despite Foucault's insistence that sovereign power is a thing of the past, it is once again displayed in the State's equally violent and symbolic reaction to the non-State, terrorist activity that has drawn its sword.[16]

Indeed, the concept of State sovereignty is still very much present in analyses of counterterrorism because of its link to national security. Therefore, the involvement of international organisations in counterterrorism questions not only whether it should be the national or the international/regional authorities that should act against the phenomenon, but also questions which branch of governance should be involved. While traditionally it was the executive that exclusively dealt with security matters, the judiciary has become increasingly involved in counterterrorism, leading to significant consequences on the nature of the response. In parallel, counterterrorism post-September 11, 2001 has exacerbated the existing conflict between the increasing security needs of States and the desire to protect human rights and procedural safeguards.

While international counterterrorism is at the heart of the debates on State sovereignty and allows a contemporary analysis of the concept, few studies have focused on the impact of counterterrorism on State sovereignty. This book aims to fill this gap by examining whether the internationalisation of counterterrorism measures through the transfer of competences to international and regional organisations, and the implementation (or lack of) of these measures, has had an impact on the sovereignty of States.[17] This book contends

16 Saul Newman, 'Terror, Sovereignty and Law: On the Politics of Violence' (2004) 5 *German Law Journal* 5, 569.

17 I use the term 'international organisations' for both global and regional organisations and I use the term as defined by the Draft Articles on the Responsibility of International Organisations, which states that an international organisation is 'an organisation established by a treaty or another instrument governed by international law and possessing its own international legal personality. International organisations may include as members, in addition to States, other entities': Article 2, Draft Articles on the Responsibility of International Organisations (ILC, Report on the Work of the Sixty-first Session (2009), UN Doc. A/64/10 at 20). These various constitutive elements can be found in literature as well, with many authors mentioning the 'public nature of international organisations [and that] the organisation has come into existence by international agreement; that is has at least one organ with a will of its own; and that it is established under international law', Henry G. Schermers and Niels Blokker, *International Institutional Law: Unity Within*

that the impact is limited by the nature of the organs adopting the measures and/or by the fact that many international instruments are widely adopted, yet poorly implemented, as they require that States adopt domestic measures that can vary widely from the original intent. As a result, States have been able to use their international counterterrorism obligations to their advantage, either by transposing their own national measures into international law, or by hiding behind international duties in order to advance their political agenda. One theme explored in this book is that regional organisations that include a court have had a more significant effect on the measures adopted both by States and international organisations because they have provided an alternative discourse to the executive-focused one.

In this respect, this book examines the counterterrorism measures adopted by the UN and four regional organisations, as well as their implementation by their Member States. Through this, the book analyses whether States have transferred sovereign competences to these organisations and whether measures adopted as a result are, in fact, implemented by the Member States, thereby impacting the domestic law and sovereignty of States. The book also focuses on the case law of regional organisations because they have significantly contributed to the understanding and procedures of the international counterterrorism regime of today. In particular, these organisations have created new standards for the conflict between various international norms and have altered the balance of power in the area of security.

2 Why Sovereignty and Which Sovereignty?

There are some theories that suggest that the concept of sovereignty has become obsolete[18] and that it should be adapted to reflect the situation of the world today.[19] However, challenges to State sovereignty show that the concept is actually relevant to relationships between States and other actors of the international community. In reality, States make claims of

Diversity (Martinus Nijhoff Publishers, 2003) 30 and Guglielmo Verdirame, *The UN and Human Rights: Who Guards the Guardians?* (Cambridge University Press, 2011) 15.

18 Pawel Frankowski, 'Liquid sovereignty in the post-modern world order', Sixth Pan-European Conference Standing Group on International Relations, Turin, September 12–15, 2007 (text available at http://www.eisa-net.org/be-bruga/eisa/files/events/turin/FRANKOWSKI-Liquid%20Sovereignty_Frankowski.pdf (last accessed 05.12.2015)).

19 J.H. Jackson, 'Sovereignty-modern: a New Approach to an Outdated Concept' (October 2003) 97 *American Journal of International Law*, 4, 782.

sovereignty regularly and the term 'sovereignty' is still very much used today and is an important element of the political discourse.[20] For example, Pakistan that argues that the US violates its territorial sovereignty, both in general terms with the use of air drones,[21] and, in particular, by killing Osama Bin Laden.[22] As well, the long-running dispute between the United Kingdom (UK) and Argentina on sovereignty over the Falkland Islands[23] and the dispute between China and Japan over the Diaoyu/Senkaku Islands[24] also show that, while it might not reflect a reality, the idea of sovereignty matters to States. While the international coalition against the Islamic State in Iraq and Syria bases the legality of its airstrikes in Iraq on the consent of the Iraqi

---

20 Michael Keating, 'Sovereignty and Plurinational Democracy: Problems in Political Science', in *Sovereignty in Transition* (Hart Publishing, 2003) 204.

21 In a leaked Wikileak cable (08ISLAMABAD3586) dated from 2008, Prime Minister Yusaf Raza Gilani Stated that drone strikes violated Pakistan's sovereignty. The cable is available at http://wikileaks.org/cable/2008/11/08ISLAMABAD3586.html (last accessed 05.12.2015). The High Court of Pakistan also held, in May 2013, that US drone strikes violate Pakistan's sovereignty because they have not been authorised by Pakistani authorities. See Judgment Sheet, Writ Petition No. 1551-P/2012 (judgment available at http://www.peshawarhighcourt.gov.pk/images/wp%201551-p%2020212.pdf (last accessed 05.12.2015)).

22 'Musharraf: Bin Laden mission violated Pakistan', *The Washington Times*, 2 May 2011, available http://www.washingtontimes.com/news/2011/may/2/musharraf-bin-laden-mission-violated-pakistan/ (last accessed 05.12.2015).

23 In 2013, a referendum, asking the residents of the Islands if they wished the Faklkand Islands to retain their status as an Overseas Territory of the United Kingdom, was accepted by 99.8% (see 'Falklands Referendum: Voters chose to remain UK territory', *BBC News*, 12 March 2013, http://www.bbc.com/news/uk-21750909 (last accessed 05.12.2015)). Nonetheless, both in June 2014 and in June 2015, the UN Decolonisation Committee adopted a resolution calling on Britain and Argentina to negotiate a solution to their dispute over the Falkland Islands, see UN Press Release 26 June 2014, available at http://www.un.org/press/en/2014/gacol3271.doc.htm (last accessed 05.12.205) and UN Press Release 25 June 2015, available at http://www.un.org/press/en/2015/gacol3283.doc.htm (last accessed 05.12.2015). Argentina's new government is also pushing for a return to the negotiating table, see 'Argentina urges UK to return to negotiating table over Falkland Islands', *The Guardian*, 4 January 2016, available at http://www.theguardian.com/uk-news/2016/jan/04/falkland-islands-argentina-urges-uk-to-return-to-negotiating-table (last accessed 07.01.2016).

24 Duncan Hollis, 'China Invokes UNCLOS in Claiming Sovereignty over the Diaoyu/Senkaku Islands', Opinio Juris, December 17, 2012, http://opiniojuris.org/2012/12/17/china-invokes-unclos-in-claiming-sovereignty-over-the-diaoyusenkaku-islands/ (last accessed 05.12.2015). See also 'Sorry, China: Japan Has the Better Claim over the Senkakus', *The National Interest*, 11 January 2015, available at http://nationalinterest.org/feature/sorry-china-japan-has-the-better-claim-over-the-senkakus-12007 (last accessed 05.12.2015).

government,[25] the latter stated that the deployment of Turkish troops on the territory violated its sovereignty.[26] These examples prove the relevance, for States, of the idea of sovereignty specifically in terms of territorial control, even if the content of the concept is flexible. Moreover, it shows the use by States of a concept that has become controversial and can be easily abused for the sake of self-interest. This is exactly why, in this book, sovereignty is used as a frame of reference for counterterrorism, an area where issues of legitimacy and power are crucial – not as an ideal concept, but rather, as the thermometer of how States consider their status, obligations and capacities in international law.

Sovereignty can be considered to have a variety of meanings;[27] it can refer to the difference between the national legal orders (where the government is sovereign or where parliamentary sovereignty prevails[28]) and the international legal order, where sovereign equality created doctrines of non-intervention and of power distribution.[29] International relations have also made significant contributions to the discussions on sovereignty.[30]

Sovereignty can refer both to the power of the State to take emergency measures in times of need[31] and to the need for protection of the rule of law.[32]

25 See letter addressed by Iraq to the UN on 22 September 2014, available at http://www.securitycouncilreport.org/atf/cf/%7B65BFCF9B-6D27-4E9C-8CD3-CF6E4FF96FF9%7D/s_2014_691.pdf (last accessed 07.12.2015).

26 See 'Iraq orders Turkey to 'immediately' withdraw troops sent across border', *The Guardian*, 2 December 2015, available at http://www.theguardian.com/world/2015/dec/05/iraq-orders-turkey-to-immediately-withdraw-troops-sent-across-border (last accessed 07.12.2015).

27 Michael Fowler and Julie Marie Bunck, *Law, Power, and the Sovereign State: The Evolution and Application of the Concept of Sovereignty* (Penn State University Press, 1995) and Josef Joffe, 'Rethinking the Nation-State – The Many Meanings of Sovereignty' (1999) 78 *Foreign Affairs* 122.

28 Albert V. Dicey, *Introduction to the Study of the Law of the Constitution* (8th ed. with new Introduction) (1915).

29 Michael Fowler, and Julie Marie Bunck, *Law, Power, and the Sovereign State: The Evolution and Application of the Concept of Sovereignty* (Penn State University Press, 1995) 11.

30 See for instance Jeremy Waldron, 'Are Sovereigns Entitled to the Benefit of the International Rule of Law', (2011) 22 *European Journal of International Law*, 2, 315 and Thomas J. Biersteker and Cynthia Weber, *State Sovereignty As Social Construct* (Cambridge University Press, 1996) for two schools of sovereignty. See also Christian Reus-Smit, 'Human Rights and the Social Construction of Sovereignty' (2001) 27 *Review of International Studies*, 519, 521.

31 Carl Schmitt, 'The leader defends the law' ("Der Führer schützt das Recht"), *Deutsche Juristen Zeitung*, 38, 1934.

32 Evan J. Criddle and Evan Fox-Decent, 'Human Rights, Emergencies, and the Rule of Law' (2012) 34 *Human Rights Quarterly*, 1, 39.

In the second half of the 20th century, sovereignty evolved to include the notion of responsibility. The emergence of the Responsibility to Protect means that 'there is a necessary re-characterization involved: from sovereignty as control to sovereignty as responsibility in both internal functions and external duties.'[33] In this context, the language of sovereignty is retained but redefined to include responsibility of the State.[34]

The study of sovereignty in this book focuses on the interactions between the national and international levels in the specific context of counterterrorism through the study of counterterrorism measures adopted by international organisations. Of note, the book does not offer a particular definition for terrorism, but rather, it focuses on the *response* of international organisations to what they consider to be terrorism. In this respect, the lack of an international definition is significant, as it shows that States retain the main responsibility for framing their responses.[35]

3 International Organisations – Conflict of Legal Orders

The increasing role of international organisations in a number of areas usually reserved to States has shed a particular light on the various meanings of sovereignty and it raises specific issues regarding the transfer and sharing of sovereign power with States.[36] In the context of counterterrorism, they also enhance

---

33 'The Responsibility to Protect' (International Commission on Intervention and State Sovereignty, December 2001) 13.

34 The Global Trust Project considers States (and other sovereigns) to hold their sovereignty in trust for humanity, which creates obligations, not only towards their own citizens, but also for foreign stakeholders. See Eyal Benvenisti, 'Sovereigns as Trustees of Humanity: On the Accountability of States to Foreign Stakeholders' (2013) 107 *American Journal of International Law*, 295.

35 There are a number of works on the issue of the international definition of terrorism, as well as the legal category that it belongs to, including Roberta Arnold, *The ICC as a New Instrument for Repressing Terrorism* (Transnational Publishers, 2004); Antonio Cassese, 'Terrorism Is Also Disrupting Some Crucial Legal Categories of International Law' (2001) 12 *European Journal of International Law*, 993; Antonio Cassese, *International Criminal Law* (2nd ed., OUP Oxford, 2008); Daniel Moeckli, 'The Emergence of Terrorism as a Distinct Category of International Law' (2008) 44 *Texas International Law Journal*; and Ben Saul, *Defining Terrorism in International Law* (Oxford University Press, 2008).

36 A large number of seminal works on international organisations and sovereignty exist which take a much broader approach, including José E. Alvarez, *International Organizations as Law-Makers* (Oxford University Press, 2006); Jan Klabbers, *Advanced Introduction to the Law of International Organizations* (Edward Elgar Publishing Limited,

certain tensions and conflicts, namely, the divide between the executive branch that intersects at the national and international levels and the judiciary which is often non-existent in international organisations; and the divide between the security needs of States, which they aim to protect, and human rights, which are given protection under international and domestic law.

International and regional organisations now constitute an inherent part of international law and some have the capacity to impose binding obligations on their Member States, including the United Nations (UN) Security Council or the European Union (EU). Some analyses therefore consider that the sovereignty of States is now shared with international organisations.[37] Yet, many do not see these obligations as stripping States of their sovereignty and have even described international organisations as strengthening the sovereignty of their Member States.[38] For Christopher Greenwood, for instance, limits on sovereignty through international organisations are, in fact, inherent fixtures of independent sovereigns and are expressions of sovereignty.[39]

Martin Loughlin further makes the distinction between, on the one hand, the concept of sovereignty itself, and, on the other hand, the components of the concept.[40] For him, international law imposed restrictions on the *exercise* of political power as opposed to on sovereignty itself. This distinction has been described as a shift from sovereignty as the ultimate right to decide to sovereignty as a set of norms and practices.[41] Therefore, if rights are transferred from a State to other actors, it does not mean a transfer of the State's sovereignty

2015); Dan Sarooshi, 'The Essentially Contested Nature of the Concept of Sovereignty: Implications for the Exercise by International Organizations of Delegated Powers of Government' (2004) 25 *Michigan Journal of International Law*, 1107; and ND White, *The Law of International Organisations* (Manchester University Press, 1996). This book focuses on their role in counterterrorism.

37 William Wallace, 'The Sharing of Sovereignty: The European Paradox' (1999) 47 *Political Studies*, 503, 506, quoted in Adriana Sinclair and Michael Byers, 'When US Scholars Speak of "Sovereignty", What Do They Mean?' (2007) 55 *Political Studies*, 2, 71.

38 International organisations can also be seen as 'voluntary associations of sovereign states'. See Alain Plantey, *International Negotiation in the Twenty-First Century* (UT Austin Studies in Foreign and Transnational Law, Routledge, 2007) 198. See also Kal Raustiala, 'Rethinking the Sovereignty Debate in International Economic Law' (2003) 6 *Journal of International Economic Law*, 4, 855.

39 Christopher Greenwood, W.G. Hart Workshop, London, 'Sovereignty in Question', June 2011.

40 Martin Loughlin, 'Ten Tenets of Sovereignty', *Sovereignty in Transition* (Hart Publishing, 2003).

41 Karen Litfin, 'Sovereignty in World Ecopolitics' (1997) 41 *Mershon International Studies Review*, 2, 167.

itself.[42] Indeed, 'a State may continue to be sovereign even though important government functions are carried out on its behalf by another State or by an international organisation.'[43] In his study of transfers of sovereignty, Guglielmo Verdirame examines supranational sovereignty, or the sovereignty functions exercised by international organisations, as existing in parallel to State sovereignty, despite the existence of transfers of functions.[44]

In this respect, the EU is a particular example of sovereignty transfers that have questioned the nature of sovereignty. Due to its '*sui generis* nature and its highly developed structures,'[45] the EU differs from other international organisations. The EU started as pragmatic steps by way of trade agreements between a few States,[46] but is now a full regional organisation with an international legal personality[47] that deals with issues ranging from education to currency.[48] The entity therefore questions State sovereignty in a specific way, as EU laws are described as constituting a 'new legal order,'[49] which are considered to have supremacy over national law.[50] Therefore, the obligations it creates might conflict with national rules and also with other international obligations.[51] Yet, the EU does not possess the *Kompetenz Kompetenz*[52] and neither do international organisations, although the Security Council has the authority to decide

42 Bruno de Witte, 'Do Not Mention the Word: Sovereignty in Two Europhile Countries: Belgium and the Netherlands', in *Sovereignty in Transition* (Hart Publishing, 2003).

43 James Crawford, *The Creation of States in International Law* (2nd ed., Oxford University Press, USA, 2006) 33.

44 Guglielmo Verdirame, 'A Normative Theory of Sovereignty Transfers' (2013) 49 *Stanford Journal of International Law*, 371.

45 Carmela Perez-Bernardez, 'The European Union Anti-Terrorism Policy in Relation to Other International Organisations', in *International Legal Dimension of Terrorism*, vol. 23, International Humanitarian Law Series (Martinus Nijhoff Publishers, 2009) 373.

46 The EU started as the European Coal and Steel Community in 1951, became the European Economic Community in 1957 and it extended its competences to common market, freedom of movement, etc. For a history of the EU's institutions and competences, see Margot Horspool and Matthew Humphreys, *European Union Law* (6th ed., Oxford University Press, 2010) 13–26.

47 Article 47 Treaty of the European Union.

48 Article 3–6 Treaty on the Functioning of the European Union (TFEU).

49 *Flaminio Costa v ENEL* [1964] ECR 585 (6/64).

50 Declaration No. 17 Concerning Primacy. Declarations annexed to the Final Act of the Intergovernmental Conference, which adopted the Treaty of Lisbon, signed on 13 December 2007.

51 Further remarks on the EU and its impact on sovereignty are included in Parts 2 and 3.

52 Hent Kalmo and Quentin Skinner, *Sovereignty in Fragments: The Past, Present and Future of a Contested Concept* (Cambridge University Press, 2010) 133.

what constitutes a 'threat to international peace and security,' and this declaration leads to the power to adopt binding decisions.[53]

In practice, international organisations have become actors who act in parallel with States, resulting in a juxtaposition of actors acting on similar areas. Due to the existence of international organisations, the *content* of State sovereignty has been altered. As well, although the concept itself still remains part of the political discourse, its practical application has changed. This can create conflicts between the various norms that coexist. However, using sovereignty as a framework of reference allows references to be made to issues of legality (are international organisations allowed to adopt counterterrorism measures?), legitimacy and efficiency (are the counterterrorism measures of international organisations well received and actually implemented in practice?).[54] It also allows taking into account the political views of States and their subsequent legal actions.

One example that illustrates some of the issues that surface in the interactions between States and international organisations is terrorism legislation. States consider that terrorism challenges their authority to provide safety for their citizens.[55] However, the increasing role of international counterterrorism questions a core competence of States. In addition, national and international security can be used to justify violations of human rights norms and terrorism is at the very centre of the discussion about security and human rights and their relation to sovereignty. Finally, within a legal order, the various branches dealing with terrorism might clash leading one to question the traditional distribution of powers that exists in a State. International law exacerbates this conflict because it gives a predominant place to the executive branch of a State. This means the existence of a variety of potential conflicts between legal orders, within legal orders, between branches, and between norms, and these all will intrinsically redefine the concept of sovereignty.

Beyond the conflict of legal orders raised by international organisations, two of the potential conflicts listed above, namely a conflict between branches of a legal order and a potential tension between security needs and human rights, allow for further dissection of the concept of State sovereignty in the

---

53 See Chapter 1, Section 2.

54 These concepts are as complex as that of sovereignty and are only refered to in this book insofar as they raise the questions of transfer of competences and of enforcement of measures.

55 Max Weber considered sovereignty to be the monopoly of power of a State whereby a State can claim the monopoly of the legitimate use of physical force within its territory. See Max Weber, 1918, Speech *Politik als Beruf* (Politics as a Vocation).

counterterrorism context. These conflicts form the backdrop of the analysis on counterterrorism and State sovereignty in this book.

4 Conflict of Branches

Domestic legal systems are traditionally divided between branches of government in a way, which, today, is often suggested as 'foster[ing] a system of checks and balances necessary for good government.'[56] The exact distribution of functions between the branches varies from one State to another.

However, when looking at the international level, this model of separation of powers is not usually replicated. Instead, the creation of international law through treaties enhances the role of the executive since it is that branch that negotiates these agreements. Dan Sarooshi summarised this situation as follows:

> Conferrals by States of powers on international organisations often affect, arguably even undermine, the separation of powers within States, especially between the executive and legislative branches of government since it is the executive branch which represents the State in the organisation when decisions are being made concerning the use of powers that may otherwise have been the power of the legislature.[57]

Further, there is a 'consensus' that the EU has

> strengthened executive power, because it is the executive which has direct access to European policy-making and policy-makers in the Council, in the European institutions and other Member States; and that national parliaments, in particular, have not succeeded in scrutinizing or controlling actions by their national governments.[58]

56 Richard Benwell and Oonagh Gay, 'The Separation of Powers' (SN/PC/06053, Parliament and Constitution Centre, 15 August 2011).

57 Sarooshi, 'The Essentially Contested Nature of the Concept of Sovereignty: Implications for the Exercise by International Organizations of Delegated Powers of Government', (2004) 1112.

58 William Phelan, 'Does the European Union Strengthen the State? Democracy, Executive Power and International Cooperation' (Centre for European Studies, Working Paper No. 95, 2003) 5.

This is exacerbated by the fact that the international judiciary is limited because its decisions are not easily enforceable. For example, there is no international court that has jurisdiction to address terrorism.[59] More generally, 'the international legal system has operated for the better part of the twentieth century without a strong international judiciary capable of fulfilling on a regular basis the traditional roles of the national judiciary – dispute settlement, law interpretation, and law application ... In short, the international rule of law has suffered from the absence of robust judicial institutions.'[60]

Therefore, because of the 'absence of a fully fledged centralised judiciary within the international legal order, domestic and regional courts play a key role in the enforcement and balancing of various international obligations.'[61] Increasingly, these courts have come to fulfil functions of norm-advancement and regime maintenance.[62]

International courts and tribunals are similar to international organisations in that they are traditionally created by intergovernmental treaties.[63] The increase in their role means that, similar to international organisations, their decisions might impact the sovereignty of States. In particular, the role of the European Court of Justice (ECJ) in assessing the nature and scope of European law and its place in national legal orders has made a significant impact on the hierarchy of norms in EU States.[64] Moreover, the impact of the

59 The International Court of Justice (ICJ) deals with inter-States disputes. The International Criminal Court (ICC) can examine terrorism under other categories of the Rome Statute, but the crime of terrorism does not exist in the Rome Statute (see Roberta Arnold, *The ICC as a New Instrument for Repressing Terrorism* (Transnational Publishers, 2004) for an analysis).

60 Yuval Shany, 'No Longer a Weak Department of Power? Reflections on the Emergence of a New International Judiciary' (2009) 20 *European Journal of International Law*, 73, 74.

61 Jure Vidmar and Erica de Wet (eds.), *Hierarchy in International Law* (Oxford University Press, 2012) 4.

62 Shany 'No Longer a Weak Department of Power? Reflections on the Emergence of a New International Judiciary', 81.

63 The ICC was created by the Rome Treaty adopted in July 1998; the European Court of Human Rights (ECtHR) was created by the European Convention for the Protection of Human Rights and Fundamental Freedoms (now the European Convention for Human Rights (ECHR)) adopted in November 1950; and the Inter-American Court of Human Rights (IACtHR) was created by the Organisation of American States (OAS) with the adoption of the American Declaration of the Rights and Duties of Man in 1948. The European Court of Justice (ECJ) was created in 1952 by the Treaty of Paris as part of the European Coal and Steel Community.

64 See *Flaminio Costa v ENEL* [1964] ECR 585 (6/64) and *Internationale Handelsgesellschaft mbH v Einfuhr – und Vorratsstelle fur Getreide und Futtermittel* (Case 11/70) [1970] ECR 1125.

European Court of Human Rights (ECtHR) on an increasing number of areas now affects even non-European States.[65] International courts can, therefore, be considered a challenge to State sovereignty not only because they replace a function of the State, but also because they possibly convict the State itself or its leaders.

However, in principle, most international courts function on the basis of complementarity or subsidiarity in order to protect State sovereignty.[66] In that context, national courts have tried to protect the separation of powers that has been blurred by the development of international organisations. The German Constitutional Court[67] sought to 'ensure that the German legislature exercised control over the content of the powers being conferred by Germany on the EU by giving the legislature the competence to specify by statute the powers being conferred.'[68] This book shows the positive impact of the inclusion of courts in the counterterrorism debate despite the various conflicts that this raises, and the effect it has on sovereignty.

5 International Security – Conflict of Norms

In cases of public emergencies or war, States are entitled to derogate from and completely suspend certain existing human rights protections so that they

65 The extraterritoriality of the ECHR has been developed in a number of cases, such as *Bankovic v Belgium*, 2001-XII Eur. Ct. H.R. 333 and *Al-Skeini v United Kingdom*, App. No. 55721/07, 53 Eur. H.R. Rep. 18 (2011).

66 According to Article 35 of the ECHR, the ECtHR only functions after all national remedies have been exhausted and the primary responsibility is placed on the States. Moreover the Court has to respect a margin of appreciation, a concept that it developed in the *Handyside* case: it is a mechanism that enables the Court to respect individual State sovereignty as part of the key concept of a confidence between the Convention organs and the contracting parties. See *Handyside v The United Kingdom*, judgment of 7.12.1976, § 48–49. The International Criminal Court (ICC) is subsidiary to national courts, which means it will only act if the State fails to do so. The Statute does not include 'complementarity' in its text, but the term has been adopted by many negotiators of the Statute, and later on by commentators, to refer to the entirety of norms governing the complementary relationship between the ICC and national jurisdictions.

67 In *Bundesverfassungsgericht* [BVerfGE][Federal Constitutional Court] 89, 155 (438–439) 1993.

68 Sarooshi, 'The Essentially Contested Nature of the Concept of Sovereignty: Implications for the Exercise by International Organizations of Delegated Powers of Government', (2004) 1112.

become inoperative.[69] Similarly, national security is considered to be a legal justification for the partial limitation of human rights in non-emergency situations,[70] except in the case of non-derogable rights.[71] These derogations and limitations can be found in human rights instruments: article 4 of the 1966 International Covenant on Civil and Political Rights[72] allows States to derogate from their obligations under the Convention for reasons of 'public emergency.' As well, the European Convention on Human Rights includes a limitation clause for some of its protected rights:

> The exercise of these freedoms, since it carries with it duties and responsibilities, may be subject to such formalities, conditions, restrictions or penalties as are prescribed by law and are necessary in a democratic society, in the interests of national security, territorial integrity or public safety, for the prevention of disorder or crime, for the protection of health or morals, for the protection of the reputation or rights of others, for preventing the disclosure of information received in confidence, or for maintaining the authority and impartiality of the judiciary.[73]

69 This section is an updated version of an analysis contained in Myriam Feinberg, 'International Counterterrorism – National Security and Human Rights: Conflicts of Norms or Checks and Balances?' *International Journal of Human Rights*, Volume 19, Number 4, 2015.

70 Henry J Steiner, Philip Alston and Ryan Goodman, *International Human Rights in Context: Law, Politics, Morals : Text and Materials* (Oxford University Press 2008) 385.

71 Some human rights are non-derogable, in which case, no exception or limit is acceptable. A definition of these peremptory norms, which create non-derogable rights, is included in the Vienna Conventions for the Law of Treaties, but the exact list of these rights is unclear- Article 54 of the Convention reads: 'Treaties conflicting with a peremptory norm of general international law (jus cogens): A treaty is void if, at the time of its conclusion, it conflicts with a peremptory norm of general international law. For the purposes of the present Convention, a peremptory norm of general international law is a norm accepted and recognized by the international community of States as a whole as a norm from which no derogation is permitted and which can be modified only by a subsequent norm of general international law having the same character', United Nations, Vienna Convention on the Law of Treaties, 23 May 1969, United Nations, Treaty Series, Vol. 1155, p. 331.

72 UN General Assembly, International Covenant on Civil and Political Rights, 16 December 1966, United Nations, Treaty Series, vol. 999, p. 171.

73 Council of Europe, European Convention for the Protection of Human Rights and Fundamental Freedoms, as amended by Protocols Nos. 11 and 14, 4 November 1950, ETS 5, article 10(2).

Similarly, many counterterrorism measures are considered necessary to protect the security of a population, even though they sometimes come at the expense of an individual or a group. This usually gives rise to a balancing exercise or the adoption of temporary measures. Following the September 11, 2001 attacks, many have argued for the adoption of an entirely new approach to counterterrorism to reflect the new nature of the terrorist threat.[74] This new approach would focus on security, often at the expense of personal freedoms and other interests.[75] For example, Thomas Poole noted that 'in the political realm, human rights are not considered as a useful weapon against the enemy but as a dangerous constraint against effective action.'[76] In a legal context post-September 11, 2001, the 'emergency' of terrorism has become the norm.[77] Of note, is that, as examined in the last section, the new approach is exacerbated at the international level for several reasons including the predominant executive branch and the lack of accountability mechanims.

Yet, against this backdrop, some authors and practitioners challenge the practice of applying conflict between these two societal features,[78] stating that 'we must reject the false choice between our values and our security.'[79]

---

74 'Blair vows hard line on fanatics', BBC News, 5 August 2005: Former British Prime Minister Tony Blair said at a press conference following the terrorist attacks in London in July 2005 that 'the rules of the game are changing', available at http://news.bbc.co.uk/2/hi/uk_news/4747573.stm (accessed January 2015).

75 'First, our highest priority is – and always will be – the safety and security of the American people. As President Obama has said, we have no greater responsibility as a government', Remarks of John O. Brennan (Director of the Central Intelligence Agency) – As Prepared for Delivery, Program on Law and Security, Harvard Law School, Cambridge, Massachusetts, Friday, September 16, 2011, http://www.whitehouse.gov/the-press-office/2011/09/16/remarks-john-o-brennan-strengthening-our-security-adhering-our-values-an (accessed January 2015).

76 Thomas Poole, 'Sovereign Indignities: International Law as Public Law' (2011) 22 *European Journal of International Law*, 2, 351.

77 For general discussions on the link between security and human rights post 9/11, read Kent Roach, The 9/11 Effect – Comparative Counter-Terrorism (Cambridge University Press, 2011); Kent Roach, 'Uneasy Neighbors: Comparative American and Canadian Counter-Terrorism' (2012) 38 *William Mitchell Law Review*; Benjamin J. Goold and Liora Lazarus, 'Sources and Trends in Post-9/11 Anti-Terrorism Laws' in Benjamin J. Goold and Liora Lazarus, eds., *Security and Human Rights* (Hart Publishing, 2007).

78 Goold and Lazarus, 'Introduction Security and Human Rights: The Search for a Language of Reconciliation', in Goold and Lazarus, *Security and Human Rights*, 2.

79 Remarks of John O. Brennan (Director of the Central Intelligence Agency) – As Prepared for Delivery, Program on Law and Security, Harvard Law School, Cambridge, Massachusetts, Friday, 16 September, 2011, http://www.whitehouse.gov/the-press-office/2011/09/16/

In particular, human rights experts have explained that it is a 'mistaken belief ... that the protection of human rights and the protection of national securities (which are both a state responsibility) are mutually exclusive, when in fact they are not.'[80] A new concept of 'human security'[81] supposes that individual liberty and human rights are not in opposition, but, rather, at the heart of security.[82] While there is a controversial aspect to human security,[83] it is said to have 'provided the theoretical foundation'[84] for the Responsibility to Protect.[85] This means that the protection of citizens, or security, has become a State obligation, not just a power, and a part of sovereignty. Indeed,

> At the heart of antiterrorism efforts is a recognition that all human beings have a right to security and to life. All governments have a responsibility to respect, ensure, and fulfill these rights and, to that end, to employ effective strategies to prevent and to punish acts of mass murder and destruction. No human rights advocate would deny this responsibility.[86]

---

remarks-john-o-brennan-strengthening-our-security-adhering-our-values-an (accessed January 2015).

80 Milena Costas-Trascasas, 'Terrorism, State of Emergency and Derogation from Judicial Guarantees', in Pablo Antonio Fernández Sánchez, *International Legal Dimension of Terrorism* (Brill, 2009) International Humanitarian Law Series, 471.

81 For a history of how the concept evolved, see Rhoda E. Howard-Hassmann, 'Human Security: Undermining Human Rights?'(2012) 34 *Human Rights Quarterly*, 1, 88.

82 Sandra Freedman, 'The Positive Right of Security', in *Security and Human Rights* (Hart Publishing, 2007) and Liora Lazarus, 'Mapping the Right to Security', in *Security and Human Rights* (Hart Publishing, 2007).

83 Moufida Goucha and John Crowley, *Rethinking Human Security* (Chichester: John Wiley & Sons, 2009) 5; Mark Duffield, *Development, Security and Unending War: Governing the World of Peoples* (London: Polity, 2007) 114.

84 Ibid.

85 The Responsibility to Protect, a new concept developed in in the early 2000s after the atrocities of Rwanda and Yugolsavia and the lack of intervention by the international community. The term was first presented in the report of the International Commission on Intervention and State Sovereignty in December 2001 and the concept was given a legal background by the UN through the Outcome Document of the 2005 United Nations World Summit (A/RES/60/1, para. 138–140) and the Secretary-General's 2009 Report (A/63/677) on Implementing the Responsibility to Protect. For an analysis of the concept, see Richard H Cooper and Juliette Voïnov Kohler (eds), *Responsibility to Protect* (Palgrave Macmillan 2009).

86 Paul Hoffman, 'Human Rights and Terrorism' (2004) 26 *Human Rights Quarterly*, 932, 949.

For Evan J. Criddle and Evan Fox-Decent, 'human rights represent the normative consequences of a state's assumption of sovereign powers, and are thus constitutive of sovereignty's normative dimension.'[87] The International Commission of Jurists supports this as follows:

> International law requires that states take all measures appropriate to guarantee the right to life, and other essential freedoms, to all within their jurisdiction. In face of the real threats that exist, states are legally bound to take appropriate counter-terrorist measures.[88]

It therefore seems counterproductive to place security in opposition to human rights, when counterterrorism measures are meant to protect the right to life. However, in practice, lawmakers, practitioners, and judges appear to be constantly faced with having to either choose between them or balance them. Through this book, the ways in which international organisations have deepened this conflict between norms due to the predominant role of the executive will be analysed. At the same time, the book will illustrate how the courts, in their role of protecting human rights, aim and increasingly manage to provide the necessary checks and balances that are needed to provide an international security that is legal and legitimate.

6 Structure and Methodology

This book focuses on the nature of counterterrorism measures since September 11, 2001 in order to assess the relationship between States and international organisations in addressing terrorism over the past decade and a half. While the role of international organisations in dealing with security issues is not a new topic, these events have raised many issues regarding State sovereignty, as States have had to decide whether to pool competences in order to address global threats, and a number of international organisations have now adopted binding measures for their Member States. The approach taken in this book is first to analyse what competences and powers have been transferred to international or regional organisations and then to examine the implementation of the international counterterrorism measures – especially those that conflict

87 Criddle and Fox-Decent 'Human Rights, Emergencies, and the Rule of Law' (2012), 41.

88 International Commission of Jurists, Addressing Damage, Urging Action. Report of the Eminent Jurists Panel on Terrorism, Counter-Terrorism and Human Rights, February 2009, Executive summary, page 1.

with one another. As part of the examination of these measures, the book looks at which actor has the primary role in their implementation and reference is made to the implementation reports for the international measures. The last part of the book consists of an analysis of the case law dealing with the conflict between various international counterterrorism measures and their respective status in order to assess which legal order – and which branch of it – has had the most significant impact on State sovereignty.

Of note here is that the lack of an agreed international definition of terrorism has not prevented States and international organisations from adopting counterterrorism measures. Terrorism has been deemed 'impossible' to define at the international level because of the variety of contexts in which it takes place.[89] This statement still rings true today, even after September 11, 2001. Yet, the *lack* of an agreed upon international definition of terrorism must be given serious consideration in the discussion of sovereignty; this lack of a definition is problematic because while States use traditional counterterrorism conventions to deal with specific crimes, they face binding obligations in counterterrorism without the benefit of a common, agreed-upon definition. On the other hand, the fact that States are still able to adopt their own definition means that they can retain the possibility to include, or exclude, certain offences. The analysis of regional counterterrorism regimes shows that States have managed to adopt common definitions through regional groupings where differences are less likely to occur, although these represent an exception and many States still rely on their own definition in order to apprehend terrorist suspects. Therefore, focus in this book is on the *response* to terrorism because it represents the steps that States are willing – or unwilling – to take in order to assert their sovereignty against challenges to their security.

This book is divided into three parts. Part 1 focuses on the impact of the September 11, 2001 attacks on the role of the UN Security Council in counterterrorism. The UN Charter granted the Security Council the role of dealing with issues of 'international peace and security'[90] and while terrorism was not originally included under its powers, the Security Council has gradually included acts of terrorism within the definition. The first mention of a terrorist act as a 'threat to international peace and security'[91] allowed the organ to adopt

89 D. Long, *The Anatomy of Terrorism* (NY: Free Press, 1990).

90 Article 24, UN Charter.

91 Resolution 748, adopted by the Security Council in 1992 in response to the 'Lockerbie' incident, mentioned Chapter 7 of the UN Charter to describe Libya's actions as a 'threat to peace and security.' An analysis of the resolution is included in Chapter 2.

binding measures under Chapter 7. These measures adopted by the Security Council and the actual enforcement of these measures by Member States are examined and compared to earlier counterterrorism efforts by the UN. In this context, it had been noted that international law, with a strong development of counterterrorism legislation, had developed a framework for counterterrorism with most of the normative work done, but that was missing enforcement mechanisms.[92]

The UN developed its counterterrorism legislation mainly through the adoption of a large number of conventions on terrorism. The success of treaties, however, is limited by the need for their ratification and enforcement by each signatory. With the Security Council stepping in as the main actor against terrorism, rules have changed culminating with Resolution 1373 (2001) that defines terrorism *per se* as a 'threat to international peace and security.'[93] This resolution has allowed the Security Council to adopt measures under Chapter 7 of the UN Charter that are immediately binding on all Member States of the organisation. As well, Resolution 1373 has created a Committee charged with monitoring the enforcement of these measures. As a result, some authors have described the role of Security Council, post-September 11, 2001, as one of a legislator[94] and this had led to questioning both its authority to act and the scope of its action.[95] The qualification of the Security Council as legislator has blurred traditional differences between national and international levels, and the balance of power between executive and judicial powers. However, the Security Council still relies on States for the definition of terrorism and therefore leaves it to its Member States to define their own regime, within the boundaries of

92 Guillaume 'Terrorism and International Law'(2004), 543.

93 UN Security Council Resolution 1373 (2001), Preamble.

94 Rosa Giles-Camero, 'Terrorism Acts as Threats to International Peace and Security', in *International Legal Dimension of Terrorism*, vol. 23, International Humanitarian Law Series (Martinus Nijhoff Publishers, 2009); Alexander Marschick, 'The Security Council's Role: Problems and Prospects in the Fight Against Terrorism', in International Cooperation in Counter-Terrorism. The UN and Regional Organisations in the Fight Against Terrorism (England-USA: Ashgate Publishing, 2006); Stefan Talmon, 'The Security Council as a World Legislature' (2005) 99 *American Journal of International Law*, 1; and Paul C. Szasz, 'The Security Council Starts Legislating' (2002) 96 *American Journal of International Law*, 901.

95 Andrea Bianchi, 'Assessing the Effectiveness of the UN Security Council's Anti-Terrorism Measures: The Quest for Legitimacy and Cohesion' (2006) *European Journal of International Law*, 881 and Bardo Fassbender, 'The UN Security Council and International Terrorism', in *Enforcing International Law Norms Against Terrorism*, Studies in International Law (Hart Publishing, 2004).

Resolution 1373. The book examines the impact on the sovereignty of its Member States and concludes that it is somewhat limited by the leeway that the Security Council still leaves to States. This conclusion includes, as well, the criticism that can be given to this system.

The events of September 11, 2001 have also had an impact on how regional organisations deal with terrorism. Part 2 of the book deals with the role of four regional organisations, namely the Organisation of American States (OAS), the Council of Europe, the EU, and the African Union (AU), in counterterrorism. These organisations reflect a geographical and structural diversity and were selected for their action against terrorism. For each organisation, the book studies the influence September 11, 2001 on its power and the type of counterterrorism regime it has developed as a result. There is a particular focus on the EU because of its 'highly developed structure [that] differentiates [it] from other organisations.'[96] The actual implementation of all regional measures allows for the analysis of the impact of the measures on the sovereignty of their Member States. While a smaller membership appears to favour the decision-making on sensitive issues such as terrorism, regional organisations use traditional treaties and agreements and face obstacles during the implementation of measures into national orders. In comparison, the nature of EU counterterrorism measures allows for a more successful implementation. At the same time, the case law of some of their courts has resulted in significant contributions. This was done by integrating the protection of human rights and procedural safeguards into the international counterterrorism legal regime. The consequences of this case law allow for the completion of the analysis in this book of the impact of regional organisations on State sovereignty.

The fact that various international organisations have acted against terrorism means that there is a potential conflict of legal regimes. This is examined in Part 3 where the focus is on the terrorism sanctions regimes that have been created, originally at the UN level and then copied by the EU and by Member States. Examples of these regimes are the sanctions imposed against Taliban and Al-Qaida with a set list created at the UN level and stemming from Resolution 1267 (1999) and the terrorism sanctions regime based on UN Resolution 1373 (2001) in which Member States create their own list of individuals and groups that they target with asset freezing. All of these regimes, as created by the UN and implemented by both the EU and Member States, originally lacked any procedural safeguards or delisting procedures. Additionally,

96 Carmela Perez-Bernardez, 'The European Union Anti-Terrorism Policy in Relation to Other International Organisations', in *International Legal Dimension of Terrorism*, vol. 23, International Humanitarian Law Series (Martinus Nijhoff Publishers, 2009) 373.

the lack of human rights protection led to increasing case law concerning terrorist sanctions. These cases, discussed in Part 3, deal with the conflict between security measures and human rights standards. These various conflicts can reshape the nature of State sovereignty in a world where security is paramount, but where human rights and the rule of law have become integral parts of counterterrorism. This book shows how some of this re-shaping is happening through the conduit of courts, which act as a balance against the ever-increasing, strong role of the executive in security issues.

The case law presented in Part 3 has had a considerable impact on the way counterterrorism measures are adapted, even by other organisations. As well, the potential conflict between the various legal orders involved in counterterrorism, and in particular, the EU's judgments, may lead to a fragmentation of international counterterrorism. Finally, the UK case law on terrorism and terrorism sanctions described in Part 3 is noteworthy. Being a Member State of both the UN and the EU, the UK is a perfect case study of a recipient of various binding obligations and its case law shows the dilemma States face when addressing terrorism.

PART 1

The United Nations Counterterrorism Framework and Its Impact on Sovereignty

CHAPTER 1

The Emergence of an International Counterterrorism Regime

The UN, with its wide membership, is, in theory, the ideal organisation to address international terrorism. Yet, originally, none of the various bodies of the organisation was specifically mandated to deal with terrorism. Moreover, in the 1960s and 1970s, terrorism was viewed as 'one of the unfortunate but necessary tactics of struggles for national liberation.'[1] The UN has since developed its action against terrorism, beginning with the adoption of multilateral treaties between its Members in the General Assembly (GA), because the Security Council was paralysed by threats of the veto during the Cold War. The adoption of these multilateral treaties allowed States to provide specific legal responses to contemporary threats. These treaties also respected State sovereignty by leaving the choice of their ratification and implementation to each State.

As a consequence, the role of the Security Council as the main actor against terrorism is a relatively new phenomenon, albeit an increasingly important one. In fact, the Security Council has now created a strong arsenal against terrorism, both through the application of its regular powers and the development of new tools and it has replaced the General Assembly as the default actor against the threat.

After September 11, 2001, the Security Council adopted, for the first time, obligations of States to prosecute suspects of specific terrorist acts and to legislate on and criminalise terrorism as a phenomenon, as opposed to reacting against a specific incident. Significantly, it also created special bodies to enhance implementation and compliance where, previously, many instruments had been in place without efficient means of supervision. In sum,

> [The] Security Council adapted to the spread of transnational terrorism by demanding more from States, intervening deeper into their domestic realm, and at the same time offering more support.[2]

1 Edward C. Luck, *UN Security Council: Practice and Promise* (Routledge, 2006) 95 and Malvina Halberstam, 'The Evolution of the United Nations Position on Terrorism: From Exempting National Liberation Movements to Criminalizing Terrorism Wherever and by Whomever Committed' (2002) 41 *Columbia Journal of Transnational Law*, 1.

2 Monika Heupel, 'Adapting to Transnational Terrorism: The UN Security Council's Evolving Approach to Terrorism' (2007) 38 *Security Dialogue*, 9.

 | DOI 10.1163/9789004299580_003

Indeed, by adopting measures against terrorism, the Security Council has possibly intervened in areas that were traditionally seen as 'domestic jurisdiction' according to Article 2(7) of the UN Charter. Therefore, contrary to the case of multilateral treaties, the actions of the Security Council can potentially be seen as a challenge to State sovereignty, and its role has been widely criticised.

1 Non-binding UN Counterterrorism Measures

Terrorism has traditionally been dealt with at the national level through criminal justice. Yet, the effects of terrorism over several States prompted them to cooperate and to develop multilateral treaties from an early stage of the UN existence. In practice, various instruments were adopted within the UN, as well as by specialised agencies, and regional groupings, to deal with terrorist acts. Because of the disagreements on the definition of the phenomenon,[3] States decided to focus on prosecuting or extraditing the authors of specifically designated acts such as hijacking, hostage taking, attacks against the safety of sea vessels, and the proliferation of nuclear weapons. There are now eighteen different conventions and their protocols that deal with terrorism.[4] As well, the lack of consensus over the definition of the phenomenon has been put aside to respond pragmatically to specific accidents that happened. This approach was described as 'sectoral'[5] and this prudence explains the success of these conventions,[6] which did not need to include the controversial issue of self-determination.

---

3 A major obstacle to an agreement on an international definition is the desire by some States to include exceptions for cases of self-determination and decolonisation. For instance, the 1999 Convention of the Organisation of Islamic Conference for Terrorism states that 'people's struggle, including armed struggle against foreign occupation, aggression, colonisation and hegemony aimed at liberation and self-determination in accordance with the principles of international law shall not be considered a terrorism crime, OIC Convention to Combat Terrorism (1999-1420H), Article 2.

4 A list of these instruments in available at https://treaties.un.org/Pages/DB.aspx?path=DB/studies/page2_en.xml (last accessed 07.12.2015).

5 Francesca Galli and Anne Weyembergh (eds.), *EU counter-terrorism offences: What impact on national legislation and case-law?* (Editions de l'Université de Bruxelles, 2012), Etudes Européennes, 15.

6 Gilbert Guillaume, 'Terrorism and International Law' (2004) 53 *International and Comparative Legal Quarterly*, 537 and Ben Saul, 'The Emerging International Law of Terrorism' (2010) *Indian Yearbook of International Law and Policy*, 163, 164.

Through these treaties, States are still considered the primary actors against terrorism.

Indeed, in practice, States can choose to ratify treaties or not. This approach characterised the period prior to the events of September 11, 2001 that corresponded to the general approach of the Cold War, that being a 'state-based, consensual manner, reflecting the traditional values of international law.'[7] As well, this approach respected sovereignty because there was no international court to implement the measures they created. Yet, it had a downside and despite the wide number of conventions, national ratification and implementation were weak. As a result, only two States were party to all of the existing conventions by 2001.[8]

In an effort to organise the many instruments on terrorism, the General Assembly created the Global Counterterrorism Strategy in 2006.[9] This marked the first time that all Member States had agreed to a common strategic and operational approach to fighting terrorism. Member States did not, however, agree on a common definition of terrorism and this restricted a truly general approach to the phenomenon. More significantly, the measures adopted by the General Assembly are not binding.

A review of the Global Counterterrorism Strategy took place at the 66th Session in July 2012.[10] It 'reaffirms the principal responsibility of Member States to implement the Strategy'[11] and encourages cooperation by 'other international, regional and subregional organisations.'[12] The Resolution also stresses in its Preamble that it is 'convinced that the GA is the competent organ, with universal membership, to address the issue of international terrorism.'[13] On the other hand, it previously affirmed 'the authority of the Security Council to mandate coercive action to maintain and restore international peace and security.'[14]

---

7 Nigel D. White, 'The United Nations and Counter-Terrorism: multilateral and executive law-making' in *Counter-Terrorism: International Law and Practice* (Oxford University Press, 2012) 54.

8 Botswana and the UK. See Eric Rosand, Alistair Milar and Jason Ipe, 'The UN Security Council's Counterterrorism Program: What Lies Ahead?' 7.

9 UN General Assembly Resolution, *The United Nations Global Counter-Terrorism Strategy*, 13 October 2010, A/RES/64/297.

10 UN General Assembly Resolution, *The United Nations Global Counter-Terrorism Strategy Review*, 29 June 2012, A/RES/66/282.

11 Ibid., §5.

12 Ibid., §17.

13 Ibid., Preamble.

14 UN General Assembly Resolution 60/1 (16 September 2005), known as the World Summit Outcome Document, §79.

Thus, the General Assembly is the organ that created the international framework for action against terrorism and the basis for the international duty of States to address the phenomenon. It still represents the forum where all States can discuss the phenomenon. Yet the General Assembly is completed, in its action, by the Security Council, which can impose binding obligations on its Member States. In the most recent years, these obligations have come at the forefront of international counterterrorism and their binding nature, without the legitimacy of the General Assembly, has renewed questions of sovereignty. The next sections – and Chapters – therefore focus on the Security Council.

2 The Security Council's Means of Action

The UN Charter gave the Security Council a broad mandate and its responsibility is the 'maintenance of international peace and security.'[15] In this context, the Security Council can adopt a variety of measures, including non-binding recommendations. The main strength of the Security Council resides in the fact that it can adopt binding decisions under Chapter 7 of the Charter. Therefore, Chapter 7 constitutes the only exception to the principle of non-intervention in State affairs.[16] As well, the Security Council can adopt enforcement measures that are legally binding on all of its Member States, provided it establishes a situation of 'threat to peace, breach of the peace, or act of aggression.'[17] The analysis in this book will focus on the Security Council's resolutions and sanctions as binding instruments for two reasons: first because they have a greater potential to affect the Member States' sovereignty; and second because they have, in fact, been adopted in the context of counterterrorism, thereby contributing to transforming them into both international phenomena and obligations.

2.1 *'Threat to International Peace and Security' – The Framework for Binding Measures Against Terrorism*

Whereas the Security Council's decisions adopted in the context of Chapter 6 for the 'pacific settlement of disputes' do not legally bind Member States, in cases of situations that qualify as a threat to international peace and security,

15 UN Charter, Article 24.

16 Kenneth Manusama, *The United Nations Security Council in the Post-Cold War Era* (Martinus Nijhoff Publishers, 2006) 26 and Luck, *UN Security Council: Practice and Promise*, 82.

17 UN Charter, Article 39.

its decisions will have a binding effect on States 'by virtue of Article 25 of the Charter.'[18] Rather than being a limitation, the 'threat to international peace and security' condition has increasingly been expanded by the Security Council in order to fit its agenda. In fact, the Security Council actually enjoys wide discretion both in determining the existence of a threat to peace and security and deciding which measure to adopt once the declaration has been made.

This qualification of what constitutes a threat to peace and security has evolved from being limited to situations where there was a threat of military action to including 'such situations as the safe delivery of humanitarian aid and the prevention of massive refugee flows in relation to geographically circumscribed crises'[19] and the creation of the two ad hoc international criminal tribunals.[20] More recently, Resolution 2177 (2014), adopted on 18 September 2014, determined that 'the unprecedented extent of the Ebola outbreak in Africa constitute[d] a threat to international peace and security.'[21] The use of this framework for situations of terrorism is therefore not surprising and the Security Council has made use of this tool in order to extend its mandate to counterterrorism and act in collective security issues.

Much discussion exists regarding the definition of peace, which the Security Council bases its mandate on.[22] A realistic view of the issue is that, in practice, 'a threat to peace seems to be whatever the Security Council says is a threat to the peace.'[23] In fact, according to Tams, 'no one seriously questions the Council's right to qualify as a 'threat to peace' situations which have nothing to do with the use of inter-State force.'[24] Criticism of this wide discretion obviously

---

18 *Prosecutor v Tadic*, Appeal on Jurisdiction, No. IT-94-1-AR72, para. 44 (2 October 1995), 35 ILM 32 (1996).

19 Andrea Bianchi, 'Assessing the Effectiveness of the UN Security Council's Anti-Terrorism Measures: The Quest for Legitimacy and Cohesion' (2006) 17 *European Journal of International Law*, 881, 889.

20 Security Council Resolution 827, 25 May 1993 and Security Council Resolution 955, 8 November 1994.

21 UN Security Council, *Security Council resolution 2177 (2014) [on the outbreak of the Ebola virus in, and its impact on, West Africa]*, 18 September 2014, S/RES/2177 (2014), Preamble.

22 For a summary of the debate, see de Wet, *The Chapter 7 Powers of the United Nations Security Council* 138, and Manusama, *The United Nations Security Council in the Post-Cold War Era*, 38.

23 Peter Malanczuk, *Akehurst's Modern Introduction to International Law* (Routledge, 1997) 426.

24 Christian J. Tams, 'The Use of Force against Terrorists' (2009) 20 *European Journal of International Law*, 359, 376.

exists, especially considering the nature of the Security Council, but no legal challenge has so far forced the Security Council to shy away from such determination.

In fact, the binding nature of Security Council's decisions is, in theory, 'accepted in advance'[25] because of Article 25 of the Charter that states that 'the Members of the United Nations agree to accept and carry out the decisions of the Security Council in accordance with the present Charter.' The exact meaning of this phrase, however, has raised a controversy over limits to the Security Council's decision since it is able to adopt any measure it considers necessary. Yet, the words 'in accordance with the present Charter' indicate that there are, in fact, some limits to the Security Council's power; hence many have considered that there is an inherent restriction in the Article.[26] Article 24(2) reads that 'in discharging these duties the Security Council shall act in accordance with the Purposes and Principles of the United Nations' which further supports that there are inherent limits to the power of the Security Council. At the same time, the absence of a definition of what these purposes and principles are has led to a number of discussions over these limits.[27] In the context of counterterrorism, the existence of limits is all the more important, because of the impact that counterterrorism measures can have on human rights. Part 3 examines how some limits have been imposed on the Security Council's power through a human rights discourse and how this has challenged the sovereignty of States.

The power to adopt binding measures is further reinforced by the Charter itself that gives express primacy to the Security Council's binding measures over other international measures in cases of conflict. The strongest tool in the Security Council's action is Article 103 of the UN Charter that states that:

25 W. Michael Reisman, 'The Constitutional Crisis in the United Nations' (1993) 87 *American Journal of International Law*, 83, 88.

26 See, among others, Erika de Wet, *The Chapter 7 Powers of the United Nations Security Council* (Hart Publishing, 2004); Bianchi, 'Assessing the Effectiveness of the UN Security Council's Anti-terrorism Measures: The Quest for Legitimacy and Cohesion'; and Kenneth Manusama, *The United Nations Security Council in the Post-Cold War Era* (Martinus Nijhoff Publishers, 2006).

27 Erika De Wet, *The Chapter 7 Powers of the United Nations Security Council* (Hart Publishing, 2004); Eric Rosand, 'Resolution 1373 and the CTC: The Security Council's Capacity-building' in *International Cooperation in Counter-Terrorism. The UN and Regional Organisations in the Fight Against Terrorism* (Ashgate Publishing, Ltd., 2006) and Michael Wood, 'The UN Security Council and International Law', Lauterparcht Lecture, 7 November 2006.

> In the event of a conflict between the obligations of the Members of the United Nations under the present Charter and their obligations under any other international agreement, their obligations under the present Charter shall prevail.

Part 3 will focus on the application of this article to counterterrorism measures. Since other actors have adopted measures to deal with terrorism, there exist conflicts between the various norms.

2.2 *Targeted Sanctions – From Punitive Measures to Concerted Framework*

Sanctions are the main non-military tool included in Chapter 7 of the UN Charter and although they are not mentioned by name, if adopted in the context of a threat to international peace and security, they are binding on all Member States of the organisation. The range of sanctions applicable in this context includes 'complete or partial interruption of economic relations and of rail, sea, air, postal, telegraphic, radio, and other means of communication, and the severance of diplomatic relations.'[28] Additionally, they can take the form of financial sanctions or arms embargoes, which has been the main form for counterterrorism.

The number of sanctions regimes greatly increased in the 1990s[29] as did the concerns about the negative consequences they could have on the civilian population:

> Broad economic sanctions strike indiscriminately and fail to make a distinction between those responsible for the threat to peace and innocent civilians and are bound to violate basic principles of procedural fairness.[30]

As a result, a number of initiatives emerged that were aimed at improving the efficiency of sanctions and reducing their negative impact on civilian populations.[31] These initiatives gave rise to the category of 'smart sanctions' or

28 UN Charter, Article 41.

29 Since the 1990s, more than twenty different sanctions regimes have been adopted. All were targeted sanctions, except for Yugoslavia in 1991 and Haiti in 1993: SC Resolution 724 (1991) and SC Resolution 841 (1993). See Guglielmo Verdirame, *The UN and Human Rights: Who Guards the Guardians?* (Cambridge University Press, 2011) 302.

30 de Wet, *The Chapter 7 Powers of the United Nations Security Council*, 223.

31 Smart sanctions, information and documents available at http://www.seco.admin.ch/themen/00513/00620/00639/index.html?lang=en; http://pcr.uu.se/research/smartsanctions/

'targeted sanctions', which can 'involve the freezing of assets and blocking the financial transactions of political elites or entities whose behaviour triggered sanctions in the first place.'[32] For instance, in 1998, the Security Council adopted travel and financial restrictions against the National Union for the Total Independence of Angola (UNITA) instead of targeting the State more generally.[33] As well, in 2004, Resolution 1556, adopted against the Sudan, imposed an arms embargo that targeted the Janjaweed militias[34] and, in the same year, Resolution 1572 imposed travel bans on specific individuals in Ivory Coast.[35]

In many cases, the use of sanctions by the Security Council corresponded to punishment for wrongdoing in international law and the changes that were made to the sanctions system were welcomed. But the evolving nature of sanctions and their increasing use for counterterrorism raises deeper questions of governance by the Security Council. Chapters 2 and 4 discuss the Security Council's increasing use of targeted sanctions as a policy tool and the issues of legality and legitimacy that result from their use.

From the onset, the UN Security Council had a number of possible tools that it used to address security threats. While it did not do so in a concentrated manner until the 1990s, it has since applied these powers to an increasing number of situations including terrorism. The involvement of the Security Council in core prerogatives of the States clearly has more potential to impact their sovereignty than the UN treaties ever did. However, the implementation rates and trends of Security Council measures must be analysed, as its decisions reflect governmental concerns and might, therefore, not challenge States' sovereignty.

---

the_stockholm_process/ and http://www.watsoninstitute.org/tfs/CD/ISD_Summary_of_Bonn_Berlin_Process.pdf (all last accessed 15.12.2015).

32 Security Council Press Release SC/7187, 25 October 2001, available at http://www.un.org/press/en/2001/SC7187.doc.htm (last accessed 15.12.2015).

33 UNSC Resolution 1173 (1998).

34 UNSC Resolution 1556 (2004) §7.

35 UNSC Resolution 1572 (2004) §9 and 11.

CHAPTER 2

Terrorism Obligations from the Security Council

1 The Definition of Terrorism as a 'Threat to International Peace and Security' – Allocation of Authority

The premise for the Security Council's concerted action against terrorism was the 1998 *Lockerbie* case, although the increasing use of sanctions facilitated this move. In response to the bombing of Pan Am Flight 103 over Lockerbie, Scotland on 21 December 1988 that mainly claimed American and British victims, the Security Council adopted Resolution 731 (under Chapter 6) that required Libya to comply with an extradition request of the main suspects by the US and the UK.[1] However, Libya refused to comply and took the matter to the ICJ, claiming that it had a right to prosecute the suspects within its own State's jurisdiction under Article 7 of the Montreal Convention.[2] Libya also claimed that it did not have to comply with the Security Council's Resolution because it had been adopted under Chapter 6 and was, therefore, not binding on Member States.[3] During the course of the ICJ's proceedings however, the Security Council adopted Resolution 748 that referred to Article 39 of the UN Charter and declared that the situation had become a threat to international peace and security.[4] In its decision regarding provisional measures, the ICJ then declared that the adoption of Resolution 748, 'despite being taken three days after the close of the [provisional measures oral] hearing, was to override the obligation of the Montreal Convention by virtue of Article 103 of the Charter.'[5]

---

1 Resolution 731 (1992) of 21 January 1992, §2.

2 Formerly known as the Convention for the Unification of Certain Rules for International Carriage by Air and adopted in 1999, the Montreal Convention contains the core international provisions applying to the international carriage of passengers, baggage, and cargo. Article 7 contains the principle known as '*aut dedere, aut judicare*', the obligation to extradite or prosecute a suspect.

3 On 3 March 1992, Libya approached the ICJ, claiming violations of its rights under the Montreal Convention and requesting provisional measures of protection under Article 41 of the ICJ Statute.

4 Preamble, SC Resolution 748 (1992) reads: 'convinced that the suppression of acts of international terrorism, including those in which States are directly or indirectly involved, is essential for the maintenance of international peace and security.'

5 ICJ, *Question of Interpretation and Application of the 1971 Montreal Convention arising from the Aerial Incident at Lockerbie*, Order-Request for the Indication of Provisional Measures (*Libyan Arab Jamahiriya v United Kingdom*) 14 April 1992, para. 39. It must be noted here, that in its

 | DOI 10.1163/9789004299580_004

Resolution 748 was seen as problematic because it blurred the distinction between Chapter 6 and 7 resolutions and, in effect, retroactively defined a situation as a threat to peace. Yet, this exercise can also been qualified as 'a rather flexible and unconventional interpretation of Article 39 of the Charter'[6] and it reflects the readiness of the Security Council to use its power under Chapter 7 of the UN Charter to address terrorism issues.

Whichever way this case is considered, it constitutes the first manifestation of terrorism acts defined as a threat to international peace and security thereby bringing the phenomenon within the mandate of the Security Council and allowing it to adopt binding decisions. In this context, the Security Council started using sanctions to put pressure on a State to act against terrorism in its territory.[7] For instance, sanctions were adopted against Libya[8] and Sudan.[9] The measures covered by these sanctions included an asset freeze, a travel ban and an arms embargo. Then, Resolution 1267, adopted in 1999, created targeted sanctions against the Taliban, and subsequently in 2000, against Al-Qaida. This resolution called on the Taliban to 'turn over' Osama bin Laden[10] and created a list of groups and individuals whose assets should be frozen by Member States.[11] Resolution 1267 is still used as the basis for one of the two major counterterrorism sanctions group of the Security Council and has been gradually expanded to include groups that are considered affiliated with Al-Qaida.[12] Under the new Resolution 2253 (2015),[13] the sanctions still include asset freezing,

---

order on provisional measures, the Court repeatedly indicated that this did not prejudge questions of law and facts to be decided in further proceedings, although the question of conflict was never solved per se following a compromise between the UK, the US and Libya.

6 David Schweigman, *The Authority of the Security Council Under Chapter 7 of the Charter: Legal Limits and the Role of the ICJ* (Kluwer Law International, 2001) 258.

7 John P. Grant, 'Beyond the Montreal Convention,' (2004) 36 *Case Western Reserve Journal of International Law*, 2–3, 453.

8 UN Security Council Resolution 748 (1992) adopted after the Lockerbie incident.

9 UN Security Council Resolutions 1054 and 1070 (1996) adopted because of Sudan's involvement in the attempted assassination of Egyptian President Hosni Mubarak.

10 UN Security Council Resolution 1267, 15 October 1999, §2.

11 Ibid., §4(b). Of note here is that in 2011, the Security Council divided the 1267 sanctions regime into two separate regimes, one targeting the Taliban (the 1988 sanctions regime) and the other targeting Al-Qaida (known as the 1989 Al-Qaeda sanctions regime). However, for the purposes of this book, reference will be made to the 1267 regime for simplicity.

12 See for instance Resolution 2178 (2014), which incorporates ISIS within the 1267 regime and Resolution 2253 which further consolidates the regimes.

13 'Unanimously Adopting Resolution 2253 (2015), Security Council Expands Sanctions Framework to Include Islamic State in Iraq and Levant', 7587th Meeting, Press Release

travel bans and arms embargoes, but their application is reinforced by a number of monitoring and enforcement measures detailed in Chapter 3.

The adoption of sanctions against terrorism paved the way for the Security Council to use its mandate more generally. This was especially true once the Security Council declared terrorism to be a threat to international peace and security. Terrorist sanctions are still a considerable part of the Security Council's counterterrorism effort, but they are now accompanied by a wider binding legal framework for domestic legislation.

2 Resolutions 1373 and 2178 – A Binding Global Framework

Immediately after September 11, 2001, the Security Council adopted Resolution 1368 that dealt with the use of force against counterterrorism. Yet, the resolution created an 'ambiguous and contradictory'[14] framework because, although its Preamble reaffirmed States' right to self-defence, the text of the resolution defined terrorism as a threat to peace and security, not as an 'armed attack' according to Article 51. In practice, the Security Council has never explicitly authorized military action against terrorism.[15] Even the latest resolution adopted after the November 2015 attacks in Paris does not explicitly authorize military force against terrorist groups,[16] though Starski argues that Resolution 2249 does amount to 'another step towards a reconfiguration of the UN collective security system.'[17] The ongoing debate over the legality of the use of force against terrorism is a complex issue and beyond the scope of this book.[18]

SC/12168, containing the full text of the resolution, available at http://www.un.org/press/en/2015/sc12168.doc.htm (last accessed 18.12.2015).

14 Antonio Cassese, 'Terrorism is Also Disrupting Some Crucial Legal Categories of International Law', (2001), 996.

15 Geoffrey S. Corn and others, *The War on Terror and the Laws of War: A Military Perspective* (Oxford University Press, 2015) 23.

16 Dapo Akande and Marko Milanovic, The Constructive Ambiguity of the Security Council's ISIS Resolution, EJIL:Talk, 21 November 2015, available *at* www.ejiltalk.org/the-constructive-ambiguity-of-the-security-councils-isis-resolution/ (last accessed 03.12.2015).

17 Paulina Starski, '"Legitimized Self-Defense" – Quo Vadis Security Coucil' EJIL Talk, 10 December 2015, available at http://www.ejiltalk.org/legitimized-self-defense-quo-vadis-security-council/ (last accessed 15.12.2015).

18 Jonathan I. Charney, 'The Use of Force against Terrorism and International Law' (2001) 95 *The American Journal of International Law*, 835; David Abramowitz, 'President, the Congress, and Use of Force: Legal and Political Considerations in Authorizing Use of

Days after September 11, 2001, the Security Council also unanimously adopted Resolution 1373, which imposes a number of binding obligations on States to deal with terrorism *per se*, as opposed to adopting punishing measures addressing the particular incident. Although the list of obligations contained in the text is lengthy, it is worth including it in its entirety in order to grasp the scope of the Security Council's action that can be contrasted with its previous measures:

> The Security Council, *Acting under Chapter 7* of the Charter of the United Nations,
>
> 1. Decides that all States shall:
>   (a) Prevent and suppress the financing of terrorist acts;
>   (b) Criminalize the wilful provision or collection, by any means, directly or indirectly, of funds by their nationals or in their territories with the intention that the funds should be used, or in the knowledge that they are to be used, in order to carry out terrorist acts;
>   (c) Freeze without delay funds and other financial assets or economic resources of persons who commit, or attempt to commit, terrorist acts or participate in or facilitate the commission of terrorist acts; of entities owned or controlled directly or indirectly by such persons; and of persons and entities acting on behalf of, or at the direction of such persons and entities, including funds derived or generated from property owned or controlled directly or indirectly by such persons and associated persons and entities;
>   (d) Prohibit their nationals or any persons and entities within their territories from making any funds, financial assets or economic resources or financial or other related services available, directly or indirectly, for the benefit of persons who commit or attempt to commit or facilitate or participate in the commission of terrorist acts, of entities owned or controlled,

---

Force against International Terrorism', (2002) 43 *Harvard International Law Journal*, 71; Michael Byers, 'Terrorism, the Use of Force and International Law after 11 September' (2002) 16 *International Relations*, 155–170; Christopher Greenwood, 'International Law and the Pre-emptive Use of Force: Afghanistan, Al-Qaida, and Iraq', (2003) 4 *San Diego International Law Journal*, 7; and Christine D. Gray, *International Law and the Use of Force* (Oxford University Press, 2008).

directly or indirectly, by such persons and of persons and entities acting on behalf of or at the direction of such persons;

2. Decides also that all States shall:
   (a) Refrain from providing any form of support, active or passive, to entities or persons involved in terrorist acts, including by suppressing recruitment of Members of terrorist groups and eliminating the supply of weapons to terrorists;
   (b) Take the necessary steps to prevent the commission of terrorist acts, including by provision of early warning to other States by exchange of information;
   (c) Deny safe haven to those who finance, plan, support, or commit terrorist acts, or provide safe havens;
   (d) Prevent those who finance, plan, facilitate or commit terrorist acts from using their respective territories for those purposes against other States or their citizens;
   (e) Ensure that any person who participates in the financing, planning, preparation or perpetration of terrorist acts or in supporting terrorist acts is brought to justice and ensure that, in addition to any other measures against them, such terrorist acts are established as serious criminal offences in domestic laws and regulations and that the punishment duly reflects the seriousness of such terrorist acts;
   (f) Afford one another the greatest measure of assistance in connection with criminal investigations or criminal proceedings relating to the financing or support of terrorist acts, including assistance in obtaining evidence in their possession necessary for the proceedings;
   (g) Prevent the movement of terrorists or terrorist groups by effective border controls and controls on issuance of identity papers and travel documents, and through measures for preventing counterfeiting, forgery or fraudulent use of identity papers and travel documents;

3. Calls upon all States to:
   (a) Find ways of intensifying and accelerating the exchange of operational information, especially regarding actions or movements of terrorist persons or networks; forged or falsified travel documents; traffic in arms, explosives or sensitive materials; use of communications technologies by terrorist groups; and the threat posed by the possession of weapons of mass destruction by terrorist groups;

(b) Exchange information in accordance with international and domestic law and cooperate on administrative and judicial matters to prevent the commission of terrorist acts;
(c) Cooperate, particularly through bilateral and multilateral arrangements and agreements, to prevent and suppress terrorist attacks and take action against perpetrators of such acts;
(d) Become parties as soon as possible to the relevant international conventions and protocols relating to terrorism, including the International Convention for the Suppression of the Financing of Terrorism of 9 December 1999;
(e) Increase cooperation and fully implement the relevant international conventions and protocols relating to terrorism and Security Council resolutions 1269 (1999) and 1368 (2001);
(f) Take appropriate measures in conformity with the relevant provisions of national and international law, including international standards of human rights, before granting refugee status, for the purpose of ensuring that the asylum seeker has not planned, facilitated or participated in the commission of terrorist acts;
(g) Ensure, in conformity with international law, that refugee status is not abused by the perpetrators, organizers or facilitators of terrorist acts, and that claims of political motivation are not recognized as grounds for refusing requests for the extradition of alleged terrorists.

This list of obligations is far from the political condemnation of terrorist acts lacking legal weight that can be found in many Security Council or General Assembly resolutions and it is much broader than the specific measures adopted by the Security Council that create targeted measures against individuals or groups. In other words, the measures adopted under Resolution 1373 are not simply punitive measures in response to a specific act; rather, they constitute an attempt at regulating terrorism at the international level. Moreover, and unlike international conventions, the obligations contained in Resolution 1373 do not necessitate the slow process of ratification and are automatically applicable in all Member States because they are taken under Chapter 7. Of note, however, because Resolution 1373 still leaves the contentious issue of a definition of terrorism to the Member States by completely avoiding the subject, its impact on sovereignty is limited.

There is merit in looking more closely at the obligations contained in Resolution 1373 in order to appreciate its scope. The first set of obligations concerns the financing of terrorism and the resolution creates a legal framework on the topic by calling for the need to freeze assets of terrorists,[19] a measure that has traditionally been seen in the use of sanctions for specific people. In Resolution 1373, the Security Council goes a step further by requesting that States criminalise terrorism financing: for the first time, it is not simply a targeted action against one individual or group, but, rather, each and every Member State must adopt specific and adequate legislation to prevent and punish any financial support to terrorism by making it a crime.[20]

The second set of obligations in the resolution deals with terrorist acts in more general terms and demands that States legislate to prevent the commission of such acts by adopting a variety of measures including, but not limited to, the suppression of recruitment, the exchange of information with other States, and the bringing of suspects to justice.[21] Although many States have, in the past, traditionally used these measures in the context of the national treatment of terrorism, as a result of Resolution 1373, all 193 States are now legally bound by international law to adopt these measures if they do not already exist in their jurisdiction.

Finally, in the last set of obligations, the Security Council encourages Member States to ratify and enforce existing international instruments against terrorism.[22] The impact that this has had on the implementation rate of international treaties will be detailed in the next section.

Resolution 1373 is ground breaking in many ways and would have constituted an exception if the Security Council had not followed this trend in its later resolutions.[23] For example, Resolution 1540 (2004) on nuclear weapons set out a new framework on actions that States are required to take with respect to weapons of massive destruction (WMD). This Resolution not only requires that States refrain from supporting non-State actors from developing and manufacturing WMD,[24] but also requires them to 'adopt and enforce effective laws'[25] that prohibit non-State actors from these actions, thereby forcing States to legislate on the matter.

Additionally, thirteen years after the attacks of September 11, 2001, the Security Council adopted another resolution with a wide scope, Resolution

19 UN SC Resolution 1373 §1(c).

20 Ibid., §1(b).

21 UN SC Resolution 1373, §2(b).

22 Ibid., §3(d) and (e).

23 In practice, since Resolution 1373 was adopted, more than thirty resolutions have been adopted by the Security Council in the fight against terrorism: Security Council Resolutions, in UN Action to counter terrorism, list available at http://www.un.org/en/terrorism/sc-res.shtml (last accessed 07.12.2015).

24 UN SC Resolution 1540 (2004) §1.

25 Ibid., §2.

2178, requiring that Member States adopt new legislation or update their national measures in order to address matters related to terrorism. Resolution 2178, adopted 24 September 2014, directly addresses the growing crisis of the Foreign Terrorist Fighter (FTF), which has taken a new significance with the rise of the Islamic State of Iraq and the Levant[26] and its ability to attract FTFs. The following summary of the obligations contained in Resolution 2178 shows, once again, the breadth of the Security Council's action. Adopted under Chapter 7 of the UN Charter, this resolution:

> 1. Reaffirms that Member States must comply with their human rights obligations when fighting terrorism and notes that a failure to do so contributes to radicalization.
> 2. Defines the term Foreign Terrorist Fighter as 'individuals who travel to a State other than their States of residence or nationality for the purpose of the perpetration, planning, or preparation of, or participation in, terrorist acts or the providing or receiving of terrorist training, including in connection with armed conflict.' …
> 6. Demands FTFs disarm and cease all terrorist acts and participation in armed conflict.
> 7. Calls upon countries to require their airlines to provide advance passenger information to detect the travel of UN-listed terrorists.
> Obligations
> 8. Requires countries to prevent and suppress recruiting, organizing, transporting, and equipping of FTFs, and the financing of FTF travel and activities.
> 9. Requires countries to have laws that permit the prosecution of:
> Their nationals and others departing their territories who travel or attempt to travel for terrorism purposes;
> The wilful provision or collection of funds by their nationals or in their territories with the intent or knowledge that they will be used to finance travel of FTFs;
> The wilful organization or facilitation by their nationals or in their territories of such travel.
> 10. Requires countries to prevent the entry or transit of individuals believed to be traveling for terrorism-related purposes.
> International Cooperation

26 The United States administration and the UN use the ISIL acronym, but the group is also known as the Islamic State of Iraq and Syria (ISIS), or Daiish for Al-Dawla Al-Islamiya fi al-Iraq wa al-Sham (also spelled Daesh in Europe).

> 11. Calls upon countries to improve international, regional, and subregional cooperation to prevent FTF travel, including through increased information-sharing…
>
> UN Engagement
>
> 17. Directs UN counter-terrorism bodies to focus attention on the FTF threat, enabling the international community to assess compliance with this resolution and to target assistance to those countries that need help enforcing its provisions.[27]

Resolution 2178 contains a number of varied obligations for States, which have to adopt or update their national measures not only in areas of criminal law, but also in administrative and civil law, in laws of armed conflict, and in matters that are beyond the strictly legal field, such as deradicalisation. Finally, as detailed in Chapter 4, the resolution includes, within operative paragraphs, the requirement of States to abide by their international human rights obligations.

The resolution was immediately compared to Resolution 1373 because of its broad scope and the fact that the Security Council is again requiring Member States to criminalise conduct relating to terrorism.[28] Resolution 2178 does fall within the legal framework of Resolution 1373, as it both affirms the authority of the Security Council to address a particular crisis in a widespread way and it contains a number of general obligations addressed to Member States in order to implement this authority. However, interestingly, it also refers to Resolution 1267 and the obligations to freeze assets of Al-Qaida suspects. In effect, Resolution 2178 compiles a number of existing UN provisions and creates new obligations on States, some of which will, again, affect individuals directly.[29]

---

27 Bureau of Public Affairs Department Of State. The Office of Electronic Information, 'FACT SHEET: UN Security Council Resolution 2178 on Foreign Terrorist Fighters' (24 September 2014), available at http://www.state.gov/j/ct/rls/other/un/ (last accessed 15.12.2015).

28 Marko Milanovic, 'UN Security Council Adopts Resolution 2178 on Foreign Terrorist Fighters' EJIL Talk, 24 September 2015, available at http://www.ejiltalk.org/un-security-council-adopts-resolution-2178-on-foreign-terrorist-fighters/ (last accessed 15.12.2015).

29 A further compilation effort was conducted through the adoption of Resolution 2253 (2015), which addresses the financing of ISIS. Its ninety-nine paragraphs and annexes add ISIS to the regime of Resolution 1267 and as examined throughout this book, reinforce the sanction regime in a number of ways. It also further ties in the various regimes on counterterrorism by clarifying the scope of Resolution 1373, reaffirming many of the Resolution 2178 measures and generally continuing the merging efforts of Resolution 2178, see 'Unanimously Adopting Resolution 2253 (2015), Security Council Expands Sanctions Framework to Include Islamic State in Iraq and Levant', 7587th Meeting, Press Release

With that, Resolution 2178 goes at least one step further than Resolution 1373, raising renewed questions regarding the role of the Security Council in the collective protection of security and prompting questions about the protection of human rights in international counterterrorism.

Against this backdrop, it is necessary to note that the sheer number and scope of obligations do not guarantee their success. Indeed, '[the obligations'] efficacy will greatly depend on the extent to which States incorporate them properly into their domestic legal orders and subsequently enforce them by means of their internal law enforcement machinery.'[30] This is exacerbated by the lack of a definition of terrorism and, as a result, the implementation of these measures will depend on each State.

Therefore, it is necessary to conduct an assessment of the concrete implementation of the terrorism obligations imposed on States, because complete disregard by Member States could show an unwillingness to transfer too many sovereign powers to the UN organisation. The next chapter focuses on the enforcement of the UN measures that were detailed in this section.

SC/12168, containing the full text of the resolution, available at http://www.un.org/press/en/2015/sc12168.doc.htm (last accessed 18.12.2015).

30 Bianchi, 'Assessing the Effectiveness of the UN Security Council's Anti-terrorism Measures: The Quest for Legitimacy and Cohesion', 882.

CHAPTER 3

Compliance and Enforcement

The success of international measures depends on their actual implementation in the national order. In the same way, the success of treaties is inherently limited by the need for their ratification and the low ratification rates that plagued counterterrorism treaties are noteworthy. To remedy this, the Security Council often referred to the terrorism conventions in its resolutions, and called on States to ratify or implement the existing conventions.[1] This seems to have produced results, as, according to the Short Ratification Status Report prepared by the United Nations Office on Drugs and Crime's Terrorism Prevention Branch, of 31 July 2007, there were eighty States party to the then twelve conventions.[2] By April 2013, however, 146 States were party to these twelve conventions and 182 were party to the 1999 Convention on the Financing of Terrorism. As well, between June and December 2012, six Member States ratified the 2005 International Convention for the Suppression of Acts of Nuclear Terrorism and some twenty States were party to all UN conventions now existing.[3] Yet, ratification alone is not sufficient. In the discussions over the adoption of Resolution 2253, the report of the Financial Task Force stated that it had

> reviewed the implementation of counter-terrorist financing measures in 196 jurisdictions...and almost all had criminalized such financing and could apply targeted financial sanctions. In the last two months alone, half of those where serious problems had been found had tabled urgent laws to address them. Yet, only 33 jurisdictions had secured convictions for terrorist financing, and most jurisdictions implemented United Nations asset freezes too slowly, with delays of between two days and one month. All must now focus urgently on implementation of the standards.[4]

1 For instance, Security Council Resolution 1269 (1999) 'calls on States...to implement' the conventions they are party to and adopt the ones that are pending.

2 Rosand, Milar, and Ipe, 'The UN Security Council's Counterterrorism Program: What Lies Ahead?' (International Peace Institute, Policy Paper October 2007) 8.

3 Figures taken from the United Nations Office for Drugs and Crime website's international legislation database. Document available at https://www.unodc.org/tldb/universal_instruments_NEW.html (last accessed 15.12.2015).

4 'Unanimously Adopting Resolution 2253 (2015), Security Council Expands Sanctions Framework to Include Islamic State in Iraq and Levant', 7587th Meeting, Press Release

 | DOI 10.1163/9789004299580_005

Yet, it is interesting to note that the binding measures adopted by the Security Council do not need ratification and or implementation. In theory, once adopted, the Chapter 7 measures are immediately applicable. States could otherwise be held responsible if they do not adopt measures, although, in practice, there is no example of punishment for non-implementation.

At the same time, the binding nature of these measures does not necessarily mean their success or strict application. Here, therefore, it is worth looking empirically at the implementation of Security Council measures and the kind of sovereignty issues they raise. The implementation of UN measures has traditionally lacked effect because of the lack of enforcement mechanisms, but this was partially remedied by the creation of implementation committees. This chapter examines implementation committees, in particular the UN's Counter-Terrorism Committee (CTC), and their impact on national legislation and policies through activities and reports.

1 Pre-September 11, 2001

As stated above, the issue of compliance is inherently present in sanctions because they all require the support of Member States for their success. In the case of sanctions against Libya following the *Lockerbie* case, these were initially well respected because the ICJ itself had declared the Resolution 748 binding on all States.[5] However, over the years, the sanctions became less and less respected by States willing to show their disagreement with the Security Council generally or, in particular, with the political situation surrounding the regime.[6] The sanctions were eventually suspended on 5 April 1999 when those accused in the *Lockerbie* case arrived in Camp Zeit for their trial and were fully lifted in 2003 after the trial ended.

SC/12168, containing the full text of the resolution, available at http://www.un.org/press/en/2015/sc12168.doc.htm (last accessed 18.12.2015).

5 *Questions of Interpretation and Application of the 1971 Montreal Convention Arising from the Aerial Incident at Lockerbie* (*Libyan Arab Jamahiriya v United States*) (Provisional Measures) [1992] ICJ Rep 3, 15.

6 In 1997, an Islamic Conference had called for an easing of the sanctions and several Arab States had authorised flights to Libya. The first European violations occurred in April 1998 when two Italian planes arrived in Tripoli. President Nelson Mandela himself decided to show his solidarity by flying to Libya in return for Libya's solidarity during the apartheid. See 'Case studies in Sanctions and Terrorism', Peterson Institute of International Economics, available at http://www.piie.com/research/topics/sanctions/libya.cfm (last accessed 15.12.2015).

In order to improve the success of sanctions and make them less controversial, Resolution 1267 established, for the first time, a committee charged with monitoring their application, which is composed of the fifteen members of the Security Council.[7] Originally known as the 1267 Sanctions Committee and later the Al-Qaida Sanctions Committee, after the adoption of Resolution 2253 (2015), it became the '1267/1989/2253 ISIL (Da'esh) and Al-Qaida Sanctions Committee.'

At the request of the Security Council, the Secretary-General also appointed, in 2004, an Analytical Support and Sanctions Monitoring Team to assist the Committee,[8] comprised of independent experts in counterterrorism and related legal issues, such as arms embargoes, travel bans, and terrorism financing.[9] The Analytical Support and Sanctions Monitoring Team's mandate, created as a temporary fixture, has regularly been extended,[10] showing the importance of implementation mechanisms for the success of counterterrorism measures. It is tasked with producing reports on the implementation of the sanctions by States[11] and cooperating with other monitoring and delisting processes.[12]

More significantly, the 1267/1989/2253 ISIL (Da'esh) and Al-Qaida Sanctions Committee keeps the 'Consolidated List' of individuals associated with Al-Qaida, the Taliban and other terrorist groups against whom sanctions are adopted. This list, originally created in 1999 is still in place today, although the listing criteria have been regularly extended, including significantly by Resolution 2253.[13] The list is accessible to the public on the website of the Committee[14] and States have to implement it in their national legal order, as reiterated by Resolutions 2178 and 2253. The implementation is monitored by the Committee, which assists States in their enforcement and requests States' implementation reports under Resolution 1455 (2003). The Committee regularly publishes reports on implementation of Resolution 1267.[15] It is now complemented by the Ombudsperson office, which deals with delisting requests

7 UN Security Council Resolution 1267, §6.

8 Security Council Resolution 1526 (2004) §7.

9 Ibid., Paragraph 4(a).

10 Resolution 2253 (2015) §89 extends its mandate for twenty-four months after the end of its current term (which finishes December 2017).

11 Resolution 2253, Annex I, §a.

12 Ibid., §b–f.

13 Resolution 2253, §3–10.

14 See https://www.un.org/sc/suborg/en/sanctions/1267/aq_sanctions_list (last accessed 15.12.2015).

15 Reports are available on the Committee's website, at https://www.un.org/sc/suborg/en/sanctions/1267/implementation-reports (last accessed 15.12.2015).

from the regime. A detailed analysis of this office and the impact it has had on international counterterrorism is included in Part 3 of this book.

A 2007 symposium report on the implementation of sanctions summarised the success of sanctions, which have both a symbolic and practical impact, as well as a 'sobering effect on targets.'[16] However, the variety of sanction regimes[17] shows that some of them were more effective and had better results than others. In particular, a comparative study of these various regimes shows that targeted sanctions and the creation of sanctions committees have improved their enforcement.[18] Building on this finding, the specific committees created for each sanctions regime were subsequently complemented by a permanent body for the specific area of terrorism that reflects the generalisation of the Security Council's action against terrorism and confirms the evolution from punishing sanctions to global counterterrorism governance.

2 The Counter-Terrorism Committee

The Counter-Terrorism Committee (CTC),[19] established by Resolution 1373, is an implementation tool that differs slightly from the previous sanctions committees. While composed of the fifteen Security Council members, as are other sanction committees, the CTC is tasked with monitoring the implementation of a series of measures that are derived from Resolution 1373 by establishing *permanent* contact with Member States. It is, therefore, a key element for the relationship between the international organisation and its Member States and much more of a two-way body than it would be if it was purely a compliance

16 Annex to the letter dated 12 December 2007 from the Permanent Representative of Greece to the United Nations addressed to the President of the Security Council: Enhancing the Implementation of United Nations Security Council Sanctions – A Symposium, 30 April 2007, United Nations, New York, S/2007/734, available at http://www.securitycouncilreport.org/atf/cf/%7B65BFCF9B-6D27-4E9C-8CD3-CF6E4FF96FF9%7D/S_2007_734.pdf (last accessed 15.12.2015).

17 According to Jeremy Matam Farrall, by 2007 there had been twenty-five regimes, in *United Nations Sanctions and the Rule of Law* (Cambridge University Press, 2007), i. As well, the current 'Sanctions Committees' portal lists sixteen regimes. See http://www.un.org/sc/committees/ (see first drop-tab 'sanctions' (last accessed 15.12.2015)).

18 David Cortright and George A. Lopez, *Sanctions and the Search for Security: Challenges to the UN Action* (Lynne Rienner, 2002).

19 The UN uses 'Counter-Terrorism' for its activities, but this book uses counterterrorism, except for direct quotes.

police. In this way, the CTC contributes to creating a counterterrorism framework within the UN.

In practice, the CTC's first action was to analyse the reports that were requested from Member States by Resolution 1373, detailing the situation of counterterrorism in their State and their implementation of Resolution 1373.[20] Subsequently, the CTC produced letters to Member States containing its views on their reports. This led to a second round of reports, consisting of the responses to these letters by the Member States. A third round of reports further increased the cooperation between the CTC and the Member States by allowing information and comments to circulate. Besides Member States, other entities, including the Organisation for Security and Co-Operation in Europe and the EU, have also submitted reports to the CTC. These reports, available on the CTC's website, show the evolution of domestic measures against terrorism,[21] as well as the strong dialogue established between the CTC and States.

At the beginning of its mandate, the work capacity of the CTC was limited, due to both a lack of expertise[22] and the slow building of the technical data representing the implementation rates. Therefore, in 2004, in order to enhance the CTC's role, the Security Council created the Counter-Terrorism Committee Executive Directorate (CTED),[23] with half of its staff being legal and human rights experts. The benefits of the CTC and the CTED's actions are recognisable, and as a result, the CTED's mandate, originally set to last until 31 December 2007, was extended a number of times and more recently, until the end of 2017.[24] The adoption of Resolution 2178 further mandates the CTC to assess the implementation of measures contained in the new resolution and to give States technical assistance and update the Security Council on their efforts.[25]

In addition to the reports further discussed in Section 3.1, an analytical tool, known as the preliminary implementation assessment (PIA), was created. The PIA is a document that was prepared by the CTC that summarises the counterterrorism situation of a State. The PIA is meant to be constantly updated by the

---

20 UN SC Resolution 1373(2001) §6.

21 See 'Other submissions' available at http://www.un.org/en/sc/ctc/resources/1373.html (last accessed 15.12.2015).

22 The fifteen members of the Committees are the fifteen members of the Security Council and are therefore government representatives with no specific expertise on counterterrorism *a priori*.

23 UN SC Resolution 1535 (2004) §4.

24 UN SC Resolution 2129 (2013) §2.

25 UN SC Resolution 2178 (2014) §24–26.

Member States themselves,[26] and is described as a 'living document to be shared with the relevant States in order to give it a sense of where it stands vis-à-vis the implementation of Resolution 1373 and 1624.'[27] Since November 2009 and according to the CTC website, it has adopted PIAs for all Member States.[28] However, none of the PIAs has been made public.[29]

Despite the fact that the creation of new bodies and tools seems to show the success of the CTC, however, a critical analysis of its concrete results must be conducted in order to assess whether it had a significant impact on the action of Member States in counterterrorism, or whether it is merely another forum for their political agenda.

3 Results and Analysis

Contrary to sanctions committees, the CTC is not tasked with creating and maintaining lists of terrorist organisations or individuals, but rather, it acts as a body of legal experts on terrorism and encourages cooperation and sharing of best practice. The CTC is composed of the Members of the Security Council, or government officials, yet reviews of the CTC's work are conducted by the Security Council itself, and this has, understandably, 'given rise to wariness and suspicion among some non-Members.'[30] In other words, since resolutions on terrorism are both adopted and reviewed by the same individuals, the independence of the reviews is inherently limited. Also, the absence of PIAs and new reports on the CTC's website has contributed to criticism about

26 Eric Rosand, Alistair Milar, Jason Ipe, and Michael Healey, 'The UN Global Counter-Terrorism Strategy and Regional and Subregional Bodies: Strengthening a Critical Partnership' (Center on Global Counterterrorism Cooperation, October 2008) 20.

27 Rosand, Milar, and Ipe, 'The UN Security Council's Counterterrorism Program: What Lies Ahead?' 20.

28 See Global Survey of the implementation of Security Council resolution 1373 (2001) by Member States, S/2009/620, available at www.un.org/en/sc/ctc/docs/gis-2009-09_en.pdf (last accessed 15.12.2015) and Global survey of the implementation of Security Council resolution 1373 (2001) by Member States, S/2011/463, 1 September 2011, available at http://daccess-dds-ny.un.org/doc/UNDOC/GEN/N11/451/21/PDF/N1145121.pdf?OpenElement (last accessed 15.12.2015).

29 The search for PIAs on the CTC website only returns one result, and while it mentions them, it does not provide access to them. See http://www.un.org/en/sc/ctc/rights.html (last accessed 15.12.2015).

30 'Global Terrorism, Task Forces on Strengthening Multilateral Security Capacity' (International Peace Institute, Blue Papers, No 4, 2009).

the lack of transparency of the CTC's procedure and the lack of referral to the Security Council of 'non-compliance' of Member States.[31]

On the other hand, the multiplication of counterterrorism bodies can explain the desire to combine all of the authority and power in the hands of the Security Council in order to have a more comprehensive framework. This is because the 'multiplication of bodies dealing with terrorism without real coordination [can] lead to diminished efficiency and legitimacy.'[32] In the UN system, there are nearly twenty-three entities that deal with terrorism; some of these bodies are comprised of legal experts, whereas others are staffed by national officials.[33] This complicated situation can be an obstacle to the effectiveness of implementation mechanisms of the Security Council. For instance, the CTC has to work with the two other terrorism committees of the Security Council, namely the 1267 and 1540 Committees. Yet, 'it took nearly two years for the CTC to begin sharing information with the other two counterterrorism-related committees.'[34] Security Council Resolution 2083 (2012) stresses the issue of coordinating numerous bodies and encourages better coordination between these, in particular through the action of the Secretary-General.[35] As well, Resolution 2178, by referring to both the 1373 and the 1267 regimes, partly merges some of the regimes' competences under the roof of the CTC. Additionally, the CTC website now also includes reports from the 1267/1989/2253 ISIL (Da'esh) and Al-Qaida Sanctions Committee on FTFs. Finally, Resolution 2253 further increases this cooperation and coordination between the various regimes.[36] All this has the potential to both simplify the complex architecture

31 Ian Johnstone, 'The UN Security Council, Counterterrorism and Human Rights' in Andrea Bianchi and Alexis Keller (eds.), *Counterterrorism: Democracy's Challenge* (Hart Publishing, 2008), Studies in International Law, 19, 337.

32 Rosand, Milar, and Ipe, 'The UN Security Council's Counterterrorism Program: What Lies Ahead?', 7.

33 There is now a Special Rapporteur on Counterterrorism and Human Rights, with specific expertise and experience in the area. However, the GA and the Security Council are composed of State representatives whose expertise is more general. Moreover, the Counterterrorism Implementation Task Force, created in 2005 by the UN Secretary-General, is composed of thirty-one entities, some of which deal with terrorism, while others are existing agencies that have become involved in counterterrorism more recently, as is the case with the International Atomic Energy Agency or the Office of the High Commissioner for Human Rights (see http://www.un.org/en/terrorism/ctitf/entities.shtml (last accessed 15.12.2015)).

34 'Global Terrorism, Task Forces on Strengthening Multilateral Security Capacity', 14.

35 Security Council Resolution 2083(2012) §56.

36 Resolution 2253, §83–85.

of the UN's counterterrorism effort and confuse the various approaches against terrorism.

The following section examines the reports, both national and from the CTC itself, of domestic counterterrorism measures, in order to assess whether States have indeed worked on enforcing the many measures adopted by the Security Council.

3.1 *State Reports on National Counterterrorism Regimes*

According to the CTC website, 191 Member States responded to the first round of reports, 144 to the second, 124 to the third, and eighty-eight to the fourth.[37] Since this analysis, and until 2006 when a decision was made not to make these reports public, seventy-three States have produced a fifth report and thirteen have filed a sixth one.[38] For some, these figures contradict usual compliance trends, as is written below:

> While international law famously has compliance problems, such problems seemed to disappear here. All 192 U.N. Member States filed at least one report with the Security Council's Counter-Terrorism Committee.[39]

Therefore, it seems that the trend in reporting, in general, has been toward an 'increased level of compliance with the Security Council and raised awareness among most States.'[40] For instance, since 2001, more than forty States have adopted new legislation on terrorism.[41] Some authors confirm this success by stressing the importance States have given to compliance in the specific context of counterterrorism.[42] This, along with the requirement to file reports

37 Results quoted in Edward, C.Luck, *UN Security Council: Practice and Promise* (Routledge, 2006) 106.

38 All reports are available at http://www.un.org/en/sc/ctc/resources/1373.html (last accessed 15.12.2015).

39 Kim Lane Scheppele, 'The International Standardization of National Security Law' (2010) 4 *Journal of National Security Law and Policy*, 437, 442.

40 Karin von Hippel, 'Improving the International Response to the Transnational Terrorist Threat', *Terrorism and the UN: Before and After September 11* (Indiana University Press, 2004) 112.

41 'New National Legislation Countering Terrorism', UNDOC, data available at https://www.unodc.org/tldb/latest_updates.html (last accessed 15.12.2015).

42 David Cortright, 'A Critical Evaluation of the UN Counterterrorism Program: Accomplishments and Challenges' (Transnational Institute, Crime & Globalisation Paper, April 2005).

within ninety days of the adoption of Resolution 1373, has enhanced the tendency of States to adopt faster measures to address terrorism.[43]

Yet, a reporting fatigue was noted after the initial enthusiasm.[44] In a 2007 report, NATO noted the obstacles States face in reporting, including the consensus decision making as well as the lack of financial and human resources, but it welcomed the awareness raised by the UN in its counterterrorism regime.[45] As was stressed in Resolution 2253, there was 'increasing concern about the lack of implementation' of counterterrorism resolutions.[46]

Finally, the *quality* of reporting should also be analysed with caution: prepared by the national governments of each State, these reports represent the States' official policies. As a consequence, 'reports from industrialised States can read as a combination of affirmations of government attention and veiled threats about how the reporting government will respond if others do not make certain cooperative changes in their own procedures.'[47] One major reason for this risk is the lack of a common definition of terrorism. It has therefore been easy for some States to use reports to the CTC to justify some of their criminal law. For instance, it has been stated that the terrorist acts listed by Cuba in its first report to the CTC can be seen as an attempt to 'justify [its] penal legislation against "saboteurs and terrorists."'[48] It is obvious that, in the absence of an agreed-upon definition of terrorism, it is the responsibility of Member States to provide their own definition and thereby adopt the measures they take in response to it. This lack of definition has been called 'the most long-standing and intractable of political challenges facing the CTC.'[49] Yet, and for the purposes of this analysis, it also means that the primary responsibility remains on States, who are sovereign over this issue. Their desire to pool competences and share good practice, and sometimes intelligence, has not led to a complete transfer of security powers to the UN.

---

43 Oren Gross and Fionnuala Ní Aoláin, *Law in Times of Crisis: Emergency Powers in Theory and Practice* (Cambridge University Press, 2006) 403.

44 Results quoted in Luck, *UN Security Council: Practice and Promise*, 106.

45 The Fight Against Terrorism: Impact and Implications for the Atlantic Alliance', NATO Committee Report, 174 PCTR 07 E rev 1, 2007 Annual Session.

46 Resolution 2253, §15.

47 Boulden, Jane and Thomas G. Weiss, eds., *Terrorism and the UN: Before and After September 11* (Indiana University Press, 2004) 112.

48 José E. Alvarez, 'The UN's "War" on Terrorism' (2003) 31 *International Journal of Legal Information*, 238, 246.

49 David Cortright, 'Can the United Nations Battle Terrorism Effectively?' USA *Magazine*, January 2005, Vol. 133 N. 2716.

3.2 CTC *Surveys on National Implementation*

In parallel, and based on State reports, the CTC itself has prepared reports on the implementation of resolutions by Member States, starting with Resolution 1373. In June 2008, the CTED published its first survey,[50] breaking down the results both by regions and subregions, as well as providing section-crossing analyses by themes and recommendations. This first survey was followed by similar surveys published in 2009[51] and 2011.[52] More recently, implementation reports have also started being published regarding Resolution 2178,[53] further merging the various counterterrorism tools of the UN.

These surveys base their information on State reports, the PIAs, communication with Member States, and the few State visits the CTED conducted[54] on behalf of the CTC 'to monitor progress, as well as to evaluate the nature and level of technical assistance a given country may need in order to implement resolution 1373 (2001).'[55] It must be noted that these visits are only possible with the consent of the State.[56] This means that a lot of the information still must come from Member States themselves and not necessarily from independent sources. For instance, in the region of the Pacific Islands, there were no State visits conducted throughout the time that three surveys were published, hence the information provided for this region needs to be analysed with caution. The CTC itself notes the limitations that this creates.[57]

The CTC surveys describe the progress and shortfalls of every region of the world in matters of counterterrorism, but also offer practical advice as to how the region should improve its action. In many cases, it is generally to 'enhance

50 Global Survey on Implementation of Resolution 1373 (2001), United Nations Counter-terrorism Committee, June 2008, S/2008/379, available at www.un.org/en/sc/ctc/docs/GIS2008.pdf (last accessed 15.12.2015).

51 Global Survey of the implementation of Security Council resolution 1373 (2001) by Member States, S/2009/620, available at www.un.org/en/sc/ctc/docs/gis-2009-09_en.pdf (last accessed 15.12.2015).

52 Global survey of the implementation of Security Council resolution 1373 (2001) by Member States, S/2011/463, 1 September 2011, available at http://www.un.org/Docs/journal/asp/ws.asp?m=S/2011/463 (last accessed 15.12.201).

53 See 'UN Documents on Foreign Terrorist Fighters' available at http://www.un.org/en/sc/ctc/news/2015-03-11_UN_documents_FTF.html (last accessed 15.12.2015).

54 The 2011 Global Surveys states that the CTED has visited sixty States, S/2011/463, §4.

55 CTED 'Working Methods,' available at http://www.un.org/en/sc/ctc/ (last accessed 15.12.2015).

56 Security Council Resolution 1963 (2010).

57 Survey of the implementation of Security Council resolution 1373 (2001) by Member States, S/2009/620, 17.

border security at points of entry' or to 'promote the adoption of legislation to fully implement the international counterterrorism instruments across the subregion.' It also touches upon more specific issues, such as taking action to 'prevent the abuse of informal worker remittance networks for the purpose of terrorist financing.'[58] Some reports adopted since Resolution 2178 specifically contain recommendations for States and provide know-how and technical assistance on how to improve their response to terrorism.[59]

Even taking into account the lack of some national reports and complete comprehensive information, a main finding of these surveys is that considerable variation exists from one region to another.[60] In part, this is due to the variation in cooperation requirements met by States, as well as the difference in resources between the various Members of the organisation. Some States face different challenges, for example, because of their geography or budget. Moreover, the lack of international definition of terrorism inherently creates variety in the legal regimes that are adopted and means that 'several States rely upon overly broad legal definitions of terrorism.'[61]

Finally, the surveys also produce results according to areas of study. These key thematic areas are identified in a Technical Guide, published in 2009,[62] and correspond to the three categories of obligations that were addressed by Resolution 1373. Thus, the surveys offer a global view of the progress that has been made on the various issues raised by Resolution 1373. Each survey stresses the increase in the adoption of new legislation in most States,[63] but still notes the lack of complete implementation. One major obstacle to the proper enforcement of new or existing legislation is the lack of financial and technical resources that some States, for example many in Africa, face.[64] The 2011 surveys also refer to the general financial climate as an extra obstacle to a lack of funding.[65]

58 Global Survey on Implementation of Resolution 1373 (2001), United Nations Counterterrorism Committee, 2009.

59 See for instance S/2015/358, Analysis and recommendations with regard to the global threat from foreign terrorist fighters (Report prepared by the 1267 Committee), available at http://www.un.org/en/sc/ctc/docs/2015/N1508457_EN.pdf (last accessed 15.12.2015).

60 2008 Implementation Survey S/2008/379, 52.

61 2011 Implementation Survey S/2011/463, 11.

62 Technical guide to the implementation of Security Council resolution 1373 (2001), 2009, available at http://www.un.org/en/sc/ctc/resources/index.html (last accessed 15.12.2015).

63 S/2008/379, 30.

64 S/2009/620, 11 and S/2011/463, 11.

65 S/2011/463, 57.

It is not surprising that, as seen above, the implementation of legislation in the context of counterterrorism has increased since the creation of the CTC. Although the number of these reports must be acknowledged and balanced against their quality, the CTC must still be credited for creating a database of information through its activities and reporting. As well, the body contributes greatly to the increase in counterterrorism measures and constitutes the enforcement arm of the Security Council's actions. Yet, although these reports reflect a concerted effort by Member States to cooperate with the Security Council in the area of counterterrorism, they also show the diversity in the content of the counterterrorism measures by the various Member States. Also, it clearly shows that States wish to remain in charge of major areas of counterterrorism for better or for worse. The Security Council's decision to adopt wide binding measures without the benefit of an international definition of terrorism raises a number of issues on its legality and legitimacy, examined in Chapter 4. However, in terms of impact on the sovereignty of its Members, this latitude still shows that the UN has not obtained the *kompetenz kompetenz* over security.

CHAPTER 4

The Scope of the Security Council's Role

During the Cold War, the Security Council's activity was curtailed because of the conflict between the US and the Former Soviet Union and the consequent threat of a veto. Therefore, 'discussion surrounding the scope of the Council's authority remained largely academic.'[1] The discussion about the legality of the Security Council's action took on a new relevance after September 11, 2001 because, for the first time, its resolutions did not aim to respond to one particular terrorist act. Rather, it required that States take action against all acts of terrorism whether present or future threats, and at the same time, it considered itself in charge of that legal framework. This has led to discussions as to whether the Security Council had acted *ultra vires*. The subject has been treated extensively. In this section, the role of the Security Council specifically with regards to sovereignty will be analysed with reference being made to these sources. Whereas the previous sections analysed this role in practice, this section will examine the role of the Security Council more generally and will look at whether its counter-terrorism role has fundamentally altered the sovereignty of its Member States. The focus in this analysis will be on Resolutions 1373 and 2178 because these impose general binding obligations on Member States on terrorism and are automatically applicable by virtue of the nature of the Security Council.

In this context, there seems to have been an assertion that Resolution 1373 constituted a 'truly legislative act'[2] because 'the Security Council rendered certain purely treaty rules on all Member States of the United Nations.'[3] It was said that Resolution 1373 started a legislative *phase* because the model of general obligations was followed in later resolutions[4] and this was confirmed more obviously by Resolution 2178. However, the book shows that while the Security Council has managed to impose a broad framework on counterterrorism, this framework requires legislative action by States, rather than constitutes legislation *per se*.

---

1 Eric Rosand, 'The Security Council As "Global Legislator": Ultra Vires or Ultra Innovative?' (2004) 28 *Fordham International Law Journal*, 542, 560.

2 Ian Johnstone, 'Legislation and Adjudication in the UN Security Council: Bringing down the Deliberative Deficit' (2008) 102 *American Journal of International Law*, 275, 283.

3 Gilbert Guillaume, 'Terrorism and International Law' (2004) 53 *International and Comparative Law Quarterly*, 543.

4 Stefan Talmon, 'The Security Council as a World Legislature' (2005) 99 *American Journal of International Law*, 175.

 | DOI 10.1163/9789004299580_006

The next two sections in this chapter will examine the legality and legitimacy of the Security Council's action. It is clear that the Security Council has a large mandate to address counterterrorism, but given its wide discretion to use Chapter 7, one must ask not only whether the Security Council has legislative powers, but also 'whether its possession of such powers is, or would be, a good thing.'[5] When States create an international organisation, they vest it with agreed-upon powers. Therefore, 'it is an established principle in the field of the law of international organisations that, but for the possibility of an act being ultra vires, the decision of an organ carries with it a prima facie presumption of validity.'[6] In practice, this perception of legality will have an impact on the fulfilment of Member States' obligations. This is true, in particular, in the case of the Security Council, where a limited number of States adopt decisions that affect other States. The nature of the Security Council has always raised questions of legitimacy because fifteen States have the power to adopt decisions that are binding on the other 178 States.[7] However, this section shows that the impact of the Security Council's role in counterterrorism on the sovereignty of its Member States is somewhat limited. On the contrary, its actions reflect a strong will of States to maintain their involvement in international security and bring their security agenda to the international level. This does not mean that the Security Council's counterterrorism regime is not problematic; the many issues it creates are raised in this chapter. The conclusions on the impact on sovereignty are an assessment of the transfer of powers and competences from States to the Security Council as much as an appreciation of the legality of the Security Council's resolutions.

---

5 Matthew Happold, 'Security Council Resolution 1373 and the Constitution of the United Nations' (2003) 16 *Leiden Journal of International Law*, 593, 595.

6 Certain Expenses of the United Nations (Article17, Paragraph 2, of the Charter) (Advisory Opinion) [1962] ICJ Rep 151, 168; Legal Consequences for States of the Continued Presence of South Africa in Namibia (South West Africa) Notwithstanding Security Council Resolution 276 (1970) (Advisory Opinion) [1971] ICJ Rep 16, 52 [110]; 22 [20]; Questions of Interpretation and Application of the 1971 Montreal Convention Arising from the Aerial Incident at Lockerbie (*Libyan Arab Jamahiriya v United States*) (Provisional Measures) [1992] ICJ Rep 3, 15 [39]-[41], quoted in Hitochi Nasu, 'Chapter 7 Powers and the Rule of Law: The jurisdictional Limits' (2007) 26 *Australian Yearbook of International Law*, 95.

7 For further analyses on the legitimacy problem of the Security Council see, among others, David D. Caron, 'The Legitimacy of the Collective Authority of the Security Council' (1993) 87 *American Journal of International Law*, 552–588; Ian Hurd, *After Anarchy: Legitimacy and Power in the United Nations Security Council* (Princeton University Press, 2008); Ian Johnstone, 'Legislation and Adjudication in the UN Security Council: Bringing down the Deliberative Deficit' (2008) 102 *American Journal of International Law*, 275–308; and Stefan Talmon, 'The Security Council as a World Legislature' (2005) 99 *American Journal of International Law*, 1.

1 The Legality of the Security Council's Actions

First, when considering the text of the Charter itself, there does not seem to be an explicit prohibition for the Security Council to act as a legislator. For example, Article 1(1) of the Charter states that the organisation's aims are to act in 'conformity with the principles of justice and international law.' Moreover, Article 24(2) states that the Security Council must act 'in accordance with the Purposes and Principles of the United Nations.' Thus the limit placed on the Security Council 'does not [exactly] make legislative action inappropriate for the Council, but does limit how the Council legislates. Hence, no legal limitation exists which forbids the Council to use Chapter 7 in a legislative capacity.'[8] Of course, this does not mean that the Security Council's powers are unlimited, but rather, that they are flexible. To this end, as previously discussed in this book, the Security Council has adopted an expanding role in counterterrorism.

The Council's actions could, therefore, potentially affect the way international norms are developed[9] because it 'erodes the principle of sovereign equality.'[10] This problem was summarised as follows:

> In addition to the obvious problem that it will be seen as serving the interests of its most powerful Members only, Council legislation circumvents the normal treaty-making process. Such action derogates from the principle that States are bound only by the law they have consented to, and it encroaches on parliamentary authority within States.[11]

These arguments converge on the idea that the Council could be 'usurping a role that States have reserved for themselves.'[12] Security is a contentious national issue and, prior to September 11, 2001, it was dealt with it at the international level by the adoption of specific instruments that addressed specific issues, leaving the onus of addressing security threats on States. Through its post-September 11, 2001 counterterrorism resolutions, though, the Security Council has been said to 'replace State capacity to develop counterterrorism

8 Keith Harper, 'Does the United Nations Security Council Have the Competence to Act as Court and Legislature' (1994) 27 *New York University Journal of International Law and Politics*, 103, 149.

9 Alexander Marschik, "The Security Council as World Legislator? Theory, Practice and Consequences of an Expanding World Power" (Institute for International Law and Justice, Working Paper 2005) 79.

10 Happold, 'Security Council Resolution 1373 and the Constitution of the United Nations', 610.

11 Ian Johnstone, 'Legislation and Adjudication in the UN Security Council: Bringing down the Deliberative Deficit' (2008) 102 *American Journal of International Law*, 275, 299.

12 Happold, 'Security Council Resolution 1373 and the Constitution of the United Nations', 610.

conventions because resolutions 1373 (2001) and 1540 (2004) obligations are coercive and therefore pre-eminent over any other legal obligations deriving from negotiations or consensus.'[13]

Like any international organisation whose mandate is dictated by States, Member States of the UN have consented to this system and have, in fact, granted the Security Council with a wide mandate for international peace and security. Member States, albeit some of them, continuously set the agenda of the Security Council on these matters and the rest of the Member States, who have given consent to this, agree on principle to implement it. Crucially, as will be further argued in this section, there was no objection, in practice, from the Member States on the measures adopted in counterterrorism.[14]

One problem is that 'creating new obligations in an area already covered by a comprehensive and almost universally accepted multilateral agreement'[15] raises the risk of creating concurrent and different norms. Traditionally, a State adopts specific legislation in order to address a lack in existing measures. While these measures might conflict with existing measures, States and regional organisations do not usually adopt measures addressing the same area on purpose, as this would inevitably lead to a conflict. This is the case in the current study, as Resolution 1373 replicates obligations included in the 1999 International Convention for the Suppression of the Financing of Terrorism. The result of this is that States that had chosen not to ratify the Convention now face these obligations through Resolution 1373 and this clearly impacts their sovereignty. It is for this reason that some have suggested that the Security Council is 'using Chapter 7 to extend some treaty obligations to subjects who have not consented them.'[16]

While Resolution 2178 does not refer to obligations contained in existing treaties, it did not emerge from a legal vacuum and it includes many of the obligations already included in previous resolutions, such as travel bans and asset freezing. Additionally, the sharing of passengers' data already exists between some Member States[17] and its inclusion in Resolution 2178 therefore reflects existing or prospected tools to address terrorism.

---

13 Rosa Giles-Camero, 'Terrorism Acts as Threats to International Peace and Security', in *International Legal Dimension of Terrorism*, vol. 23, International Humanitarian Law Series (Martinus Nijhoff Publishers, 2009) 64.

14 Nigel White, 'The United Nations and Counter-Terrorism: multilateral and executive law-making' in Sambei, Arvinder, Anton Du Plessis and Martin Polaine, *Counter-Terrorism Law and Practice. An International Handbook* (Oxford University Press, 2009) 72.

15 See Harper, 'Does the United Nations Security Council Have the Competence to Act as Court and Legislature', 129.

16 Giles-Camero, 'Terrorism Acts as Threats to International Peace and Security', 64.

17 While Passenger Name Record (PNR) agreements are still a contentious issue within the EU, the organisation has such agreements with the US, Canada and Australia. See http://

More generally, the resolution does reflect changes and standards in national legislation and the general attitude of States towards counterterrorism. In effect, Resolution 2178 brings together, in one place, the various obligations created over time by various UN Security Council resolutions. It also fills a lacuna in international law, as it provides the framework to deal with the new threat of the FTF. By intervening in this matter, the Security Council closes gaps that could emerge due to the new nature of the threat. Moreover, the resolutions by the Security Council confirm that States 'have obligations to refrain from engaging in and to prevent acts of international terrorism.'[18] It is even considered that the obligation to fight terrorism could be part of customary international law and that UN resolutions 'may serve as evidence of a common opinio juris.'[19] For Proulx, 'the existence of [the obligation to prevent terrorism] is so widely recognised that it poses no problems and should not fuel a futile or circuitous debate.'[20]

One further issue with such wide action by the Security Council is that its action is supposedly 'only justifiable on the basis of its specific – and limited – purpose.'[21] Unlike previous resolutions, Resolutions 1373 and 2178 impose obligations to fight (international) terrorism *per se*, all the while obviously providing responses to specific attacks or threats. In the case of Resolution 2178, there are references to specific terrorist groups that are of concern.[22] Yet, most of the operative paragraphs focus on terrorists or terrorist groups generally, without specifying or defining the terms. In doing so, the resolution has the potential to become a general tool to address terrorism, as did Resolution 1373, while immediately allowing the targeting of groups and individuals of concern under direct reference to Resolution 1267. Resolution 2178 collates all the existing UN measures to address terrorism, and requires States to adopt a

---

ec.europa.eu/justice/data-protection/international-transfers/pnr-tftp/pnr-and-tftp_en.htm (last accessed 15.12.2015).

18 Kimberley Trapp, 'Terrorism and the International Law of State Responsibility' in *Research Handbook on International Law and Terrorism* (Edward Elgar Publishing Limited, 2014) 40.

19 Kai Ambos and Anina Timmermann, 'Terrorism and Customary International Law', *Research Handbook on International Law and Terrorism* (Edward Elgar Publishing Limited, 2014) 30.

20 Vincent-Joël Proulx, *Transnational Terrorism and State Accountability: A New Theory of Prevention* (Hart Publishing, 2012) 22.

21 Martti Koskenniemi, 'The Police in the Temple: Order, Justice and the UN: A Dialectal View' (1995) 6 *European Journal of International Law*, 325, 339.

22 In the preamble, the resolution refers to 'entities such as the Islamic State in Iraq and the Levant (ISIL), the Al-Nusrah Front (ANF) and other cells, affiliates, splinter groups or derivatives of Al-Qaida' and some of the Operative Paragraphs refer specifically to Al-Qaida associates.

new combination of measures in criminal law, financial law and terrorist sanctions, to name a few. Therefore, Resolution 2178 is clearly a complex legal instrument and it can appear even more controversial than Resolutions 1373 or 1267. Resolution 2178 is also even more intrusive into national legislation than is Resolution 1373, as the list of its obligations is longer and more specific and consists of a combination of criminal, civil and administrative measures. It both crystallises existing measures whose legitimacy have previously been questioned and goes at least a step further in terms of the breadth of the new measures it requires from Member States. As a result, the intervention of the Security Council into core constitutional and criminal matters is quite dramatic and this has led to the consistency of counterterrorism becoming greatly enhanced along with the concerns of legality.

It must be stressed, however, that Resolutions 1373 and 2178 do not legislate *per se* on terrorism. Rather, they require States to do so and are not meant to be 'directly effective supranational legislation.'[23] Indeed, paragraph 1(b) of Resolution 1373, requiring Member States to criminalise the financing of terrorism, 'is the only one of the eleven binding paragraphs in Resolution 1373 that actually requires specific action from States'[24] and this obligation is actually a transposition of obligations from the 1999 International Convention for the Suppression of the Financing of Terrorism. The rest of the resolution leaves discretion to the Member States on the specific implementation of the general obligations. Although the obligations contained in Resolution 2178 are more detailed than in 1373, both resolutions, in effect, provide a framework and require States to take action against terrorism, but do not tell them how to define terrorism or what penalties they should adopt against terrorism suspects. As well, though Resolution 2178 uses language such as 'take the necessary steps' that indicates that the idea of criminalising terrorism must be recognised internationally, it leaves the appropriate legal terrorism regimes to be taken to the Member State. This is partially because a number of measures concern criminal law, which is defined at the domestic level, and resolutions will therefore require criminalisation of certain behaviours but will not specify penalties. In effect, this resembles the obligation of goal, rather than that of means, imposed by some European measures on the State.[25]

The lack of definition of key terms in these resolutions is an interesting point for the Security Council's mandate in counterterrorism. Prior to September 11,

---

23 White, 'The United Nations and Counter-Terrorism: multilateral and executive law-making', 72.

24 Rosand, 'The Security Council As 'Global Legislator'', 584.

25 See Chapter 6, Section 4.

2001, this had not stopped the Security Council from defining specific incidents and attacks as threats to international peace and security. Yet, these instances referred to particular attacks.[26] In contrast, after September 11, 2001 and with the adoption of Resolution 1373, the Security Council declared international terrorism, *per se*, to be a threat to international peace and security. Clearly, this resolution was a response to the attacks, yet because of the linguistics of the text, it generalised the Security Council's scope of action to any acts of international terrorism without actually defining terrorism itself. In Resolution 2178, the Security Council went a step further by defining 'terrorist acts' as a threat to international peace and security. This progression has led to two significant, yet somewhat contradictory, consequences for Member States: first, the Security Council is now mandated to address and use enforcement action against any acts it deems to be terrorist, even when they are not necessarily international in nature, creating further questions about its intrusion into national affairs; and second, by not defining terrorism, the responsibility of defining terrorism is left to each Member State, thereby allowing for a flexible framework in those States with varied legal cultures. This schizophrenic situation means that although the Security Council creates a binding framework for action against terrorism, it requires States to devise the specific measures they want in their own territory.

Currently, the Security Council is granted the flexibility to address ever-changing threats. This flexibility is visible in the varied legal genre of the obligations contained in Resolution 2178: it is a complex legal instrument that includes a number of obligations of different legal nature. For example, Article 6 of Resolution 2178 requires States to adopt criminal legislation to deal with FTFs. Articles 2 and 8 provide for administrative and civil measures to restrict travel, training and support for terrorism and prevent radicalisation. Article 3 requires cooperation on data information and the last few articles require cooperation and technical assistance between States. In other words, such an all-compassing instrument reflects all the tools necessary to address terrorism and stresses the need for non-legal measures instead of limiting itself to one legal category of measures to fight terrorism. On the other hand, though, this complexity has been criticised for the confusion that it creates.[27] Martin

---

26 See, for instance, UN Security Council Resolution 748 (1992) adopted after the Lockerbie incident and which imposed sanctions on Libya; UN Security Council Resolutions 1054 and 1070 (1996) against Sudan after its involvement in the attempted assassination of Egyptian President Hosni Mubarak; and UN Security Council Resolution 1267, 15 October 1999, which imposes sanctions against Taliban.

27 Martin Scheinin, 'The Council of Europe's Draft Protocol on Foreign Terrorist Fighters Is Fundamentally Flawed' (*Just Security*, 18 March 2015), available at http://justsecurity

Scheinin notes that 'the Security Council seeks to extend the notions of terrorism and terrorist training to broad situations of armed conflict, without any analytical effort to identify the legal consequences.'[28] With the controversy surrounding air strikes against ISIS[29] and the debate in the US over the legal basis for authorising the use of force against ISIS,[30] Resolution 2178's lack of definition and inclusion of measures of various legal nature do not provide a clear-cut answer as to the legal regime that applies to terrorist groups. This only serves to reinforce the differences that exist between different national cultures of counterterrorism. As well, it pushes the boundaries of the measures States can adopt to deal with the phenomenon, which is something that, on a pragmatic level, provides the necessary flexibility to deal with new and emerging threats, but at the same time, can also lead to abuse.

Whereas there does not seem to be a clear obstacle to the adoption of resolutions such as Resolutions 1373 and 2178 by the Security Council, the criticism that is addressed to the scope of its action raises the question of its legitimacy to act against terrorism. This is important because a legitimacy deficit can lead to poor enforcement, thereby negating that competences have truly been transferred to the Security Council.

2 The Legitimacy of the Security Council's Actions

According to Bardo Fassbender, the power that is given to the Security Council indicates that the Charter is similar to a world constitution,[31] if it is possible to

.org/21207/council-europe-draft-protocol-foreign-terrorist-fighters-fundamentally-flawed/ (last accessed 15.12.2015).

28 Ibid.

29 For a summary of the legal issues surrounding the international coalition against ISIS, see Jonathan Horowitz, 'A Legal Map of Airstrikes in Syria (Part 1), *Just Security*, December 7, 2015, available at https://www.justsecurity.org/28167/legal-map-airstrikes-syria-part-1/ (last accessed 15.12.2015).

30 William C. Banks, Myriam Feinberg and Daphné Richemond-Barak, An ISIL AUMF? Counterterrorism and Congressional Authorization in the United States, I-CONnect, Dec. 18, 2014, available at www.iconnectblog.com/2014/12/an-isil-aumf-counterterrorism-and-congressional-authorization-in-the-united-states/ (last visited 17 Nov. 2015); Myriam Feinberg, Guest Post: 'New Battlefields, Old Laws' – Debate on the Future of the 2001 AUMF, Opinio Juris Sept. 28, 2014, available at opiniojuris.org/2014/09/28/guest-post-new-battlefields-old-laws-debate-future-2001-aumf/(last visited 17 Nov. 2015).

31 Bardo Fassbender, 'The United Nations Charter as Constitution of the International Community' (1997) 36 *Columbia Journal of Transnational Law*, 529, 594 (claiming that

liken the UN system to a national system where the Security Council would act as the executive branch.[32] The move from punishing sanctions to counterterrorism governance that emerges post-September 11, 2001 seems to confirm this trend. Yet, there are concerns that a Security Council that legislates would lead to a 'concentration of all three functions as lawmaker, judge and executioner [that] represents a recipe for abuse of power or the very definition of tyranny.'[33]

The problematic nature of the Security Council's action on terrorism is reinforced by the fact that its resolutions target individuals directly, not only by way of asset freezing measures, but also by other measures that are likely to affect them directly, raising complex human rights issues. There were originally strong currents of opinion that hold that the human rights perspective should not 'unduly burden the Council's agenda.'[34] This idea was supported by the existence of many human rights mechanisms within the rest of the UN.[35] Resolution 1373 was an example of this trend, as it does not even mention human rights. Moreover, there has always been an argument that in cases of emergency, the curtailment of human rights might become a necessity[36] and the events of September 11, 2001 certainly prompted discourses that human rights were second to international security.

The controversial nature of the Security Council acting in areas of security is exacerbated if there is no means to review its actions. Even before the events of September 11, 2001, scholars had questioned the idea of balancing the acts of the Security Council by those of another body. For example, many analysed the role of the ICJ in this area.[37] In practice, the ICJ can either deal with inter-States

---

Article 2(6) and Article 103 of the Charter 'give a strong hint of its constitutional character').

32 Thomas M. Franck, 'The "Powers of Appreciation": Who Is the Ultimate Guardian of UN Legality' (1992) 86 *American Journal of International Law*, 519.

33 N D White, 'The United Nations System: Conference, Contract or Constitutional Order?' (2000) 4 *Singapore Journal of International and Comparative Law* 281, 293.

34 As summarised by E.J. Flynn, 'The Security Council's Counter-Terrorism Committee and Human Rights' (2007) 7 *Human Rights Law Review* 371, 371.

35 Including the Human Rights Council, formerly Human Rights Commission, the offices of Special Rapporteurs on Human Rights issues, etc.

36 See Introduction, Section 4.

37 Dapo Akande, 'The International Court of Justice and the Security Council: Is there Room for Judicial Control of Decisions of the Political Organs of the United Nations?' (1997) 46 *International and Comparative Law Quarterly* 309–343; Jose E. Alvarez, 'Judging the Security Council' (1996) 90 *American Journal of International Law* 1; Vera Gowlland-Debbas, 'Relationship between the International Court of Justice and the Security Council in the Light of the Lockerbie Case,' (1994) 88 *American Journal of International Law* 643 and Jonathan A. Frank, 'A Return to Lockerbie and the Montreal Convention in the Wake

disputes,[38] or can give Advisory Opinions, as requested by other UN organs.[39] The ICJ declared however that it did 'not possess powers of judicial review or appeal in respect of the decisions taken by the United Nations organs concerned.'[40] It stated that, contrary to national systems, where the validity of governmental acts can be reviewed, this is not the case at the international level despite proposals made during the drafting of the UN Charter.[41] In essence, because of the powers of the Security Council under Chapter 7, a review by the ICJ would be 'narrowly construed'[42] and would only happen incidentally during a dispute between two States, such as when the ICJ gave precedence to the Security Council in the *Lockerbie* case or if an organ asked for an Advisory Opinion, which is non-binding. Therefore, 'for an ICJ decision to effectively invalidate a Council decision, states would generally have to give the Court's decision more pervasive force than the law requires.'[43] The possibility of the international court reviewing the acts of the Security Council was seen as 'threaten[ing] to unravel the whole system of binding enforcement action under Chapter 7.'[44] While separate opinions written for the *Lockerbie* case consider that the Court could or should review acts of other organs of the UN,[45] so far, in practice, the Court has not decided to do so.

It must be noted that there are other bodies that can balance the Security Council's actions and these have done so. In particular, in 2006, the GA included human rights directly in its Global Counterterrorism Strategy mandate, which also included the right for victims of terrorism acts to obtain compensation.[46]

---

of the September 11 Terrorist Attacks: Ramifications of Past Security Council and International Court of Justice Action' (2002) 30 *Denver Journal of International Law and Policy*.

38 Article 36, Statute of the International Court of Justice.

39 UN Charter Article 96.

40 *Legal Consequences for States of the Continued Presence of South Africa in Namibia (S.W. Africa) Notwithstanding Security Council Resolution 276*, 1971 I.C.J. 16 (Jun. 21, 1971), §89.

41 *Certain Expenses of the United Nations (Article 17, Paragraph 2, of the Charter)*, Advisory Opinion, I.C.J. Reports 1962, 168.

42 Ioana Petculescu, 'The Review of the United Nations Security Council Decisions by the International Court of Justice' (2005) 52 *Netherlands International Law Review*, 167, 173.

43 *Alvarez*, 'Judging the Security Council', 5.

44 Dapo Akande, 'The International Court of Justice and the Security Council: Is there Room for Judicial Control of Decisions of the Political Organs of the United Nations?' (1997) 46 *International and Comparative Law Quarterly*, 309, 336.

45 See the Separate Opinion by Judge Rezek, Judgment of 27 February 1998, §3.

46 Article I.8 of the United Nations General Assembly Adopts Global Counterterrorism Strategy: 'To consider putting in place, on a voluntary basis, national systems of assistance

More significantly, some regional courts have taken upon themselves to review the legality of the Security Council's actions. The role of regional and national courts in this respect is to provide the checks and balances that are necessary for a democratic counterterrorism regime, which can be lacking if the Security Council acts alone. This has led to some crucial results, including the creation of the Ombudsperson in the 1267 sanctions regime, which introduces some checks and balances into the Security Council's counterterrorism regime.[47] Additionally, Resolution 2178 stresses the necessity for Member States to 'comply with', 'respect' and 'conform with' their human rights obligations. Significantly, this is the case, not only in the Preamble, but also in operative paragraphs 5, 11 and 17. This is crucial because it means that the protection of human rights now becomes part and parcel of the obligation to fight terrorism, in tandem with the specific obligations of the resolution and courts can, therefore, carry out a balancing exercise between the obligations included in it. This was reiterated by Ben Emmerson, the current UN Special Rapporteur on the promotion and protection of human rights and fundamental freedoms while countering terrorism. Indeed, for Emmerson, human rights are not only an important part of international law that cannot be set aside, but more importantly, he thinks that 'by actively promoting and protecting human rights, States contribute to preventing terrorism.'[48] Human rights have now become part of the Security Council's mandate in counterterrorism and the protection of human rights has, in fact, become a *tool* for counterterrorism – Resolution 2253 affirms, in its Preamble, that 'security, and human rights are mutually reinforcing and are vital to an effective and comprehensive approach to countering terrorism,' although the reference to human rights obligations is only included in one of the operative paragraphs of the resolution.[49] For a review of the changes in human rights protection that have occurred due to the pressure inflicted by courts on the Security Council, refer to Part 3.

---

that would promote the needs of victims of terrorism and their families and facilitate the normalization of their lives. In this regard, we encourage States to request the relevant United Nations entities to help them to develop such national systems. We will also strive to promote international solidarity in support of victims and foster the involvement of civil society in a global campaign against terrorism and for its condemnation. This could include exploring at the General Assembly the possibility of developing practical mechanisms assistance to victims.'

47 See Chapters 10, 11 and 12 and the analysis of the *Kadi* case by the ECJ.

48 Press Release, 'Human rights must always be protected, even when countering terrorism – UN experts', document available at http://www.ohchr.org/EN/NewsEvents/Pages/DisplayNews.aspx?NewsID=15846&LangID=E (last accessed 15.12.2015).

49 Resolution 2252, §22.

Finally, some have suggested that State practice could amount to countermeasures, by refusing to comply with obligations stemming from the Security Council.[50] Not going as far, this book aims to show how crucial State practice is in determining transfer of competences and implementation and the next section shows the role of States in adopting and enforcing Security Council resolutions.

3 Do States Care?

Both Resolutions 1373 and 2178 were adopted unanimously. Resolution 2178 was co-sponsored by 104 States[51] and was introduced at a summit presided over by United States President Barack Obama and opened by UN Secretary-General Ban Ki-moon. Clearly, the resolutions were adopted when States felt the need to respond to a serious threat and unanimity is always easier to obtain in the aftermath of attacks. However, these resolutions also represent the will of States to address a threat through the coordinated response of the Security Council and the idea that terrorism calls for a strong global answer:

> security and stability are obviously public goods… The provision of such a good raises a collective action problem.[52]

With Chapter 7 resolutions from the Security Council, there is a 'marked decrease in margin of appreciation which States enjoy in setting their own counter-terrorism priorities and determining appropriate measures to meet those priorities.'[53] However, 'the limit of the Council's powers is reached when the Council orders sanctions or military intervention and no one will respond.'[54] States have the power to disregard the Security Council's decisions and might thereby face sanctions if they do so. Yet, Jean-Paul Laborde, the Executive Director of the CTED noted that, despite the possibility of imposing sanctions against Member States that do not abide by their Security Council obligations,

---

50 Antonios Tzanakopoulos, *Disobeying the Security Council: Countermeasures against Wrongful Sanctions* (Oxford University Press, 2011).

51 Thelistcanbefoundathttps://drive.google.com/file/d/oB4XISuoPj6voclgfTk5fWGRROWs/edit (last accessed 15.12.2015).

52 Eyal Benvenisti, 'The US and the Use of Force: Double-Edged Hegemony and the Management of Global Emergencies' (2004) 15 *European Journal of International Law*, 677, 681.

53 Trapp, 'Terrorism and the International Law of State Responsibility', 44.

54 Jose E. Alvarez, 'Judging the Security Council', 2.

non-compliance has not happened in the context of Resolutions 1373 and 1267.[55] He stressed that 'a resolution of the Council is a resolution for Member States, for empowering Member States, but also imposing on Member States measures which are necessary to counter the phenomenon of the foreign terrorist fighters.'[56]

In practice, many States did not consider Resolution 1373 to be problematic and, rather, 'a number of Council Members cited the flexibility the Council was allowing States to implement the provisions of the Resolution.'[57] In fact,

> Partly as a result of Resolution 1373, and the work of its offspring, the Counter-Terrorism Committee…almost every country has taken steps to enhance its counter-terrorism machinery, whether in the form of adopting anti-terrorism legislation, strengthening border controls, becoming party to international treaties related to terrorism, or becoming proactive in denying safe haven to terrorists and their supporters.[58]

These results are confirmed by studies that analyse the success of the CTC's mode of reporting.[59] For instance, since 2001, States have adopted more than

---

55 'Strategies for Countering Violent Extremism', interview of Jean-Paul Laborde by Joanne J. Myers, the Carnegie Council for Ethics in International Affairs, November 24, 2014, transcript and video available at http://www.carnegiecouncil.org/studio/multimedia/20141124/index.html (last accessed 15.12.2015).

56 Ibid.

57 Rosand, 'The Security Council As "Global Legislator"', 585: Rosand quotes 'the Spanish Ambassador [that] said that the resolution "was not intrusive as it gives States leeway on how to internally interpret its implementation"' (see Statement by Mr. Arias, Representative of Spain, to the United Nations, U.N. SCOR, 59th Sess., 4950th mtg. at 7, U.N. Doc. S/PV.4950 (2004)); the French Ambassador [that] added that the Council was simply 'establishing the goals, but leaving each State free to define the penalties, legal regulations, and practical measures to be adopted' to fulfill them (see Statement by Jean-Marc de La Sabliere, Representative of France, to the United Nations, U.N. SCOR, 59th Sess., 4950th mtg. at 8, U.N. Doc. S/PV.4950 (2004)) and Pakistan [that] made it clear that the flexibility the Council allowed States in implementing the resolution was part of the reason that it could join other Council Members in supporting the text (see Statement by Munir Akram, Representative of Pakistan, to the United Nations, U.N. SCOR, 59th Sess., 4950th mtg. at 15, U.N. Doc. S/PV.4950 (2004)).

58 Rosand, 'The Security Council As "Global Legislator"', 548.

59 See David Cortright and others, 'An Action Agenda for Enhancing the United Nations Program on Counter-Terrorism' (Fourth Freedom Forum and the Kroc Institute for International Peace Studies 2004), kroc.nd.edu/sites/default/files/an_action_agenda.pdf, last accessed (15.12.2015).

fifty new measures on terrorism.[60] In practice, States have not reacted negatively and, rather, more and more States adopt legislation, usually immediately after the adoption of the resolutions[61] as seen from the following examples: in November 2014, France adopted a new piece of legislation on counterterrorism that includes, among other provisions, a travel ban for French citizens suspected of terrorism;[62] the UK adopted the Counter-Terrorism and Security Act 2015,[63] which provides for the seizure and retention of a passport of a person suspected of leaving the UK for the terrorism activities and the temporary exclusion of individuals if they are suspected of terrorism activities outside of the UK; New Zealand approved a new temporary law on counterterrorism, which allows for the cancellation of passports for up to three years for those suspected of involvement in terrorism;[64] and Australia itself has adopted the Counter-Terrorism Legislation Amendment (Foreign Fighters) Act 2014.[65]

This is not to say that these measures are not problematic legally and it is clear that a number of them might be contrary to fundamental freedoms.[66]

---

60 'New National Legislation Countering Terrorism', UNDOC, data available at https://www.unodc.org/tldb/latest_updates.html (last accessed 07.12.2015).

61 In June 2012, the Philippines adopted legislation on the financing of terrorism known as the Terrorism Financing Prevention and Suppression Act 2012. The Preamble states that 'The State, likewise, recognizes and adheres to international commitments to combat the financing of terrorism, specifically to the International Convention for the Suppression of the Financing of Terrorism, as well as other binding terrorism-related Resolutions of the United Nations Security Council pursuant to Chapter 7 of the Charter of the United Nations (UN).'

62 LOI n° 2014–1353 du 13 novembre 2014 renforçant les dispositions relatives à la lutte contre le terrorisme (1), Article L2241.

63 Counter-Terrorism and Security Act 2015, available at http://www.legislation.gov.uk/ukpga/2015/6/contents/enacted (last accessed 18.12.2015).

64 See 'Foreign fighters bill passes 94 – 27', *nzherald.com*, 9 December 2014, available at http://www.nzherald.co.nz/nz/news/article.cfm?c_id=1&objectid=11371580 (last accessed 18.12.2015).

65 Text available at http://www.comlaw.gov.au/Details/C2014A00116/CanPrint (last accessed 18.12.2015).

66 See Steven Thiru, 'Anti-terrorism or punishing all dissent?', FMT, 5 April 2015 criticising the new counterterrorism law in Malyasia; Paul Peachey, 'Anti-terror Bill: Teresa May criticised for producing "a chilling recipe for injustice"', The Independent, 24 November 2014, http://www.independent.co.uk/news/uk/politics/antiterror-bill-teresa-may-criticised-for-producing-a-chilling-recipe-for-injustice-9880754.html regarding the UK bill; and, 'France Enacts Controversial New Anti-Jihadist Law', Vice News, 6 November 2014, https://news.vice.com/article/france-enacts-controversial-new-anti-jihadist-law on the French law (all accessed 15.12.2015).

Yet, in terms of State sovereignty, Security Council resolutions still allow its Member States wide flexibility. For example, there have already been some warnings expressed about the lack of political will of some States to prevent the threat of FTFs.[67] Put another way, 'as strong as the resolution is, it is not self-enforcing. Responsibility falls to UN member states individually, bilaterally, and multilaterally to develop ways of meeting the resolution's obligations.'[68] Zachary Goldman therefore suggests that the following diplomatic tools will need to be used for Resolution 2178 to be successful:

(1) Consistent pressure at the highest levels designed to overcome domestic political obstacles to robust enforcement of UNSCR 2178 in States that are the origin or transit points for foreign fighters;
(2) Sustained information-sharing to help States with less effective intelligence services identify networks of facilitators operating in their countries; and
(3) Working-level assistance, including by UN organs like the Counterterrorism Executive Directorate, to build effective border control and interdiction processes.[69]

The acceptance by States of the Security Council's expanding role has prompted it to continue in this vein, as has been seen from later resolutions that also address terrorism in a very broad way. 'Security Council Resolution 1373 was thus not a unique aberration, an *ultra vires* act remedied by acquiescence, but the beginning of a continuing practice.'[70] The Council's actions can represent a natural evolution of the organisation. It also reflects the changes in international counterterrorism that occurred in the past decade, adjusting where States felt the Security Council should incorporate human rights protection.

67 Zachary Goldman, 'The Foreign Fighter Resolution: Implementing a Holistic Strategy to Defeat ISIL', *Just Security*, 29 September 2014, http://justsecurity.org/15721/foreign-fighter-resolution-implementing-holistic-strategy-defeat-isil/ (last accessed 15.12.2015).

68 Sean Davis, 'Responding to Foreign Terrorist Fighters: A Risk-Based Playbook for States and the International Community' (Global Center on Cooperative Security 2014), November 2014, available at http://www.globalcenter.org/publications/responding-to-foreign-terrorist-fighters-a-risk-based-playbook-for-states-and-the-international-community/ (last accessed 15.12.2015).

69 Zachary Goldman, 'The Foreign Fighter Resolution: Implementing a Holistic Strategy to Defeat ISIL' http://justsecurity.org/15721/foreign-fighter-resolution-implementing-holistic-strategy-defeat-isil/ (last accessed 15.12.2015).

70 Marschik, 'The Security Council as World Legislator? Theory, Practice and Consequences of an Expanding World Power', 19.

While it is obvious that Resolution 1373 was ground-breaking and its legitimacy can be questioned, is it is not obvious whether the Security Council acted *ultra vires*. The evolution of counterterrorism within the UN has been criticised, and it is right to question the breadth of the Security Council's decisions. The existence of a wide obligation to prevent terrorism, as is found in Resolutions 1373 and 2178, creates a risk of counterterrorism legislation inflation and abuse by fostering a climate of emergency.

For our purposes, the Security Council resolutions show that, while States have granted the Security Council competence to determine the scope of international counterterrorism, they remain in charge of its application. In fact, creating international measures that allow them to adopt the measures they want gives them an added legitimacy, as they, *a posteriori*, can point to a Security Council resolution that authorises them to adopt new measures.[71]

The UN, which presents sovereignty as the pinnacle of the international system,[72] began requesting that States adopt legislation in order to improve counterterrorism. At the same time, however, State practice shows that States have accepted this new role. Yet, the Security Council counterterrorism resolutions still put the onus on States for the details of their counterterrorism regimes, including the very important issue of definition. Many States have chosen to update their counterterrorism regimes or have created such regimes. In 2004, the UN stated:

> States are still the front-line responders to today's threat...greater effort must be made to enhance the capacity of States to exercise their sovereignty responsibly.[73]

In other words, the Security Council acts like a global actor that created a global framework on counterterrorism, which gives it the authority to request that States adopt measures on counterterrorism, yet leaves the detail of these measures to States, with all the issues it creates regarding human rights. In

71 On a similar level, and while it is not a resolution adopted under Chapter 7 that authorises the use of force, States have used Resolution 2499, UN Security Council, *Security Council resolution 2249 (2015) [on terrorist attacks perpetrated by ISIL also known as Da'esh]*, 20 November 2015, adopted after the 13 November 2015 Paris attacks, as a basis for the legitimacy to conduct airstrikes against ISIS in Syria.

72 UN Charter, Article 2 (7).

73 Report of the High-Level Panel on Threats, Challenges and Change, 'A More Secure World: Our Shared Responsibility', UN Doc A/59/565 (2004), 2 December 2004, 18.

effect, States have granted the Security Council competence to require some standards in international security, thereby providing themselves with an international basis for their own domestic legislation. While this can be highly problematic, in terms of sovereignty impact it continues to represent an intergovernmental model of governance. Creating an obligation where the main responsibility remains on States reaffirms a sovereignty of absolutism. On the other hand, creating limits and accountability on States for their actions is a real challenge to this kind of sovereignty. Limits and accountability are present when there are mechanisms to review the decisions adopted by the organisation. These mechanisms, missing in the case of the UN with regards to the Security Council, are present in regional organisations, which have also become increasingly active in addressing terrorism. Part 2 therefore examines the role of regional organisations, which have had a crucial role in counterterrorism, both through the emergence of regional standards of counterterrorism and through the imposition of limits on the executive.

PART 2

The Role of Regional Organisations in International Counterterrorism

CHAPTER 5

The Mandate of Regional Organisations for Terrorism

After the Second World War, a series of regional organisations were created in a spirit of 'tolerance and peace.'[1] Apart from the OAS that emerged at the end of the 19th century, the EU and NATO were created in the same decade as the UN. Additional regional organisations, for example the Organisation of African Unity (OAU), now the African Union (AU) and the Association of Southeast Asian Nations were created during the 1960s following decolonisation. Throughout the late 1980s, additional organisations, such as the Asia-Pacific Economic Cooperation and the Mercado Común del Sur (MERCOSUR or Southern Common Market), were formed. In this chapter, the focus will be on the following regional organisations: the EU, the Council of Europe, the OAS and the AU. These organisations were selected because of their degree of activity concerning the specific context of counterterrorism. They also reflect a geographical and structural variety of regional organisations.[2]

It is important to note that none of these regional organisations was specifically created to deal with security and terrorism issues. Moreover, security being a core domestic issue, it is not included, *a priori*, in their competences. Yet, in its founding document, the UN recognised that regional organisations were to have a 'formal role in contributing to international peace and security.'[3] In addition, many of their Member States experienced terrorist attacks often impacting several of their territories, and regional organisations became increasingly involved in cooperative counterterrorism.

The rationale behind the creation of regional organisations is one of 'shared values, interests, history, experience and objectives.'[4] For this reason, regional organizations arguably have a 'high degree of legitimacy…and confidence among their Members.'[5] This, in turn, will tend to lead to increased implementation and

1 Preamble, United Nations, *Charter of the United Nations*, 24 October 1945, 1 UNTS XVI.

2 For a study of the counterterrorism regime of the Organisation of Islamic State, as well as its relation with the UN's system, see Katja Samuel, *The OIC, the UN, and Counter-Terrorism Law-Making: Conflicting or Cooperative Legal Orders?* (Hart 2013).

3 Louise Fawcett, 'Regional Governance Architecture and Security Policy' (Dialogue on Globalization Briefing Papers, Friedrich Ebert Stiftung February 2006) 3.

4 Lawrence Scheinman (ed.), 'Implementing Resolution 1540: The Role of Regional Organisations' (United Nations Institute for Disarmament Research 2008) 4.

5 Ibid.

 | DOI 10.1163/9789004299580_007

enforcement. Yet, even regional organisations function on the basis of transfer of competences. According to the ICJ:

> International organizations are governed by the 'principle of speciality', that is to say, they are invested by the States which create them with powers, the limits of which are a function of the common interests whose promotion those States entrust to them.[6]

Member States have not relinquished general competences to regional organisations. Instead, power is allocated to regional organisations by their Member States, either by the constitutive document, or by way of general principles of power attribution. Moreover, because most international and regional organisations are based on an inter-governmental structure, their main means of action is through the adoption of treaties that are decided by their Members States who must then implement them in their legal order.

The next two sections examine the mandate of regional organisations, first with regards to whether their Member States have transferred competences and sovereignty and second with regards to the UN Security Council in view of its wide mandate on international counterterrorism.

1 Relationships with Member States: Distribution of Powers

The power to act for regional organisations will depend both on what competences its Members are ready to relinquish, and, once the organisation has adopted measures, on what place these measures have in the national hierarchy of measures.

For instance, the OAS 'has no powers other than those expressly conferred upon it by this Charter, none of whose provisions authorizes it to intervene in matters that are within the internal jurisdiction of the Member States.'[7] The EU has exclusive competences over certain areas, such as custom unions or the monetary policy for States whose currency is the euro.[8] On the other hand, it only has a shared competence with Member States for many other areas, including agriculture, social policy, or more relevant here, for the area

6 *Advisory Opinion on the Legality of the Use by a State of Nuclear Weapons in Armed Conflict*, ICJ Reports, 1996, p. 78, §25.

7 Article 1, Organization of American States (OAS), *Charter of the Organisation of American States*, 30 April 1948.

8 Article 3 TFEU details the areas of exclusive competence of the EU.

of security.[9] Therefore, the distribution of competences between States and regional organisations is based on the concept of primacy and the concept of subsidiarity.

The primacy of Member States' domestic law and legislation as a fundamental right and duty is preserved in Article 13 of the OAS Charter.[10] Yet, only eight Member States' constitutions provide for the primacy of international treaty provisions over constitutional and domestic law.[11] There is nothing in the Constitutive Act of the AU regarding the status of its decisions and treaties on Member States. Therefore, each Member State incorporates the AU treaties as it would any other international treaty, and therefore, the status of regional law in national law varies from one State to another.[12] As for the Council of Europe, it does not proclaim the principle of primacy of its decisions in its statute so the status of its treaties depends on the incorporation of international treaties by the Member States.[13]

On the other hand, primacy in the context of the EU is fundamental and is part of the treaties[14] following jurisprudence by the courts. The ECJ established the concept in *Costa v ENEL* by stating that EU treaties had supremacy over

9 Shared competence areas are included in Article 4 TFEU.

10 'The political existence of the State is independent of recognition by other States. Even before being recognized, the State has the right to defend its integrity and independence, to provide for its preservation and prosperity, and consequently to organize itself as it sees fit, to legislate concerning its interests, to administer its services, and to determine the jurisdiction and competence of its courts. The exercise of these rights is limited only by the exercise of the rights of other States in accordance with international law.'

11 These States are Colombia, Ecuador, El Salvador, Guatemala, Haiti, Honduras, Mexico and Paraguay.

12 Section 231 (4) of the 1996 South African Constitution states: 'Any international agreement becomes law in the Republic when it is enacted into law by national legislation: but a self-executing provision of an agreement that has been approved by Parliament is law in the Republic unless it is inconsistent with the Constitution or an Act of Parliament'; Article 144 of the 1990 Namibian Constitution states: 'Unless otherwise provided by this Constitution or Act of Parliament, the general rules of public international law and international agreements binding upon Namibia under this Constitution shall form part of the law of Namibia'; and Article 32 of the Tunisian Constitution states: 'Treaties do not have force of law until they have been ratified. Duly ratified treaties have an authority superior to that of the laws.'

13 For instance, since a constitutional reform in Turkey, Article 90 of the Constitution now provides for the priority of international human rights treaties over conflicting national law, thus placing them on a level between the Constitution and ordinary law.

14 Declaration No. 17 Concerning Primacy. Declarations annexed to the Final Act of the Intergovernmental Conference, which adopted the Lisbon Treaty, signed on 13 December 2007.

national legislation.[15] By way of the direct effect doctrine developed by the ECJ in the 1960s,[16] the obligations and rights included in the organisations' treaties, or primary legislation, now apply directly to individuals. The EU also adopts secondary legislation,[17] for example, regulations, directives and decisions, which are all legally binding on Member States, as well as recommendations, which are not binding. Regulations are directly applicable meaning that once they have become EU law, they apply immediately in all EU Member States and do not need implementation by the Member States. In comparison, directives must be implemented by each EU Member State through its own domestic legislative process, although they leave States some discretion as to the details of the measures to adopt.[18] As the German Federal Constitutional Court stressed, the EU does not have 'competence to extend competences.'[19]

The OAS and the AU do not specifically refer to the subsidiarity principle.[20] On the other hand, for competences that are shared between Member States and the EU, the principle of subsidiarity applies. One of the main consequences of the Lisbon Treaty, which entered into force in December 2009, is that every EU legislative or executive proposal must now pass the subsidiarity test.[21] Article 5(3) TEU now defines the principle of subsidiarity as follows:

> Under the principle of subsidiarity, in areas which do not fall within its exclusive competence, the Union shall act only if and in so far as the objectives of the proposed action cannot be sufficiently achieved by the Member States, either at central level or at regional and local level, but can rather, by reason of the scale or effects of the proposed action, be better achieved at Union level.

---

15 *Flaminio Costa v ENEL* [1964] ECR 585 (6/64).

16 Case 26/62 *van Gend en Loos v Netherlands Inland Revenue Administration* [1963] ECR 1.

17 Horspool and Humphreys, 104.

18 Article 288 TFEU states that 'A directive shall be binding, as to the result to be achieved, upon each Member State to which it is addressed, but shall leave to the national authorities the choice of form and methods.'

19 *Lisbon* Case, BVerfG, cases 2 BvE 2/08 and others from 30 June 2009.

20 The principle is a 'power allocation principle that expresses a preference for the allocation and exercise of governmental functions at the lowest level of governance', see Isabel Feichtner, 'Subsidiarity', Max Planck Encyclopaedia of Public International Law, available at http://opil.ouplaw.com/view/10.1093/law:epil/9780199231690/law-9780199231690-e1477?rskey=LCjeSX&result=1&prd=EPIL (last accessed 12.01.2016).

21 2nd Protocol 2 to the European Treaties on the application of the principles of subsidiarity and proportionality, C310/107, 2004.

Finally, the ECtHR itself is an example of the principle of subsidiarity, as is stated in Article 1 of the European Convention on Human Rights:

> The primary responsibility for implementing and enforcing the rights and freedoms guaranteed by the Convention is laid on the national authorities. The machinery of complaint to the Court is thus subsidiary to national systems safeguarding human rights.[22]

More details about the respective powers of regional organisations are included in the discussion of their specific role in counterterrorism in Chapter 6.

States have transferred or are sharing some of their competences with the regional organisations they have created. Yet, the organisations have not entirely replaced the national entity, in particular in the context of security.[23] Moreover, when it comes to international security, one actor has, on principle, prime responsibility for its protection.

2 Relationship with the United Nations – Threats to Peace and Security: A Mandate for Counterterrorism?

While the distribution of powers between an organisation and its Member States is crucial to establish the organisation's role, the existence of other international organisations can create situations of overlapping jurisdiction. This is the case in particular with the Security Council. The main interaction between the UN and the regional organisations occurs when decisions must be made regarding what amounts to 'threats to peace and security' and how to respond to these threats.

Chapter 8 of the UN Charter, 'Regional Arrangements,' governs the relationship between the UN and the regional organisations. More specifically, Article 52 of the UN Charter gives the primary role to regional organisations for the

22 In practice, all national remedies must have been exhausted before anyone can apply to the ECHR. See article 35(1) of the European Convention on Human Rights.

23 Of note here, the specific case of the EU has created an entire literature on the topic of sovereignty. See among others, Dimitris N Chryssochoou, 'The European Synarchy: New Discourses on Sovereignty' (2009) 1 *Göttingen Journal of International Law*, 115; Neil Walker, 'Late Sovereignty in the European Union', *Sovereignty in Transition* (Hart Publishing, 2003); Theodore Konstadinides, *Division of Powers in European Union Law: The Delimitation of Internal Competence between the EU and the Member States* (Kluwer Law International, 2009); and Michael Newman, *Democracy, Sovereignty and the European Union* (C. Hurst & Co. Publishers, 1996).

'pacific settlement of local disputes'. In this instance, according to the text, the role of the UN is secondary. However, terrorism today usually covers several States and is therefore often not a 'local dispute'. An even more crucial point is that if a threat to international peace or security is to be identified by the Security Council, it is the Security Council that is supposed to assume the primary role and decide what coercive measures should apply. In this context, the Security Council can 'utilise such regional arrangements or agencies for enforcement action under its authority. But no enforcement action shall be taken under regional arrangements or by regional agencies without the authorization of the Security Council.'[24]

This is particularly significant in this analysis because the Security Council has defined terrorism as a threat to international peace and security, meaning that, on principle, it has the main power to act against any kind of terrorism and does not need to include regional arrangements. Moreover, under Article 103 of the UN Charter, the Security Council has primacy over other international or regional actors if they have chosen to act in that area too. Finally, regional organisations themselves have specified their powers vis-à-vis the UN in their constitutive instruments. For instance, the Preamble of the OAS Charter states that the Member States 'resolve to persevere in the noble undertaking that humanity has conferred upon the United Nations, whose principles and purposes they solemnly reaffirm.' According to Article l(c) of the Statute of the Council of Europe, '[p]articipation in [this organization] shall not affect the collaboration of its Members in the work of the United Nations and of other international organisations or unions to which they are parties.' Finally, Article 3(5) of the Treaty of the European Union (TEU), titled 'Relationship with the UN', affirms 'the strict observance and the development of international law, including respect for the principles of the United Nations Charter.' The Constitutive Act of the AU states that the objectives of the organisations are to 'encourage international cooperation, taking due account of the Charter of the United Nations,'[25] which means that the organisation would follow the UN's rules of competence.

This leads to the question of whether regional organisations have any role in the context of counterterrorism and, if they do, which will prevail in case of a conflict between the international and regional measures? The next three chapters clearly demonstrate that regional organisations *have* adopted counterterrorism measures and that, in some cases, these have had a significant impact on domestic legislation. The conflicts between the various international and regional measures will be detailed in Part 3 of this book.

---

24 Article 53(1), UN Charter.

25 Article 3(e), Constitutive Act of the African Union.

CHAPTER 6

Regional Counterterrorism Measures

Although none of the regional organisations examined here was expressly created with the purpose of acting against terrorism, they have gradually become involved in countering the threat. The response from regional organisations came, on the one hand, from their own initiative in the adoption of binding documents, but also, because of their own obligations under the UN Security Council decisions. Terrorism sanctions adopted because of the Security Council's resolutions will be analysed in Chapter 9.

1 The Organisation of American States

The first Inter-American convention relating to terrorism dates back to 1971 and addressed acts of terrorism against internationally protected persons, especially diplomats.[1] For the first time, the 1971 OAS Convention imposed an explicit obligation to prevent terrorism by preventing the use of a territory for the preparation of terrorism acts, which was copied in later UN conventions. Two special conferences in 1996 and 1998 led to the signature of the Commitment of Mar del Plata, which called for the establishment of a Committee on Terrorism. The Inter-American Committee against Terrorism, known as CICTE, was consequently created in 1999.[2] Its significance increased with the signature of a new treaty, adopted by the OAS in 2002, known as the Inter-American Convention against Terrorism.[3] With the adoption of this treaty, the OAS 'became one of the first group of nations to adopt an anti-terrorism treaty in the wake of September 11.'[4] After the September 11, 2001 attacks, all of the Members expressed their support to the US with the resolution known as the 'Terrorism Threat to the

1 The Inter-American Convention to Prevent and Punish the Acts of Terrorism Taking the Forms of Crimes against Persons and Related Extortion That Are of International Significance, Washington, 1971.

2 Assembly General Resolution AG/RES.1650 (XXIX-0/99).

3 OAS Convention against Terrorism, AG/RES 1840 (XXXII.0/02) signed by thirty Member States at the General Assembly in Bridgetown, Barbados on 3 June 2002 and entered into force in July 2003.

4 Enrique Lagos and Timothy D. Rudy, 'Latin Americas: Views on Contemporary Issues in the Region Preventing, Punishing and Eliminating Terrorism in the Western Hemisphere: A Post 9/11 Inter-American Treaty' (2003) 26 *Fordham International Law Journal*, 402.

 | DOI 10.1163/9789004299580_008

Americas' by stating that 'these terrorist attacks against the United States of America are attacks against all American States.'[5]

The Inter-American Convention against Terrorism does not contain a definition of terrorism, in line with most international measures. Rather, Article 2 includes a list of international instruments to which Member States 'shall endeavour to become a party.' In Articles 4, 5, and 6, the text sets a list of specific obligations 'binding governments of the Western Hemisphere.'[6] According to Article 4:

> Each State party, to the extent it has not already done so, shall institute a legal and regulatory regime to prevent, combat, and eradicate the financing of terrorism and for effective international cooperation with respect thereto, which shall include:
>
> a. A comprehensive domestic regulatory and supervisory regime for banks, other financial institutions, and other entities deemed particularly susceptible to being used for the financing of terrorist activities. This regime shall emphasize requirements for customer identification, record-keeping, and the reporting of suspicious or unusual transactions.
>
> b. Measures to detect and monitor movements across borders of cash, bearer negotiable instruments, and other appropriate movements of value. These measures shall be subject to safeguards to ensure proper use of information and should not impede legitimate capital movements.
>
> c. Measures to ensure that the competent authorities dedicated to combating the offenses established in the international instruments listed in Article 2 have the ability to cooperate and exchange information at the national and international levels within the conditions prescribed under its domestic law. To that end, each State party shall establish and maintain a financial intelligence unit to serve as a national centre for the collection, analysis, and dissemination of pertinent money laundering and terrorist financing information. Each State party shall inform the Secretary General of the Organization of American States of the authority designated to be its financial intelligence unit.

In order to apply this rather detailed Article, States are called, under Article 5, to 'take such measures as may be necessary to provide for the identification, freezing or seizure for the purposes of possible forfeiture, and confiscation or

---

5 RC.24/RES.1/01, 19 September 2001.

6 Enrique Lagos and Timothy D. Rudy, 'Latin America: Views on Contemporary Issues in the Region-Preventing, Punishing and Eliminating Terrorism in the Western Hemisphere: A Post-9/11 Inter-American Treaty', 422.

forfeiture, of any funds or other assets constituting the proceeds of, used to facilitate, or used or intended to finance, the commission of terrorist offences.' Finally, Article 15 imposes on States to respect their human rights obligations under international law 'in particular the Charter of the United Nations, the Charter of the Organization of American States, international humanitarian law, international human rights law, and international refugee law.'

The essence of the Inter-American Convention against Terrorism is cooperation, rather than the harmonisation of national regimes, as can be seen from the fact that at least five of its Articles are devoted to cooperation between and among governments. In other words, it contributes to raising awareness to the phenomenon at the regional level and encourages the adoption of national legislation. In practice, the CICTE deals specifically with cooperation between Member States, and creates a forum for discussion and cooperation.[7]

Because the Inter-American Convention against Terrorism does not include wide-ranging obligations or an actual definition of terrorism, but rather focuses on cooperation, it corresponds to a type of 'conventions [that] reiterate the limited approach of the multilateral sectoral anti-terrorism convention in a regional context and are not particularly controversial.'[8] The OAS counterterrorism framework shows a desire by Member States to coordinate actions at the regional level against terrorism. It reflects the pragmatic need for cooperation in addressing the threat, without a strict binding nature. In terms of sovereignty, Member States have not transferred competences to the organisation, which instead functions as a cooperation forum. The enforcement of these measures will be detailed in the next Chapter.

2 The African Union

The AU replaced the OAU in 2000 and inherited much of its instruments and principles. The silence of the OAU on terrorism and the absence of reference to terrorism threat in the organisation's Charter are linked to the history of

7 Programs in eight areas are being developed, namely, airport security, customs and border protection, cyber-security, legislation against terrorism, port security, terrorist financing, terrorism policy engagement and tourism security (see http://www.oas.org/en/sms/cicte/programs.asp (last accessed 16.12.2015)). 'In 2005 alone there have been eight national and Regional Seminars on Counter terrorist Legislation in different capitals in Latin America.' Fawcett 'Regional Governance Architecture and Security Policy', 6.

8 Ben Saul, 'Criminality and Terrorism', *Counter-Terrorism: International Law and Practice* (Oxford University Press, 2012) 135.

self-determination of the OAU.[9] The first measure that referred to terrorism was OAU Resolution 213 on the Strengthening of Cooperation and Coordination among African States, July 1992.[10] The pace accelerated after the 1998 attacks in Nairobi and Dar el Salam and the AU has now adopted a broad-based normative framework to combat terrorism via its 1999 Convention on the Prevention and Combating of Terrorism, 2004 Protocol to the Convention, and 2002 Plan of Action on the Prevention and Combating of Terrorism, which 'confirm[s] the role of the Union as a standard setter.'[11] It also has a Peace and Security Council, in charge of enforcing the organisation's measures, and a Special Representative in charge of Counter-Terrorism Cooperation, appointed in 2010. More significantly, the 1999 Convention on the Prevention and Combating of Terrorism includes the following definition of terrorist acts:

> 'Terrorist act' means:
> (a) any act which is a violation of the criminal laws of a State Party and which may endanger the life, physical integrity or freedom of, or cause serious injury or death to, any person, any number or group of persons or causes or may cause damage to public or private property, natural resources, environmental or cultural heritage and is calculated or intended to:
> (i) intimidate, put in fear, force, coerce or induce any government, body, institution, the general public or any segment thereof, to do or abstain from doing any act, or to adopt or abandon a particular standpoint, or to act according to certain principles; or
> (ii) disrupt any public service, the delivery of any essential service to the public or to create a public emergency; or
> (iii) create general insurrection in a State.
> (b) any promotion, sponsoring, contribution to, command, aid, incitement, encouragement, attempt, threat, conspiracy, organizing, or procurement of any person, with the intent to commit any act referred to in paragraph (a) (i) to(iii).[12]

9 Martin Ewi and Anton Du Plessis, 'Counter-Terrorism and Pan-Africanism: From Non-Action to Non-Indifference', *Research Handbook on International Law and Terrorism* (Edward Elgar Publishing Limited, 2014) 736.

10 Resolution 213 on the Strengthening of Cooperation and Coordination among African States, July 1992 [AHG/Res.213 (XXVIII)].

11 Ewi Martin and Kwesi Aning, 'Assessing the Role of the African Union in Preventing and Combating Terrorism in Africa' (2006) 15 *African Security Review* 3, 41.

12 Article 1(3), 1999 Terrorism Convention.

It is important to note that the text describes what constitutes a terrorist act rather than terrorism. As well, terrorism is defined in the above Article as a violation of national criminal law. The absence of a more detailed definition means that the decision is still left to Member States as to which acts constitute a violation of their particular criminal laws. The 1999 Convention on Prevention and Combating Terrorism includes a list of obligations for Member States, including, in its annex, a list of international instruments the signing of which they are required to 'consider, as a matter of priority.'[13] In order to fight terrorism, States are required to review their national laws and criminalise terrorist acts, as defined, with 'appropriate penalties.'[14] However, there is no detail as to what appropriate penalties mean.

A Protocol to the Convention to 'enhance the effective implementation' of the 1999 Convention on Prevention and Combating Terrorism was signed in 2004.[15] The necessary fifteen ratifications were obtained in January 2014 and the Protocol was set to enter into force in February 2014.[16] In July 2011, the AU also adopted an African Model Law on Counter Terrorism 'to facilitate the elaboration of necessary domestic legislation',[17] which will be further discussed in Chapter 7. As a regional organisation, the AU has adopted a number of treaties to deal with terrorism, which means State sovereignty is, *a priori*, left unchallenged as States can choose to ratify and implement treaties.

3 The Council of Europe

Common action against terrorism in Europe has traditionally been found in bilateral action or cooperation between a small number of States and informal groups.[18] The most advanced cooperation has been taking place in the past

13 Article 2(b), OAU Convention on the Prevention and Combating of Terrorism, 1999.

14 Article 2(a), (c), (d), OAU Convention on the Prevention and Combating of Terrorism, 1999.

15 Document available at http://www.au.int/en/treaties (last accessed 08.12.2015).

16 See ratification list: http://www.au.int/en/sites/default/files/treaties/7787-sl-protocol_on_terrorism.pdf (last accessed 08.12.2015). The website of the AU does not, however, list the protocol as entered into force.

17 Ewi and Du Plessis, 'Counter-Terrorism and Pan-Africanism: From Non-Action to Non-Indifference', 752.

18 For instance, the Club de Berne, dating back to the mid-1960s and composed of the heads of European security agencies. The Club de Berne, however, is not part of the EU, but rather, is a sharing of intelligence forum between members of the EU, Norway and Switzerland. See 'EU Commission Keen to Set up New Counter-terrorism Office', *Euobserver.com*, 31 March 2011, http://euobserver.com/institutional/32104 (accessed

twenty years between France and Spain[19] in order to tackle the problems raised by the armed separatist organisation, Euskadi ta Askatasuna (ETA).[20] However, very early regional case law also exists on counterterrorism.[21] The Council of Europe has had an important role in framing regional counterterrorism through human rights protection.

The Council of Europe has the authority to adopt conventions, which will then need to be ratified and enforced in order to be binding. The organisation has produced 200 instruments on various subjects, including three specific conventions on terrorism.[22] It first addressed terrorism with the adoption of the 1977 European Convention on Terrorism, the first instrument in Europe at the time. This convention focused on extradition, and like most international organisations' counterterrorism measures, did not define terrorist acts, but rather, left the definition to Member States. This convention was updated by a Protocol signed in 2003, as a result of the September 11, 2001 attacks.[23] The actual approach to the phenomenon of terrorism changed with the May 2005 adoption of the Council of Europe's Convention on the Prevention of Terrorism. Its purpose, set out in Article 2, is:

> To enhance the efforts of Parties in preventing terrorism and its negative effects on the full enjoyment of human rights, in particular the right to life, both by measures to be taken at national level and through international

16.12.2015); 'EU Intelligence Services Opening up to Collaboration', *Intelligence Quarterly*, 21 January 2011, http://www.intelligencequarterly.com/2011/01/eu-intelligence-services-opening-up-to-collaboration/ (accessed 16.12.2015).

19 'Other types of cooperation', France Diplomatie, available at http://www.diplomatie.gouv.fr/en/country-files/spain/spain-and-france/other-types-of-cooperation-6347/ (last accessed 16.12.2015).

20 A summary of the history of the terrorist organisation and the legal responses can be found on the Council of Foreign Relations database, at http://www.cfr.org/separatist-terrorism/basque-fatherland-liberty-eta-spain-separatists-euskadi-ta-askatasuna/p9271 (last accessed 08.12.2015).

21 *Lawless v Ireland* (1961) 1 EHRR 1, for example.

22 Namely, the European Convention on the Suppression of Terrorism 1977, the Council of Europe Convention on the Prevention of Terrorism 2005 and the Council of Europe Convention on Laundering, Search, Seizure and Confiscation of the Proceeds from Crime and on the Financing of Terrorism, 2005.

23 The Preamble of the Protocol refers to the Committee of Ministers of the Council of Europe's Declaration of 12 September 2001 and its Decision of 21 September 2001 on the Fight against International Terrorism, which both condemn the September 11, 2001 attacks.

> co-operation, with due regard to the existing applicable multilateral or bilateral treaties or agreements between the Parties.[24]

Once again, the Council of Europe's Convention on the Prevention of Terrorism does not define the terrorism offence *per se*. Rather, it states that the 'terrorist offence means any of the offences within the scope of and as defined in one of the treaties listed in the Appendix.'[25] This convention, however, not only criminalizes terrorism, but also the acts that may lead to it, such as incitement, recruitment and training, and provides for 'a much broader and improved framework of investigative and judicial cooperation' among European States.[26] It also includes the obligation to investigate and prosecute those suspected of being involved in terrorism and, importantly, creates the obligation to provide support for victims of terrorism.[27]

The Convention on the Prevention of Terrorism is now completed by a Protocol, adopted in May 2015, to implement UN Security Council Resolution 2178 on FTFs.[28] Both the 2005 Convention and its 2015 Protocol have had an important impact on Member States as many of its measures have then been copied by EU counterterrorism measures.[29]

Very soon after the events of September 11, 2001, the Council of Europe also published Guidelines on human rights and the fight against terrorism.[30] These Guidelines offer advice and good practice examples on how to respect human rights while countering terrorism. They do not have a legally binding force, but

---

24 Council of Europe, *Council of Europe Convention on the Prevention of Terrorism*, 16 May 2005, ETS No. 196, Article 2.

25 Ibid., Article 1(1).

26 Victor Comras, 'Europe's New Anti Terrorism Convention Strong on Substance, Short on Adherents', *Counterterrorism Blog*, 6 June 2007, available at http://counterterrorismblog.org/2007/06/europes_new_anti_terrorism_con.php (last accessed 16.12.2015).

27 Council of Europe, *Council of Europe Convention on the Prevention of Terrorism*, 16 May 2005, ETS No. 196, Article 13.

28 Council of Europe: Committee of Ministers, *Additional Protocol to the Council of Europe Convention on the Prevention of Terrorism*, 19 May 2015.

29 See note 406. Moreover, a proposal for a new EU directive on counterterrorism, tabled in December 2015 incorporates a number of measures included in the 2015 Protocol to the Council of Europe 2005 Convention, see Proposal for a Directive of the European Parliament and of the Council on combating terrorism and replacing Council Framework Decision 2002/475/JHA on combating terrorism, available at http://www.statewatch.org/news/2015/dec/eu-council-dir-terrorism-comparison-table-15279-15.pdf (last accessed 07.01.2016).

30 Guidelines on human rights and the fight against terrorism adopted by the Committee of Ministers on 11 July 2002 at the 804th meeting of the Ministers' Deputies.

are considered by Member States to 'trace inter alia the absolute limits established to protect human rights. Exceeding these limits cannot be justified even in the fight against terrorism.'[31]

The existence of such an instrument shows the importance, for the Council of Europe, of the necessity to protect human rights when countering terrorism. In this respect, the most important Council of Europe instrument is the European Convention of Human Rights (ECHR) and its fourteen protocols,[32] which is implemented by the ECtHR. While it does not address terrorism *per se*, it has become crucial in this context. Judgments of the ECtHR are binding on the Member States[33] and its jurisdiction is to deal with inter-State disputes and with cases brought by individuals against their government once all national remedies have been exhausted. As seen through its judgments, the ECtHR also has had an important impact on counterterrorism, which will be discussed in further detail in Chapter 8.

4 The European Union

The EU is the regional organisation that has the most comprehensive counterterrorism regime but it is not the purpose of this book to examine all the legal issues that arise from this complex framework.[34] This section shows the breadth of the measures adopted by the EU after September 11, 2001 and the competences that have been transferred by States, and it examines them in terms of their sovereignty impact as seen from the following: the 1997 Treaty of

---

31 'Fighting Terrorism in the Council of Europe', website of the General Foreign Office of Germany, available at http://www.auswaertiges-amt.de/EN/Aussenpolitik/GlobaleFragen/TerrorismusOK/TerrorismusbekaempfungER_node.html (last accessed 16.12.2015).

32 Council of Europe, The European Convention on Human Rights, Rome 4 November 1950 and its Five Protocols: Paris 20 March 1952, Strasbourg 6 May 1963, Strasbourg 6 May 1963, Strasbourg 16 September 1963 and Strasbourg 20 January 1966.

33 Article 46(1) ECHR.

34 A number of works have been written on the subject of EU counterterrorism, including, among others, Raphael Bossong, *The Evolution of EU Counter-Terrorism: European Security Policy After 9/11* (Routledge, 2012); Rik Coolsaet, 'EU Counterterrorism Strategy: Value Added or Chimera?' (2010) 86 *International Affairs*, 857; and Cian C. Murphy, *EU Counter-Terrorism Law: Pre-Emption and the Rule of Law* (Hart Publishing, 2012). Moreover, a multi-year project examined the impact, legitimacy and effectiveness of EU counterterrorism; see Final Report Summary SECILE (Securing Europe through Counter-Terrorism – Impact, Legitimacy and Effectiveness), European Commission, available at http://cordis.europa.eu/result/rcn/164039_en.html (last accessed 14.01.2016).

Amsterdam, that resulted in the EU being 'for the first time vested with an explicit internal security mandate,' through Article 2 that creates an 'area of freedom, security and justice'; Article 29 TEU that establishes the objective of providing citizens with a 'high level of safety' within the Area of Freedom, Security and Justice (AFSJ);[35] and through the integration of the Schengen Aquis.[36] Yet, there remains in the EU, a '"hidden agenda" of minimising sovereignty costs.'[37] This tension will be examined here.

The EU, which was first directly affected by international terrorism in Madrid in 2004 and London in 2005, has developed an 'extensive multidimensional approach that combines legislative and operational, repressive and preventive, internal and external, as well as institutional, measures.'[38] The EU now has a Security Strategy[39] that includes terrorism as one of its 'key threats' and it has developed a Plan of Action on Terrorism, which was originally created in 2007 and amended several times;[40] an Internal Security Strategy 2010–2014;[41] and the European Agenda on Security 2015–2020.[42] The Plan of Action contains 200 individual measures[43] and is, therefore, the 'most comprehensive plan ever adopted by the EU on an internal or external security threat.'[44] The SECILE

35 For an analysis of the AFSJ, see Neil Walker (ed.), *Europe's Area Of Freedom, Security, And Justice* (Oxford University Press, USA, 2005).

36 The Schengen Acquis consists of the 1985 Schengen Agreement, the 1990 Convention, and the measures implementing the Convention. Under the Schengen agreement, European States have abolished border controls for internal borders and created a unique visa system for international travel.

37 Bossong, *The Evolution of EU Counter-Terrorism: European Security Policy After 9/11*, 55.

38 Jörg Monar, 'The EU's Approach post-September 11: Global Terrorism as a Multidimensional Law Enforcement Challenge' (2007) 2 *Cambridge Review of International Affairs*, 2, 267.

39 European Security Strategy (often referred to as the 'Solana Strategy') on 12 December 2003, full text available at http://www.consilium.europa.eu/uedocs/cmsUpload/78367.pdf (last accessed 16.12.2015).

40 European Council 'European Action Plan on Combating Terrorism', March 2007, document available http://register.consilium.europa.eu/doc/srv?l=EN&f=ST%207233%20 2007%20REV%201 (last accessed 16.12.2015).

41 The EU Internal Security Strategy in Action – COM(2010) 673 final, available at http://eur-lex .europa.eu/legal-content/EN/TXT/?uri=URISERV%3Ajl0050 (last accessed 08.12.2015).

42 The European Agenda on Security – COM (2015) 185 final, available at http://ec.europa.eu/ dgs/home-affairs/e-library/documents/basic-documents/docs/eu_agenda_on_security _en.pdf (last accessed 08.12.2015).

43 Jörg Monar, 'Common Threat and Common Response? The European Union's Counter-Terrorism Strategy and its Problems' (2007) 42 *Government and Opposition*, 292, 303.

44 Jörg Monar, 'The EU's approach post-September 11: global terrorism as a multidimensional law enforcement challenge', 267.

project concluded that 'since 2001, the EU has been very active in counter-terrorism, having produced 239 counter-terrorism measures between Autumn 2011 and Summer 2013, 88 of which are "legally binding".'[45] Moreover, the counterterrorism regime of the EU benefits from the existence of institutions such as EUROPOL, the European Police Office, and EUROJUST, the EU's Judicial Cooperation Unit. EUROPOL's aims are to coordinate intelligence and information,[46] while those of EUROJUST are prosecution and investigation.[47] These organisations, however, focus mainly on law enforcement and do not consist of a merging of criminal regimes. The 2015–2020 Agenda is also proposing a new Counter-Terrorism Center, in addition to its existing Counterterrorism Coordinator.[48] The Solidarity Clause introduced in 2009 states that

> 1. The Union and its Member States shall act jointly in a spirit of solidarity if a Member State is the object of a terrorist attack or the victim of a natural or man-made disaster. The Union shall mobilise all the instruments at its disposal, including the military resources made available by the Member States, to:
>
> (a) – prevent the terrorist threat in the territory of the Member States;
> – protect democratic institutions and the civilian population from any terrorist attack;

45 See Final Report Summary – SECILE (Securing Europe through Counter-Terrorism – Impact, Legitimacy and Effectiveness).

46 EUROPOL is the EU's law enforcement agency. In terrorism, it provides support 'in the form of analysis and analytical products, threat assessments, information exchange and the annual EU Terrorism Situation and Trend Report (TE-SAT), which presents facts and figures on terror arrests in the EU, as well as new trends in terrorist activity.' See https://www.europol.europa.eu/content/page/mandate-119 (last accessed 16.12.2015).

47 EUROJUST is the EU's judicial cooperation unit. It 'stimulates and improves the coordination of investigations and prosecutions between the competent authorities in the Member States and improves the cooperation between the competent authorities of the Member States, in particular by facilitating the execution of international mutual legal assistance and the implementation of extradition requests.' See http://eurojust.europa.eu/about/background/Pages/mission-tasks.aspx (last accessed 16.12.2015).

48 The role was established in 2004 after the Madrid attacks. See European Council – Declaration on combating terrorism, 25 March 2004, 7906/04, 29 March 2004, available at http://data.consilium.europa.eu/doc/document/ST-7906-2004-INIT/en/pdf (last accessed 09.12.2015). The current coordinator is Gilles de Kerchove, appointed in 2007. See Press release S256/07, available at http://www.consilium.europa.eu/en/policies/fight-against-terrorism/counter-terrorism-coordinator/ (last accessed 09.12.2015).

– assist a Member State in its territory, at the request of its political authorities, in the event of a terrorist attack[49]

The Solidarity Clause has not been invoked so far and it is interesting to note that, after the Paris attacks in November 2015, France invoked the mutual defence clause[50] that provides that 'if a Member State is the victim of armed aggression on its territory, the other Member States shall have towards it an obligation of aid and assistance by all the means in their power, in accordance with Article 51 of the United Nations Charter.'[51]

A significant contribution of the EU as a regional organisation after September 11, 2001 came with the adoption of two Framework Decisions on 13 June 2002 by the Council of Ministers.[52] The text of the Framework Decisions did not refer explicitly to the September 11, 2001 attacks, but the EU website quotes the events as the catalyst to the document.[53] The document identifies terrorism as 'one of the most serious violations of the universal values…and principles…on which the EU is founded,' thereby justifying its regional action.

The first Framework Decision created a European Arrest Warrant (EAW), harmonizing the rules of extradition and lowering the threshold for extradition requests. The EAW is an example of mutual recognition of judicial decisions within the EU. Moreover, this Framework Decision does away with the political exception, which traditionally prevents extradition, and makes double criminality an option. Thus, the EAW allows a wider range of acts to fall under its scope despite the variety of existing criminal systems. Yet, the EAW is not a harmonisation of the criminal law of the Member States, but rather, a coordination of different regimes. Indeed, the EAW functions on the basis of national law for the definition of terrorism.[54] Similarly, a European Evidence

---

49 Article 222 TFEU.

50 'France 'at war' inaugurates EU's mutual defence clause', *EurActiv.com*, 17 November 2015, available at http://www.euractiv.com/sections/global-europe/france-war-inaugurates-eus-mutual-defence-clause-319531 (last accessed 17.12.2015).

51 Article 42(7) TEU.

52 According to Art. 34 (2) (b) of the TEU, Framework Decisions serve the purpose of approximating of the laws and regulations of the Member States. They shall be binding upon the Member States as to the result to be achieved but shall leave the choice of form and methods to the national authorities. With the Lisbon Treaty, Framework Decisions disappear, but existing decisions are not abandoned. The Framework Decisions were subject to an optional jurisdiction of the ECJ according to Article 35 TEU.

53 'Terrorist Offences' in Justice, Freedom and Security Section of Europa, the website of the EU.

54 Article 2(1), Council Framework Decision 2002/584/JHA of 13 June 2002 on the European arrest warrant and the surrender procedures between Member States.

Warrant was created in 2008,[55] which aims to 'replace the system of mutual assistance in criminal matters between Member States for obtaining objects, documents and data for use in criminal proceedings.'[56] Similar to the EAW, this instrument favours coordination of national regimes rather than integration.

More importantly, the second Framework Decision creates a common definition of terrorism, applicable throughout the organisation. Article 1(1) sets out a three-part definition of terrorism consisting of the context of an action, the aim of the action and the specific acts being committed as follows:

> Each Member State shall take the necessary measures to ensure that the intentional acts referred to below in points (a) to (i), as defined as offences under national law, which, given their nature or context, may seriously damage a State or an international organisation where committed with the aim of:
> – seriously intimidating a population, or
> – unduly compelling a Government or international organisation to perform or abstain from performing any act, or
> – seriously destabilising or destroying the fundamental political, constitutional, economic or social structures of a State or an international organisation

It is interesting to note that, except for two offences,[57] the penalties for what is defined as terrorism are left to Member States. The only requirement is that the offences must be extraditable and that the penalty must be heavier than it would be without the required special intent for terrorism. Generally, this Framework Decision also contains obligations for Member States to 'criminalise certain behaviours.'[58] However, the text does not define the term 'punishable,' and leaves it to Member States to decide whether to make the offences

55 Council Framework Decision 2008/978/JHA of 18 December 2008 on the European evidence warrant for the purpose of obtaining objects, documents and data for use in proceedings in criminal matters.

56 Europa, Summaries of European Legislation, available at http://europa.eu/legislation_summaries/justice_freedom_security/judicial_cooperation_in_criminal_matters/jl0015_en.htm (last accessed 16.12.2015).

57 Article 5(3) Framework Decision 2008/978/JHA is a fifteen-year minimum custodial sentence for leading a terrorist group and an eight-year sentence for other offences relating to involvement with a terrorist group.

58 Mark Pieth, 'Criminalising the Financing of Terrorism' (2006) 4 *Journal of International Criminal Justice*, 5, 1077.

criminal or not,[59] but makes a provision for the 'protection of, and assistance to victims.'[60] In addition, Article 1(2) states that 'this Framework Decision shall not have the effect of altering the obligation to respect fundamental rights and fundamental legal principles as enshrined in Article 6 of the Treaty on European Union.'[61]

A Framework Decision from 2008 amends this Framework Decision,[62] and includes provisions from the Council of Europe 2005 Terrorism Convention, which some EU Member States had already implemented in their domestic order.[63] The Framework Decision creates three new offences linked to terrorism: public provocation to commit a terrorist offence, recruitment to terrorism and training for terrorism.[64] In addition, a proposal was tabled in December 2015 for a new Directive on counterterrorism before the Council of the EU, which includes many measures to implement the Council of Europe 2015 Protocol to the 2005 Convention.[65] As the Protocol aims to implement UN Security Council Resolution 2178, many EU States have already adopted some of these measures. With an EU Directive however, these measures would need to be implemented by all EU Member States.[66]

Framework Decisions, with their obligation of goal, allow States to adopt their own domestic legislation to implement them. For Saul, the 2002 Terrorism

59 'Amendment of the Framework Decision on combating terrorism', Press Release, EU, 18 April 2008.

60 Article 10, Council Framework Decision of 13 June 2002 on combating terrorism,

61 Article 6(1) of the TEU states as follows: 'The Union recognises the rights, freedoms and principles set out in the Charter of Fundamental Rights of the European Union of 7 December 2000, as adapted at Strasbourg, on 12 December 2007, which shall have the same legal value as the Treaties.'

62 Council Framework Decision 2008/919/JHA of 28 November 2008 amending Framework Decision 2002/475/JHA on combating terrorism.

63 See Report from the Commission to the European Parliament and the Council on the implementation of Council Framework Decision 2008/919/JHA of 28 November 2008 amending Framework Decision 2002/475/JHA on combating terrorism {SWD(2014) 270 final, available at http://ec.europa.eu/dgs/home-affairs/e-library/documents/policies/crisis-and-terrorism/general/docs/report_on_the_implementation_of_cfd_2008-919-jha_and_cfd_2002-475-jha_on_combating_terrorism_en.pdf (last accessed 16.12.2015).

64 See Article 1(1) of FD 2008 amending Article 3.

65 Proposal for a Directive of the European Parliament and of the Council on combating terrorism and replacing Council Framework Decision 2002/475/JHA on combating terrorism, available at http://www.statewatch.org/news/2015/dec/eu-council-dir-terrorism-comparison-table-15279-15.pdf (last accessed 07.01.2016).

66 Although due to the nature of EU directives, each State will be able to adapt the obligation to fit their own legal order.

Framework Decision 'raises concerns for the rule of law,'[67] because it contains a very loose definition and therefore, it can result in broad legal rules. The implementation of Framework Decisions will be examined in the next chapter.

Finally, the use of administrative measures in the shape of sanctions has increased significantly in the context of terrorism and the EU has played a significant role in these measures. The question of whether regional organisations have the power to impose sanctions has divided academics and politicians[68] but, in practice, the EU started adopting sanctions against third States and non-State actors in the early eighties. Over time, and especially after the creation of the Common Foreign and Security Policy in the early nineties, this practice 'increased in frequency and sophistication, so that it is now possible to speak of an *EU sanctions policy*.'[69] The EU has clarified its position in a 2008 Parliament Resolution[70] and created a framework with the Basic Principles on the Use of Restrictive Measures (Sanctions) adopted by the Council of the organisation in 2003. Article 215 Treaty on the Functioning of the European Union (TFEU) now provides for sanctions against States, but also 'natural or legal persons and groups or non-State entities'. This basis has been carefully drafted in order to include all types of targets, including non-State actors, and this provides an 'explicit legal basis' for smart sanctions.[71] Some measures of this type have been taken against terrorist suspects within the framework of the Common Foreign and Security Policy. In this context, the EU

---

67 Ben Saul, 'Criminality and Terrorism' in A. Salinas de Frias, K. Samuel and N. White (eds.), *Counter-Terrorism: International Law and Practice* (Oxford, United Kingdom: Oxford University Press, 2012) 161.

68 For instance, Christina Eckes argues that the EU does not possess the competence to adopt individual sanctions in Christina Eckes, *EU Counter – Terrorist Policies and Fundamental Rights – The Case of Individual Sanctions*, Oxford Studies in European Law (Oxford University Press, 2009) even though the European Courts have not expressly denied this competence. See for instance: Court of Appeal, *A, K, L, Q, G v HM Treasury* [2008] EWCA Civ 1187 and Joined Cases C-402/05 P & C-415/05 P and *Kadi & Al Barakaat v Council of the European Union and EC Commission*, 3 C.M.L.R. 41 (2008).

69 Clara Portela, 'Where and Why Does the EU Impose Sanctions ?' (2005) n° 17 *Politique européenne*, 83.

70 European Parliament Resolution, 'The Evaluation of EU Sanctions as part of the EU's actions and policies in the area of human rights' (2008/2031 (INI), September 4, 2008) Paragraph C.

71 Stephan Griller and Jacques Ziller, *The Lisbon Treaty: EU Constitutionalism Without a Constitutional Treaty?* European Community Studies Association of Austria (ECSA Austria) Publication Series (Springer, 2008).

has created a 'consolidated list'[72] of suspects and organisations that face financing measures. Sanctions against terrorist suspects are the subject of Part 3 of this book.

The EU counterterrorism framework is the most advanced among regional organisations, but there are failings in the creation of a true EU intelligence-sharing platform.[73] As well, despite the following quote from the EU summit of February 2015 outcome that 'Member States have the primary responsibility for addressing terrorism',[74] the EU recent norms or proposed measures have been criticised for being too intrusive.[75] In particular, the current debate on the passenger name record (PNR) agreement within the EU is dividing many Member States over the issues it raises on privacy.[76]

The regional model of counterterrorism, therefore, does not present, *a priori*, a serious challenge to the State as the main actor, except for the EU. Similar to the case of the UN, because most measures are adopted by the executive branch of the organisation or through inter-governmental treaties, the regional counterterrorism measures mainly reflect domestic policy and may, in fact, act to provide even more basis for States to increase their action against terrorism. Therefore, as with the UN, the question of the practical application of these regional regimes in the legal order of their Member States must be addressed in order to assess their success and their impact on Member States' sovereignty.

---

72 EU External Action, Consolidated list of persons, groups and entities subject to EU financial sanctions, available at http://eeas.europa.eu/cfsp/sanctions/consol-list_en.htm (last accessed 01.07.13).

73 Cian Murphy details the intelligence efforts of the EU and questions its efficiency, in Murphy *EU Counter-Terrorism Law: Pre-Emption and the Rule of Law*, 32.

74 Council of the European Union 6044/15, Outcome of the Council Meeting, 3367th Council meeting, Brussels, 9 February 2015, text available at http://www.consilium.europa.eu/en/meetings/fac/2015/02/outcome-of-the-council-meeting_fac_150209_pdf/ (last accessed 16.12.2015).

75 See Fionnuala Ní Aoláin, 'Europe's Newest Attempts at Anti-Terror Regulation Could Shake the Foundations of the EU', *Just Security*, 7 February 2015, available at http://justsecurity.org/20077/european-regulates-again-counter-terrorism/ (last accessed 16.12.2015).

76 See 'EU moves on air passenger deal to track foreign fighters', Mail Online, 24 February 2015, available at http://www.dailymail.co.uk/wires/ap/article-2966901/EU-moves-air-passenger-deal-track-foreign-fighters.html and 'EU PNR proposal is "neither proportionate nor appropriate"', The Parliament Magazine, 11 March 2015, available at https://www.theparliamentmagazine.eu/articles/feature/eu-pnr-proposal-neither-proportionate-nor-appropriate (both last accessed 16.12.2015).

CHAPTER 7

Compliance and Implementation

The analysis of the powers of regional organisations shows a clear increase in focus towards counterterrorism. However, many organisations have adopted counterterrorism measures through traditional conventions that require ratification and implementation at the national level. The implementation of these documents is a concern for regional organisations that do not have the same infrastructure as States or the binding power of the Security Council. In question, therefore, is the impact on the sovereignty of the Member States. This chapter will examine the ratification rates, as well as the types of measures States have adopted, if any.

1 The Organisation of American States

Although all but one Member State of the OAS signed the Inter-American Convention on Terrorism in 2002,[1] to date, only twenty-four of the thirty-five Member States have ratified it.[2] The instrument was adopted very soon after September 11, 2001 and the wide-ranging signatures reflect the symbolic reaction to terrorist attacks, which is in contrast to the absence of ratifications since 2008.

A number of Member States of the OAS have updated their counterterrorism regimes since the adoption of the Inter-American Convention on Terrorism. For example, Colombia created a Financial Information and Analysis Unity in 2002, and El Salvador adopted its Special Law Against Acts of Terrorism, which entered into force in 2006.[3] It was also noted that Colombia 'frequently

1 The Commonwealth of Dominica did not sign the Convention in 2002, but later acceded to it.

2 Bahamas, Barbados, Belize, Bolivia, Haiti, Jamaica, St Kitts and Nevis, St Lucia, St Vincent and the Grenadines and Suriname signed the Convention in 2002, but have not ratified it. The ratification status of the Convention, as well as a list of reservations can be found at http://www.oas.org/juridico/english/sigs/a-66.html (last accessed 16.12.2015).

3 State Reports on Terrorism, US Department of State, available at http://www.state.gov/j/ct/rls/crt/2002/ and http://www.state.gov/j/ct/rls/crt/2006/ (both last accessed 16.12.2015). This law has since been criticised by human rights institutions. See Human Rights Watch, 'El Salvador: Terrorism Law Misused Against Protesters', July 30, 2007, available at https://www.hrw.org/news/2007/07/30/el-salvador-terrorism-law-misused-against-protesters (last accessed 16.12.2015).

 | DOI 10.1163/9789004299580_009

integrated the recommendations of the UN and OAS into its security decisions.'[4] Yet, others still fail to have appropriate legislation. As seen by the US Financial Action Task Force, Bolivia and Ecuador have been identified as jurisdictions with 'structural deficiencies in their anti-money laundering/countering terrorist finance (AML/CFT) regime.'[5] As well, in 2007, the Egmont Group, an informal group of financial intelligence units, had suspended Bolivia from their Membership because of continued lack of adequate legislation against terrorist financing.[6]

The main issue with the Inter-American system is that there is no specific legal obligation to comply with its Convention on Terrorism, or any enforcement mechanism. Article 16 *encourages* 'technical cooperation and training programs at the national, bilateral, subregional, and regional levels and in the framework of the Organisation of American States to strengthen the national institutions responsible for compliance with the obligations assumed under this Convention,' and periodic meetings are requested,[7] but there is no mention of penalties for violations.

The OAS has been successful in creating a framework for counterterrorism and encouraging cooperation, and, as detailed in Chapter 8, its judicial system has also contributed in some ways to enforcing this framework. However, the practical application of the obligations on Member States is still underdeveloped and the impact on the sovereignty of its Member States is rather limited.

2 The African Union

In 2004, the framework created by the AU had 'yet to be implemented by many of its 53 Member States.'[8] Ten years after these remarks, the ratification itself is rather high, but scepticism has been expressed regarding whether some African States have adopted terrorism legislation as a result of Security Council

4 See report from the US State Department, available at http://www.state.gov/j/ct/rls/crt/2011/195546.htm (last accessed 16.12.2015).

5 FATF Public Statement – 19 October 2012 (see http://www.fatf-gafi.org/topics/high-riskandnon-cooperativejurisdictions/documents/fatfpublicstatement-19october2012.html#Bolivia (last accessed 16.12.2015)).

6 State Reports on Terrorism, US Department of State, available at http://www.state.gov/j/ct/rls/crt/2009/index.htm (last accessed 16.12.2015).

7 Article 18, Inter-American Convention against Terrorism.

8 Ademola Abass, *Regional Organisations and the Development of Collective Security: Beyond Chapter 8 of the UN Charter* (Hart Publishing, 2004).

Resolution 1373 rather than the regional instrument.[9] As of January 2013, the latest available ratification date,[10] fifty of the fifty-four States had signed the 1999 Convention on the Prevention and Combating of Terrorism and forty-one had ratified it, whereas only fifteen States had ratified the 2004 Protocol to the Convention.[11]

Despite the signing of the 1999 Convention on the Prevention and Combating of Terrorism, a 'glaring omission is the lack of enforcement mechanism of the instrument.'[12] The Convention only requires, in its Article 2, to notify the Secretary-General of all the legislative measures that State Parties have taken and the penalties imposed on terrorist acts within one year of ratification of, or accession to, the Convention. In September 2002, the AU adopted a Plan of Action on the Prevention and Combating of Terrorism in Africa. The Peace and Security Council is in charge of implementing the counterterrorism measures of the African Union, but its only action so far – in January 2015 – has been to authorise a Multinational Joint Task Force (MNJTF) to act against Boko Haram.[13] Moreover, the African Model Law on Counter Terrorism was adopted specifically to assist Member States in implementing the provisions contained in the various continental and international counter-terrorism instruments.[14] A study of implementation in African countries summarises the situation as follows:

> The key political factors limiting ratification relate to the priorities and perceived level of importance of counter-terrorism efforts especially when weighed against other pressing demands facing many African countries. More specifically, ratification in Africa is hampered

9 J. Shola Omotola, 'Assessing Counter-Terrorism Measures in Africa: Implications for Human Rights and National Security' (2008) 2 *Conflict Trends*, 44.

10 Status lists of OAU/AU Treaties, Conventions, Protocols & Charters, available at http://www.au.int/en/treaties (last accessed 16.12.2015).

11 See ratification list: http://www.au.int/en/sites/default/files/treaties/7787-sl-protocol_on_terrorism.pdf (last accessed 08.12.2015). The website of the AU does not, however, list the protocol as entered into force.

12 J. Cilliers and Kathryn Sturman, eds. 'Africa and Terrorism, Joining the Global Campaign' (Monograph Series No 74, ISS, 2002).

13 Communiqué of the 484th meeting of the PSC on the Boko Haram terrorist group, 30 January 2015, available at http://www.peaceau.org/en/article/communique-of-the-484th-meeting-of-the-psc-on-the-boko-haram-terrorist-group (last accessed 09.12.2015).

14 Decision on the Report of the Peace and Security Council on its Activities and the State of Peace and Security in Africa, Assembly of the African Union Decision 369 (XVII) (30 June–1 July 2011).

> because states do not see counter-terrorism as a sufficient priority, resist the manner in which the agenda is presented, face internal political struggles to bring legal measures forward, or (for mainly historical reasons) entertain reservations about the discourse of counter-terrorism.[15]

The AU's counterterrorism regimes reflects a counterterrorism regime that is protective of the sovereignty of its Member States as it created a regional framework to address the threat, which is largely ratified, but not actually implemented due to a number of factors stressed by the quote above. There is an increasing sense of the need for a common response to the terrorism threat, but the many pressing issues plaguing the African continent, do not make this common response a priority.

3 The Council of Europe

To date, thirty-four out of forty-seven States have ratified the 2005 Convention on the Prevention of Terrorism, while three have not even signed it.[16] In practice, however, this convention has had an impact on other regional instruments.[17] The 2003 Protocol to the 1977 European Convention on Terrorism introduces the role of a European Committee on Crime Problems, as 'responsible for following the application of the Convention'. However, the Protocol has not yet entered into force due to a lack of ratification.[18]

It is too early to assess the implementation of the 2015 Protocol that does not have ratification thus far,[19] but the Protocol cites Resolution 2178, which Member States of the Council of Europe must implement as Members of the

15 Jolyon Ford, *African Counter-Terrorism Legal Frameworks a Decade after 2001* (Institure for Security Studies 2011) vi.

16 All parties to the 1977 European Convention on Terrorism need to ratify the Protocol in order that it enters into force. A number of these States have not ratified the convention and its ratification status can be accessed at http://www.conventions.coe.int/Treaty/Commun/ChercheSig.asp?NT=196&CM=1&DF=&CL=ENG (last accessed 09.12.2015).

17 The EU 2008 Framework Decision includes some provisions from the Council of Europe 2005 Convention on the Prevention of Terrorism and therefore, in theory, now all EU States also have to implement these provisions.

18 See http://www.coe.int/en/web/conventions/full-list/-/conventions/treaty/190/signatures?p_auth=nMofqmM9 (last accessed 09.12.2015).

19 See http://www.coe.int/en/web/conventions/full-list/-/conventions/treaty/217/signatures?p_auth=nMofqmM9 (last accessed 16.12.2015).

UN. Therefore, a number of States are already in effect implementing some of its measures because of their Resolution 2178 obligations.[20]

In 2003, the Council of Europe appointed a group of inter-governmental experts, known as the Committee of Experts on Terrorism, or CODEXTER,[21] whose role is to coordinate the implementation of the Council of Europe's actions against terrorism. In order to do so, the CODEXTER prepares State profiles, outlining the counterterrorism situation in each State of the organisation, and consistently updating them to reflect changes in national legislation.[22] More importantly, the committee prepared the draft for the 2005 Convention on the Prevention of Terrorism and regularly report on the status of its implementation. The CODEXTER reports concern specific areas of the Convention on the Prevention of Terrorism,[23] and contain updates to State profiles. Moreover, the CODEXTER regularly compiles a ratification list for the international instruments included in the Annex of the Convention on the Prevention of Terrorism.

Instruments by the Council of Europe might need implementation, but a comprehensive framework has been developed. Moreover, the organisation has had an important impact on counterterrorism through the role of its court, which will be discussed in Chapter 8.

4 The European Union

The EU's counterterrorism regime is based on a Framework Decision and not a convention, hence the application of its measures does not depend on ratification

20 A report was published by the Law Library of Congress, which includes the laws adopted by States on FTFs, which is available at 'Treatment of Foreign Fighters in Selected Jurisdictions', http://www.loc.gov/law/help/foreign-fighters/index.php (last accessed 09.12.2015).

21 Committee of Experts on Terrorism was created in 2003 and replaced the Multidisciplinary Group on International Action against Terrorism (GMT). Information on this committee can be found at http://www.coe.int/t/dlapil/codexter/default_EN.asp and http://www.coe.int/t/dlapil/codexter/about_en.asp (both last accessed 16.12.2015).

22 For instance, at the December 2010 meeting, CODEXTER updated the State profile of Slovakia to include its new provisions of the criminal code concerning terrorism (see report available at http://www.coe.int/t/dlapil/codexter/Source/meetings/codexter_m19_report_en.pdf (last acessed 16.12.2015)).

23 For instance, ongoing activities of the CODEXTER related to the monitoring of the specific provisions of the Convention CETS No 196, in particular, the freedom of expression and '*apologie du terrorisme*' report, November 2009; Second Thematic Review – Recruitment for terrorism, April 2009; and Protection and compensation of victims of terrorism: Exchange of best practices, November 2008. All documents available at http://www.coe.int/t/dlapil/codexter/working-documents.asp (last accessed 06.01.2016).

first but, rather, on implementation directly. This is important because it means that the EU terrorism measures are less dependent on the will of Member States, as they must adopt measures against terrorism even though they are free to decide how. The EU requires implementation reports from its Member States, as does the Security Council. This implementation requirement is significant in a regional landscape that favours intergovernmental treaties to deal with terrorism without real enforcement power. In this respect, the EU is closer to the Security Council, in terms of both the binding nature of some of its measures and its implementation requirement. Yet, each Member State still assesses the terrorist threats in a national perspective, and similar to the UN system, implementation *reporting* does not automatically mean enforcement of regional measures.

In practice, Article 11 of the 2003 EU Framework Decision requested that Member States submit a report to the General Secretariat of the Council and to the Commission by 31 December 2002. A 2004 Commission's report noted that, as of December 2002, only five Member States had provided the Commission with information on implementation and only two of them actually included the relevant transposing provisions.[24] The 2004 report stated that by 2001, only eight out of fifteen Member States included terrorism as a separate crime,[25] while other States were punishing terrorist acts as a common offence or an *infraction de droit commun*. The report also raised the issue of the lack of information, which 'led to a delay in the production of the report.'[26]

A second report on the implementation of the Framework Decision was published in November 2007.[27] This report covered all Member States and distinguished between those that had already been assessed in the previous report and those that were being evaluated for the first time. Among the latter

24 'Commission evaluates the Implementation of the Framework Decision on Terrorism', EC04-142EN, June 2004, available at http://www.eu-un.europa.eu/articles/fr/article_3565_fr.htm (last accessed 16.12.2015). The document, Report from the Commission based on article 11 of the Council Framework Decision of 13 June 2002 on combating terrorism {SEC(2004)688} COM/2004/0409 final is available at http://eur-lex.europa.eu/legal-content/EN/TXT/PDF/?uri=CELEX:52004DC0409&from=EN (last accessed 07.01.2016). The 2004 report only applies to twelve Member States, as the others had not provided information.

25 Implementation report, 2004, 'Assessment', page 6.

26 'Commission evaluates the Implementation of the Framework Decision on Terrorism', EC04-142EN, June 2004, 'level of transposition.'

27 Report from the Commission of 6 November 2007 based on Article 11 of the Council Framework Decision of 13 June 2002 on combating terrorism COM (2007) 681, available at http://eur-lex.europa.eu/LexUriServ/LexUriServ.do?uri=CELEX:52007DC0681:EN:NOT (last accessed 16.12.2015).

group, the Commission stressed that only eight had a separate category of crime for terrorist offences.[28] As for the previously assessed States, the assessment was based on the findings of the previous report and the complementary information they had provided. The Commission reported a 'higher level of compliance'[29] in this group. As well, the Commission noted that, in general, most States had 'satisfactor[ily] achieved implementation of the main provisions contained in the Framework Decision,'[30] but bemoaned the lack of improvement for the shortcomings that were raised in the first report.[31]

Although no further report by the Commission exists for the 2002 Framework Decision, a report from the EU Counter-Terrorism Coordinator, dated 30 November 2010, stressed that all Member States had 'completed' the implementation of the Framework Decision and that national legislation is in place.[32] After this report, the Commission financed a conference about the impact of the Framework Decisions on the national legislation and case law. The findings of this conference, which took place in May 2011,[33] were published in a more general report on EU counterterrorism measures.[34] This report found that 'the most relevant effect of the Framework Decision 2002 was to impose the duty to incriminate terrorist offences as such, since some of the Member States, and perhaps even the majority, did not provide for any specific punishment for acts of terrorism.'[35]

For Cian Murphy, who produced a detailed analysis of the reports divided by elements of the Framework Decision, these reports 'demonstrate the failure

28 2007 Commission Report, Article 1: The Czech Republic, Estonia, Greece, Hungary, Latvia, Malta, the Netherlands and Slovakia. At the time of the report, Cyprus was amending its legislation to comply.

29 2007 Commission Report, Conclusions.

30 Ibid.

31 Ibid.

32 Council of the European Union, 'Addendum to Note', 15893/10 ADD 1 REV 1, Brussels, 1 December 2010.

33 'EU Counter-Terrorism Offences: What Impact on National Legislation and Case-law?' Conference organized by ECLAN (European Criminal Law Academic Network) and the Institute for European Studies (Université Libre de Bruxelles), with the financial support of the European Commission (DG Justice) and the Ministry of Justice of the Grand Duchy of Luxembourg Brussels, Albert Borschette Conference Centre (27 May 2011) and Institut d'Etudes Européennes, ULB (28 May 2011).

34 Francesca Galli, Anne Weyembergh, Marianne Dony and François Foret, *EU counter-terrorism offences: What impact on national legislation and case-law?* (Éditions de l'Université de Bruxelles, 2012).

35 Pedro Caeiro, 'Concluding Remarks' in *EU counter-terrorism offences: What impact on national legislation and case-law?*, 305.

of Member States to correctly implement the law'.[36] A number of reasons are responsible for this failure including the following: States implemented the Framework Decision by transcribing literally the definition into national law 'which causes substantial problems with regard to interpretation of the law by national judiciary;'[37] the minimum rule principle of the Framework Decision led to an '"over-implementation" of European legislation on substantive criminal law,' which made a common definition of terrorism 'virtually impossible;'[38] and a number of States claimed that they did not need to implement the Framework Decision because their counterterrorism legislation was sufficient.[39] Oren Gross and Fionnuala Ní Aoláin summarise implementation as follows:

> Unfortunately, as two surveys of state incorporation of the Framework Decision reveal, state practice has generally been to use the Decision as a means to augment and further legislate and not as a minimal base-line.[40]

A 2014 report, which analyses the implementation of the 2008 Framework Decision, confirms these trends.[41]

---

36 Cian Murphy, *EU Counter-Terrorism Law: Pre-Emption and the Rule of Law*, 55.

37 Jorn Vestergaard, 'Denmark: Criminal Law as an Anchorage Point for Proactive Anti-Terrorism Legislation', in *EU counter-terrorism offences: What impact on national legislation and case-law?*,193.

38 Pedro Caeiro, 'Concluding Remarks', 307.

39 Henri Labayle, 'Les Infractions Terroristes En Droit Pénal Français: Quel Impact Des Décisions-cadres de 2002 et 2008?' in *EU Counter-terrorism Offences: What Impact on National Legislation and Case-law?* (Editions de l'Université de Bruxelles, 2012), 51; Manuel Cancio Melia, 'The Reform of Spain's Antiterrorist Criminal Law and the 2008 Framework Decision', in *EU Counter-terrorism Offences: What Impact on National Legislation and Case-law?* (Editions de l'Université de Bruxelles, 2012) 100; and John R Spencer, '"No Thank You, We've Already Got One!" Why EU Anti-Terrorist Legislation Has Made Little Impact on the Law of the UK', in *EU counter-terrorism offences: What impact on national legislation and case-law?* (Editions de l'Université de Bruxelles 2012) 119.

40 Oren Gross and Fionnuala Ní Aoláin, *Law in Times of Crisis: Emergency Powers in Theory and Practice*, 2006, 417.

41 See the Report from the Commission to the European Parliament and the Council on the implementation of Council Framework Decision 2008/919/JHA of 28 November 2008 amending Framework Decision 2002/475/JHA on combating terrorism {SWD(2014) 270 final}, available at http://ec.europa.eu/dgs/home-affairs/e-library/documents/policies/crisis-and-terrorism/general/docs/report_on_the_implementation_of_cfd_2008-919-jha_and_cfd_2002-475-jha_on_combating_terrorism_en.pdf (last accessed 10.12.2016).

Other reports from the Commission deal with the implementation of the Framework Decision on the EAW.[42] A July 2007 report, evaluating the measures adopted by Member States to transpose the Framework Decision into national law from 2005 until 1 June 2007, stated that the EAW was a 'success'[43] and that it was now 'standard practice' within the EU. In practice, the Commission reported that 6900 warrants were issued in 2005 alone. It also examined the transitional measures adopted by States, and whether or not they were suitable.[44] The report recalled the difficulties of implementation, particularly in Germany and Cyprus that held, in two cases, that the provisions were contrary to their constitutions.[45] These States, as well as France and Poland, had to amend their constitutions to comply with the provisions of the Framework Decision.[46]

A 2011 Commission report[47] gave information on the number of warrants issued and executed since the first report,[48] as well as on the implementation status. It noted that twelve Member States[49] had not made amendments to their respective legislations, although they were recommended to do so in previous Council and Commission reports. The report stressed that these

42 'Report from the Commission on the implementation since 2005 of the Council Framework Decision of 13 June 2002 on the European arrest warrant and the surrender procedures between Member States', COM (2007) 407 final, July 2007, document available at http://register.consilium.europa.eu/doc/srv?l=EN&f=ST%2011788%202007%20INIT (last accessed 16.12.2015).

43 Ibid.

44 Czech Republic adopted an amendment to the law of transposition that came into force on 1 July 2006 in order to give full retroactive effect to the EAW. On the other hand, Article 30(1) of the Italian Law states that its provisions apply only to requests for execution of European arrest warrants issued and received after its entry into force on 14 May 2005, which does not conform with the Framework Decision.

45 Decision of the Constitutional Court (DE) of 18.7.2005, BvR 2236/04, also available in 58 NJW (Neue Juristische Wochenschrift) 2289 (2005) and A. No. 294/2005, Supreme Court of Cyprus, 7 Nov. 2005.

46 The Polish Code of Criminal Procedure was amended following a Constitutional reform in July 2006.

47 Report from the Commission to the European Parliament and the Council on the implementation, since 2007, of the Council Framework Decision of 13 June 2002 on the European arrest warrant and the surrender procedures between Member States, COM (2011) 175 final, 11 April 2011, available at http://eur-lex.europa.eu/LexUriServ/LexUriServ.do?uri=COM:2011:0175:FIN:EN:PDF (last accessed 16.12.2015).

48 54 689 EAWs were issued and 11 630 EAWs were executed between 2005 and 2009.

49 Belgium, Cyprus, Denmark, Germany, Greece, Spain, Finland, Italy, Malta, Netherlands, Sweden and the UK.

omissions were 'even more regrettable' in the case of those Member States that were expressly mentioned in the 2007 Report as 'requiring an effort to comply fully with the Council Framework Decision.'[50] Despite qualifying the EAW as a 'success' in the previous report, the Commission considered the situation slightly less optimistic in 2011[51] and it stressed that there was still much work to do.

A reform proposal of the EAW system was presented in 2014 by the European Parliament, which noted the following:

> Whereas Framework Decision 2002/584/JHA has for the most part been successful in meeting its aim of speeding up surrender procedures throughout the Union compared to the traditional extradition system among Member States and constitutes the cornerstone of mutual recognition of judicial decisions in criminal matters...;
>
> Whereas problems have however arisen in its operation, some specific to Framework Decision 2002/584/JHA and resulting from gaps in the Framework Decision such as failing to explicitly include fundamental rights safeguards or a proportionality check as well as from the incomplete and inconsistent implementation thereof; whereas other problems are shared with the set of mutual recognition instruments due to the incomplete and unbalanced development of the Union area of criminal justice.[52]

The reform proposal of the EAW system also asked the Commission to 'request from Member States comprehensive data relating to the operation of the EAW mechanism and to include such data in its next implementation report with a view to proposing appropriate action if any problems are found.'[53] There have not been any reports since.

Regional organisations have not adopted measures with a binding nature comparable to the adoption of measures by the Security Council under Chapter 7. The exception is the EU counterterrorism system, because it has the ability to adopt binding measures, even if the measures create an obligation of result,

50 Cyprus, Denmark, Italy, Malta, Netherlands and the UK.

51 'Confidence in the application of the EAW has been undermined by the systematic issue of EAWs for the surrender of persons sought in respect of often very minor offences', 2011 report, page 7.

52 European Parliament resolution of 27 February 2014 with recommendations to the Commission on the review of the EAW (2013/2109(INL)), Preamble §B and C.

53 Ibid., §9.

rather than a strict obligation of means to achieve it. At the same time, as previously noted, because of existing national legislation against terrorism, implementation has not been perfect. It must also be stressed that the EU's counterterrorism effort 'was never intended to replace the Member States' own endeavours. Rather, it complements the national level.'[54] As Gijs de Vries, former EU Counter-Terrorism Coordinator stated, 'the role of the EU in fighting terrorism, as defined by the Council, is to assist the Member States, not to supplant them.'[55] But this assisting role might lead to a legitimising role of domestic agendas. What this means is that the Member States continue to retain full national sovereignty in these fields because they have not transferred exclusive competence to the EU. Rather, they are still able to pursue their national anti-terrorism policies and use the framework of the Framework Decisions. The Member States of the EU agree on a 'shared approach,'[56] but 'the EU's ability to tackle terrorism is limited.'[57]

Although regional organisations are able to create a common framework on counterterrorism and set an agenda for its apprehension of terrorists, they still rely on domestic measures for the practical application of these standards. The ratification rates of regional counterterrorism instruments are generally satisfying, but do not necessarily translate in national implementation. On the other hand, and contrary to the UN situation, the regional organisations examined in this book have a judicial body that can review the measures adopted by the organisation and/or have a human rights mandate. These two aspects are particularly crucial for counterterrorism, as outlined in the Introduction. The role of regional courts in counterterrorism is discussed in the next chapter.

---

54 Rik Coolsaet, 'EU Counterterrorism Strategy: Value Added or Chimera?'(2010) 86 *International Affairs* 4, 872.

55 Gijs de Vries, 'The European Union's role in the fight against terrorism', address in Royal Irish Academy, Dublin, 25 November 2004, available at http://www.consilium.europa.eu/uedocs/cmsUpload/Dublin_November_25-2004.pdf (last accessed 16.12.2015).

56 Daniel Keohane, 'The Absent Friend: EU Foreign Policy and Counter-Terrorism' (2008) 46 *Journal of Common Market Studies*, 1, 129.

57 Daniel Keohane, 'The EU and Counter-terrorism' (Centre for European Reform, Working Papers, May 2005) 2.

CHAPTER 8

The Role of Regional Courts in Counterterrorism

For the regional organisations focused on in this book, having a court is important for sovereignty either because the court might review the actions of the executive branch, thereby providing the checks and balances that are usually absent in inter-governmental organisations or because the regional courts have a mandate on human rights, which is relevant in international counterterrorism. It is noteworthy that some of the regional courts have come to play a fundamental role in counterterrorism and this chapter, as well as the next ones, show the crucial impact that regional courts have had on both counterterrorism and State sovereignty. Although the human rights mandate of the AU's judicial system is an important issue, its role will not be expanded on here, as it has not developed a sufficient case law on terrorism.[1]

1 The Organisation of American States

The judicial system of the OAS has a mandate for human rights based on the American Declaration of the Rights and Duties of Man, adopted in 1948,[2] and the American Convention on Human Rights (ACHR), adopted in 1969.[3] The main organs of the system are the Inter-American Commission on Human

1 The AU's human rights system is fast developing and authors have written about it (see, for example, Rachel Murray and Debra Long, *The Implementation of the Findings of the African Commission on Human and Peoples' Rights* (Cambridge University Press, 2015)). It does not refer to cases on terrorism however. Only one case was brought to the African Commission on Human and People's Rights, but it was rejected as inadmissible (see ACommHPR, *Mohammed Abdullah Saleh Al-Asad v Djibouti*, Communication No. 383/2010, 55th Ordinary Session, 14 October 2014). Ewi and du Plessis show in an analysis of the role of the AU on terrorism, that a more significant role is undertaken by 'Sub-Regional' criminal justice systems (see Martin Ewi and Anton Du Plessis, 'Criminal Justice Responses to Terrorism in Africa: The Role of the African Union and Sub-Regional Organizations', *Counter-Terrorism: International Law and Practice* (Oxford University Press, 2012) 1016).

2 American Declaration Of The Rights And Duties Of Man (Adopted by the Ninth International Conference of American States, Bogotá, Colombia, 1948).

3 American Convention On Human Rights (Adopted at the Inter-American Specialized Conference on Human Rights, San José, Costa Rica, 22 November 1969).

 | DOI 10.1163/9789004299580_010

Rights (IACHR) and the Inter-American Court of Human Rights (IACtHR).[4] The IACHR's principal function is to promote the defence of human rights on the continent. This is done by regularly visiting Member States to assess their human rights situation and preparing reports on the human rights assessments in the OAS. The IACHR also hears cases, stemming from petitions that can emanate from any person or group of persons,[5] but its decisions are not binding.[6] In addition, the IACHR has the authority to issue precautionary measures against a State[7] and has 'invoked this mechanism with a significant degree of success.'[8] In 2005, the IACHR reiterated the binding nature of these measures, stating that it was an 'international obligation that Member States have to comply with precautionary measures issued by the Inter-American Commission on Human Rights.'[9] Finally, the IACHR can decide to take the case to the IACtHR.[10] To date, twenty-two of the twenty-four States parties to the ACHR have accepted the jurisdiction of the IACtHR.[11] Under the ACHR, either the IACHR or a State party can bring a case before the Court, but not an individual.[12]

---

4 The IACHR was established in 1959 and was incorporated into the Charter by the 1967 amendments. It is composed of seven commissioners, elected from the OAS Member States. The IACtHR, composed of seven judges, held its first hearing in 1979.

5 Article 23, Rules of Procedure, Document available at http://www.oas.org/en/iachr/mandate/Basics/rulesiachr.asp (last accessed 16.12.2015).

6 Donald T. Fox, 'Inter-American Commission on Human Rights Finds United States in Violation' (1988) 82 *American Journal of International Law*, 3, 602.

7 Article 25, Rules of Procedure.

8 Brian D. Tittemore, 'Guantanamo Bay and the Precautionary Measures of the Inter-American Commission on Human Rights: A Case for International Oversight in the Struggle Against Terrorism' (2006) 6 *Human Rights Law Review*, 2, 381.

9 IACHR Resolution 1/05, 8 March 2005, Paragraph 1, available at http://www.cidh.org/resolution1.05.htm (last accessed 16.12.2015).

10 Article 45, Rules of Procedure.

11 Antigua and Barbuda; Bahamas; Belize; Canada; Guyana; St. Kitts & Nevis; St. Lucia and St. Vincent; and Grenadines are not parties to the Convention. The United States signed the Convention in 1977, but never ratified it. As for Trinidad and Tobago, they originally signed the Convention on 28 May 1991, but suspended its ratification on 26 May 1998 over the death penalty issue. In 1999, under President Alberto Fujimori, Peru announced it was withdrawing its acceptance of the IACHR's jurisdiction. This decision was reversed by the transitional Peruvian government of Valentin Paniagua in 2001. Venezuela announced, in September 2012, its decision to withdraw from the Convention after the Venezuelan government condemned its decision in the case of *Diaz Pena* (see Press release on the OAS website, available (in Spanish) at http://www.oas.org/es/centro_noticias/comunicado_prensa.asp?sCodigo=C-307%2F12 (last accessed 16.12.2015)).

12 Article 61(1), American Convention on Human Rights.

A year after the events of September 11, 2001, the IACHR decided 'to undertake a study by which it would reaffirm and elaborate upon the manner in which international human rights requirements regulate State conduct in responding to terrorist threats.'[13] This led to the production of a report on terrorism and human rights published in 2002. In the report, the IACHR stressed that:

> In no uncertain terms ... ensuring fundamental human rights in these situations does not contradict the obligation of member states to protect their populations from terrorist violence. To the contrary, the very purpose of anti-terrorist initiatives is to preserve the fundamental rights and democratic institutions that terrorism seeks to undermine and destroy.[14]

The report then analysed some specific rights in their application to counterterrorism and, for each right, described the situation regarding international instruments and the case law referred to by the IACHR in that respect.[15] The IACHR has also ruled on the legality of domestic norms and standards.[16]

It was noted that the IACtHR has 'tripled the number of cases that it resolves annually,'[17] contributing to a focus on human rights for the region. Of course, the IACtHR and IACHR only have jurisdiction over the ACHR and will, therefore, not consider potential violation of the Terrorism Convention of 2002 by Member States. However, the IACHR has been particularly active in addressing the issues raised by counterterrorism legislation of its Member States[18] and trying to adjust the balance between security and the protection of fundamental

---

13 Executive Summary, Report on Terrorism and Human Rights, OEA/Ser.L/V/II.116, Doc. 5 rev. 1 corr., 22 October 2002.

14 Preface, Report on Terrorism and Human Rights, OEA/Ser.L/V/II.116, Doc. 5 rev. 1 corr., 22 October 2002.

15 On the rule of *non bis in idem*: IACtHR, *Loayza Tamayo* Case, September 19, 1997, Series C N° 33, §66; on the right to life and the use of force against individuals: IACtHR *Neira Alegría* Case, Judgment of 19 January 1995, Series A N° 20, §4.

16 See, for example, the Report on the Situation of Human Rights in Peru (1993), OEA/Ser.L/V/II.83, Doc. 31, 85th Session, 12 March, 1993 and the Report on the Situation of Human Rights in Peru (2000) OEA/Ser.L/V/II.106, Doc. 59 rev., 2 June 2000, §80, 168.

17 James Cavallaro and Stephanie Brewer, 'Reevaluating Regional Human Rights Litigation in the Twenty-First Century: The Case of the Inter-American Court' (2008) 102 *American Journal of International Law* 4, 768.

18 For an analysis of these cases, see Sergio Garcia Ramirez, 'The Inter-American Court of Human Rights' Perspective on Terrorism', *Counter-Terrorism: International Law and Practice* (Oxford University Press, 2012) 785–810.

freedoms. For instance, it has taken an active role in the controversy over Guantanamo Bay. In March 2002, the IACHR received a request for precautionary measures by the Council for Constitutional Rights, the Human Rights Clinic at Columbia Law School and the Centre for Justice and International Law, regarding the treatment, by the United States, of 245 prisoners detained at Guantanamo Bay.[19] The IACHR imposed the precautionary measures on the US,[20] and asked the government to adopt measures for a US court to determine the legal status of the detainees. Further measures were taken and expanded by the IACHR over the years.[21] On 30 September 2014, former prisoner Djamel Ameziane filed a petition with the IACHR seeking reparations from the US government for human rights violations.[22] However, the US disputes this jurisdiction and the precautionary measures.[23] Other OAS States have temporarily refused to comply with judgments of the IACHR,[24] 'asserting that the Court's orders were an intrusion upon state sovereignty,'[25] but they eventually complied with the judgment.[26]

19 A copy of the 24 February 2002 request for precautionary measures is available at: http://humanrights.ucdavis.edu/projects/the-guantanamo-testimonials-project/testimonies/prisoner-testimonies/ameziane_iachr_petition.pdf (last accessed 16.12.2015).

20 Guantanamo Bay Precautionary Measures Communication of 12 March 2002 from IACHR President Juan E. Mendez to US Secretary of State Colin Powell ('Guantanamo Bay Precautionary Measures of March 12, 2002') (2002) 96 *American Journal of International Law* 730; 11 IHRR 1037 (2004). See also Annual Report of the IACtHR 2002, Chapter III(C)(1) para. 80.

21 For an analysis of the measures until 2006, see Tittemore, 'Guantanamo Bay and the Precautionary Measures of the Inter-American Commission on Human Rights.'

22 For a summary of the case, as well as updates, see *Ameziane v Obama/Ameziane v United States*, Center for Constituional Rights, available at https://ccrjustice.org/home/what-we-do/our-cases/ameziane-v-obama-ameziane-v-united-states (last accessed 13.12.2015).

23 Following the various precautionary measures imposed by the IACHR, the US has disputed its jurisdiction over detainees at Guantanamo Bay. See for instance, the US' response to the Precautionary Measures of 2002, delivered on 12 April 2002 available at http://www.state.gov/s/l/38642.htm (last accessed 16.12.2015). See also *Hanidan v Rumsfeld* 415 F 3d 33 (DC Cir. 2005) in re Guantanamo Detainees 355 F. Supp. 2d 311 (DDC 2005) and *Boumediene v Bush* 2005 US Lexis 14580 (DC Cir. 2005).

24 Castillo Petruzzi, Compliance with Judgment, Inter-Am. Ct. H.R. (ser. C) No. 59, at 3, para. 3 (17 Nov. 1999).

25 Cavallaro and Brewer 'Reevaluating Regional Human Rights Litigation in the Twenty-First Century: The Case of the Inter-American Court', 789.Legislative Res. No. 27152 (July 8, 1999); see Letter from Fernando de Trazegnies Granda, Minister for Foreign Affairs, Republic of Peru, to Ce´sar Gaviria, Secretary General, OAS (8 July 1999), available at http://www.umn.edu/humanrts/iachr/Annuals/app16-99.html (last accessed 16.12.2015).

26 'Peru will comply with Inter-American court ruling, says Humala', *Peru this week*, 26 September 2012, available at http://www.peruthisweek.com/news-2878-Peru-will-comply-with-Inter-American-court-ruling-says-Humala/ (last accessed 16.12.2015).

The activities of the IACHR and the IACtHR allow a focus on human rights matters in the continent's counterterrorism regimes. Yet, their authority is partially disputed, mainly by the US, and better implementation remains necessary for their success.

2 The Council of Europe

The ECtHR has issued many important cases in the context of terrorism.[27] Many of these cases focus on the human rights of terrorist suspects, including a developed case law concerning the interdiction to extradite a terrorist suspect to a State where he might face torture.[28] Other such cases deal with fair trial and detention rights[29] and whether national legislation on terrorism is compatible with the Council's counterterrorism regime in place at the time.[30] Moreover, the scope of Article 2 of the ECHR on the right to life has been widened progressively and now includes an obligation to investigate. This obligation was discussed first in the *McCann* case, and then again in 2003 in the non-admissibility decision in *Menson,* where the court held that 'the absence of any direct State responsibility for the death of an individual who was not in the State's custody or detention did not exclude the applicability of Article 2.'[31] As well, in the *Osman* case, the ECtHR held that:

> States have a positive obligation to protect the life of their citizens. They should do all that could be reasonably expected from them to avoid a real and immediate risk to life of which they have or ought to have knowledge.[32]

The cases of the ECtHR contribute to the idea that counterterrorism has become an international obligation on States, but it also furthers the idea that

---

27 See for instance *McCann and others v United Kingdom* (21 ECHR 97 GC); *Lawless v Ireland,* No. 1/61, Judgment of 1July 1961, ECHR.

28 In *Trabelsi vs. Italy,* Application no. 50163/2008, Decision, 13.4.2010, the ECHR found Italy in violation of Article 3 of the Convention in respect to the expulsion of a Tunisian man accused of being a Member of a terrorist organisation.

29 In *A v UK* (2009) 49 EHRR 29, [2009] All ER (D) 203 (Feb.), the ECHR held that the detention of terrorist suspects based 'solely or to a decisive degree on closed material' always amounts to a breach of procedural fairness as guaranteed by the ECHR.

30 *Murray v The United Kingdom* 14310/88; [1994] ECHR 39; (1994) 19 EHRR 193.

31 *Menson and others v UK* (2003) 37 EHRR CD 220.

32 *Osman v United Kingdom* (23452/94) [1999] 1 F.L.R. 193.

the obligation to prevent risks for the lives of citizens does not mean unlimited powers against terrorist suspects. For example, in *A v UK*, the ECtHR held that the detention of terrorist suspects based 'solely or to a decisive degree on closed material' always amounts to a breach of procedural fairness as guaranteed by the ECHR.[33] The decision was 'irrespective of domestic exigencies and procedural safeguards such as the use of special advocates and private hearings questioning the veracity of the evidence.'[34] As well, the obligation of non-refoulement[35] that was stated in the *Soering* case[36] was confirmed in the *Saadi* case, where the ECtHR unanimously noted that involvement in terrorism did not affect an individual's absolute rights under Article 3.[37]

Finally, recent cases on extraordinary renditions show that the ECtHR is ready to investigate even the most secret activities by States to deal with terrorism.[38] An analysis of rendition cases show that the attempts before domestic courts to obtain redress for renditions have been rather unsuccessful due to national security obstacles[39] and therefore, the involvement of European courts is crucial. The next section further shows that European courts have attempted to balance national (and international) security interests with the protection of human rights.

While the ECtHR has adopted many decisions on terrorism, it faces the general problem when it comes to the actual implementation of its judgments. While the supervision of this implementation is conducted by the

33 *A v UK* (2009) 49 EHRR 29, [2009] All ER (D) 203 (Feb.).

34 Philippe Sands and Pierre Klein, *Bowett's Law of International Institutions* (6th Edition, Thomson Reuters, 2009).

35 This means the obligation to not return an individual to a country where that individual is likely to be subjected to treatment, which would violate Article 3.

36 In the *Soering* case, the Court established that the extradition of a German national to the US to face charges of capital murder violated Article 3 of the Convention guaranteeing the right against inhuman and degrading treatment: *Soering v United Kingdom* 11 Eur. Ct. H.R. (ser. A) (1989).

37 *Saadi v Italy*, Appl. No. 37201/06, Council of Europe: European Court of Human Rights, 28 February 2008.

38 The first case was *El Masri v the former Yugoslav Republic of Macedonia* [GC], no. 39630/09, ECHR 2012, Judgment of 13 December 2012. Two cases followed against Poland namely, *Al Nashiri v Poland*, no. 28761/11, Judgment of 24 July 2014 and *Husayn (Abu Zubaydah) v Poland*, no. 7511/13, Judgment of 24 July 2014. Other cases are currently pending before the ECtHR (see http://www.echr.coe.int/Documents/FS_Secret_detention_ENG.PDF (last accessed 14.12.2015)).

39 Silvia Borelli, 'Extraordinary Renditions, Counter-Terrorism and International Law', in *Research Handbook on International Law and Terrorism* (Edward Elgar Publishing Limited, 2014) 369.

Committee of Ministers,[40] in practice, each State is in charge of implementing ECtHR judgments that apply to it.[41] In this context, it is noted that the 'number of cases still awaiting the finalisation of the execution process after more than five years has increased.'[42] Some Member States have also complained about 'infringement' by the ECtHR of their national sovereignty[43] and, in general, show a disappointing implementation rate of ECtHR rulings.[44] In December 2015, Russia adopted a new law giving the constitutional court the right to declare international court orders unenforceable in Russia if they contradict the constitution.[45] This, in effect, means that a local court can chose which decisions of the ECtHR it implements. The UK is also regularly vocal against the ECtHR.[46] Yet, figures show that 99 percent of cases brought against the UK before the ECtHR are struck out[47] and in practice, 'the

40 Article 46(2) ECHR.

41 Article 46(1) of the European Convention on Human Rights.

42 Supervision of the execution of judgments and decisions of the European Court of Human Rights, Annual Report 2011, Page 10; document available at http://www.coe.int/t/dghl/monitoring/execution/Source/Publications/CM_annreport2011_en.pdf (last accessed 16.12.2015).

43 Dimitry Medvedev said, 'We never gave away a part of our sovereignty that would allow an international court or foreign court to carry out decisions that violate our national legislation.' See 'Russian Legislation Takes Aim At Human Rights Court In Strasbourg', Radio Free Europe, June 2011, available at http://www.rferl.org/content/russia_legislation_takes_aim_european_human_rights_court/24248275.html (last accessed 16.12.2015).

44 In January 2011, the Parliamentary Assembly of the Council of Europe passed a special resolution where it found that 'nine countries are failing to implement the rulings of the European Court of Human Rights (ECHR) in a timely fashion'. See 'Turkey among worst performers in implementing ECtHR rulings', *Today's Zaman*, 28 January 2011, available at http://www.todayszaman.com/diplomacy_turkey-among-worst-performers-in-implementing-ecthr-rulings_233707.html (last accessed 16.12.2015).

45 'Russia passes law to overrule European human rights court', *BBC News*, 4 December 2015, available at http://www.bbc.com/news/world-europe-35007059 (last accessed 14.12.2015).

46 See the Sixth Report of the Independent Reviewer Pursuant to Section 14(3) of the Prevention of Terrorism Act 2005, Lord Carlile of Berriew Q.C., 3 February 2011; Prime Minister David Cameron has said he is 'fed up' with the fact that Omar Othman cannot be deported to Jordan: 'Abu Qatada release: Cameron "fed up"', BBC News, 13 November 2012; and the Justice Secretary said there was a 'need for major changes to the way the European human rights framework operates.' (See *Abu Qatada* case is reason to change human rights laws, says Justice Secretary', The Telegraph, 13 November 2012, available at http://www.telegraph.co.uk/news/uknews/law-and-order/9675236/Abu-Qatada-case-is-reason-to-change-human-rights-laws-says-Justice-Secretary.html (last accessed 16.12.2015)).

47 Figures available for download at http://ukhumanrightsblog.com/2013/01/24/european-court-of-human-rights-struck-out-99-of-uk-cases-in-2012/analysis_statistics_2012_eng/ (last accessed 16.12.2015).

vast majority of human rights judgments are now generated by [the UK's] own courts.'[48]

In the specific context of counterterrorism, the ECtHR has mainly aimed to protect human rights and procedural standards for terrorist suspects, thereby giving an important focus to what had otherwise been put aside by States and international organisations in their fight against terrorism. Chapter 9 will show how the ECtHR has tried to constructively integrate human rights into the framework of administrative measures taken by States and the UN against terrorist suspects.[49]

3 The European Union

In contrast to the other regional courts considered here, the ECJ has a very wide mandate that is not limited to human rights issues. Rather, it deals with many different types of cases including agriculture, trade, citizenship and family law to name a few, and covers 'all the law of the European Union.'[50]

A variety of cases of importance can be noted. These include, of course, the cases on supremacy and primacy of EU law that developed the new European legal order. The ECJ established the concept of primacy in *Costa v ENEL* by stating that EU treaties had supremacy over national legislation.[51] This followed the creation of the concept of a 'new legal order', which was integrated within the national legal systems in *NV Algemene Transporten Expeditie Onderneming van Gend en Loos v Nederlandse Administratie der Belastingen*.[52] Such integration means that the then European Community (EC) law was directly applicable to both the Member States and their nationals. The ECJ based its argument on Article 189 of the EEC Treaty, which stated that EC regulations had an 'obligatory' value and were 'directly applicable within each Member State.'[53] The principle of supremacy was later confirmed and

48 Adam Wagner, 'Context Is Everything – European Court of Human Rights Struck Out 99% of UK Cases in 2012', *UK Human Rights Blog*, 24 January 2013, available at http://ukhumanrightsblog.com/2013/01/24/european-court-of-human-rights-struck-out-99-of-uk-cases-in-2012/ (last accessed 16.12.2015).

49 See *Al-Jedda v United Kingdom* [2011] ECHR 1092 (7 July 2011). A detailed analysis follows in Chapter 10.

50 Horspool and Humphreys, *European Union Law*, 76.

51 *Flaminio Costa v ENEL* [1964] ECR 585 (6/64).

52 Case 26/62 *NV Algemene Transport- en Expeditie Onderneming van Gend en Loos v Nederlandse Administratie der Belastingen* [1963] ECR 1.

53 Ibid.

expanded in *Internationale Handelsgesellschaft mbH v Einfuhr- und Vorratsstelle für Getreide und Futtermittel*[54] where the Court stated the primacy of EC law over national constitutional law. In these cases, the courts of the EU developed the doctrines that now regulate the relationships between the organisation and its Member States.[55] In that respect, the EU, through its judicial branch, has had a significant impact on the sovereignty of its States.

Yet, it is mostly the Council and the Commission of the EU that have been involved in creating a counterterrorism regime in the EU and this echoes the strong role of the executive at the national level for all security matters. Traditionally, the European Parliament and the ECJ had not been involved. As well, the ECJ does not have jurisdiction over the Common Foreign and Security Policy, except to review the legality of decisions on restrictive measures for combating terrorism.[56] In this context, the EU judicial branch has competence to hear individual complaints of alleged human rights violations.[57] Moreover, if a Member State fails to implement a judgment of the ECJ, the Commission can bring infringement proceedings against it[58] and the ECJ itself can impose financial penalties on the Member State.[59]

In practice, until September 11, 2001, less than ten judgments had been decided that directly focused on terrorism. However, since September 11, 2001, more than fifty judgments were given on terrorism-related issues.[60] In particular, since the EU has developed a regime of administrative measures against terrorist suspects, an important case law has developed that looks at the legality of these measures through the prism of human rights.[61] While originally

54 *Internationale Handelsgesellschaft mbH v Einfuhr- und Vorratsstelle fur Getreide und Futtermittel* (Case 11/70) [1970] ECR 1125.

55 A Declaration attached to the Treaty of Lisbon describes the doctrine of supremacy of Union Law over national law: Declaration No. 17 Concerning Primacy. Declarations annexed to the Final Act of the Intergovernmental Conference which adopted the Treaty of Lisbon signed on 13 December 2007: 'The Conference recalls that, in accordance with well settled case law of the Court of Justice of the European Union, the Treaties and the law adopted by the Union on the basis of the Treaties have primacy over the law of Member States, under the conditions laid down by the said case law.'

56 The Court can review compliance with Article 40 TEU and the legality of decisions adopted under Article 263(4) TFEU.

57 Article 263 TFEU.

58 Article 260 TFEU.

59 Article 260(2) TFEU.

60 General search for EU cases is available at http://curia.europa.eu/jcms/jcms/j_6/ (last accessed 14.12.2015).

61 The detailed analysis of this case law is the subject of Chapter 10.

human rights were not specifically part of the EU's mandate, the organisation came to develop its own jurisprudence following national case law on human rights safeguards.[62] In *Internationale Handelsgesellschaft*, the ECJ held that the respect for human rights was an 'integral part of the general principles of law protected by the Court of Justice.'[63] Human rights were given a legal basis by the Lisbon Treaty, which gives legal binding effect to the European Charter of Fundamental Rights[64] and provides for the accession of the EU to the ECHR.[65] The most important case on the relationship between the human rights standards protected by the EU and the demands of the EU's counterterrorism regime is the *Kadi* case, decided by the ECJ in 2008.[66] The case will be analysed in Chapter 10.

The action of regional organisations in the context of international security has traditionally been limited by the role of the Security Council, which has the sole jurisdiction for international peace and security, as well as States' desire to maintain national security as a domestic competence. However, many of these organisations were affected by terrorism because of the experiences of their own Member States'. As a result, from an early stage of their existence, some of them adopted common measures to facilitate prosecution between States, including extradition treaties. In practice, counterterrorism was mainly conducted through bilateral State action and cooperation.

Significantly, and contrary to the Security Council whose decisions are not subject to judicial review by other organs of the UN, regional organisations have, from the start, provided some balance to counterterrorism needs with other values. The need to protect and promote human rights while countering terrorism is included in all regional documents. Moreover, some of the regional organisations have made human rights the focus of their action and regional courts have increased the scope of human rights protection. It might be said that the main success of the regional organisations in the context of counterterrorism is that it provides a framework that favours national action while protecting shared values. If human rights are considered to be 'inherent to

62 *Solange I* [1974] 2 CMLR 540.

63 Case C-11/70 *Internationale Handelsgesellschaft* [1970] ECR 1125, 1134.

64 Protocol on the application of the Charter of Fundamental Rights of the European Union to Poland and to the United Kingdom.

65 Protocol relating to Article 6(2) of the Treaty on European Union on the accession of the Union to the European Convention on the Protection of Human Rights and Fundamental Freedoms. This is currently under negotiations.

66 Joined Cases C-402/05 P and C-415/05 P *Kadi and Al Barakaat International Foundation v Council of the European Union and Commission of the European Communities* [2008] ECR I-6351.

external sovereignty,'[67] regional organisations have managed to create counterterrorism regimes that include human rights and this should be welcomed. The impact of this case law has been fundamental on the Member States of these organisations that can face financial penalties in case of non-application.

At the same time, the increasing role of regional organisations in issues of counterterrorism has the potential to conflict with the primary role of the Security Council and the review mechanisms present in regional systems have contributed to these conflicts. As David Bonner stated, the 'rules of the game'[68] of counterterrorism have not actually changed since the beginning of the century. For him, what is different is that courts 'have started applying an enhanced level of scrutiny in an area they once characterised as too sensitive for judicial involvement.'[69] This role is crucial in the context of counterterrorism because it has had an impact, not only on Member States of regional organisations, but also on the UN itself, in part through conflicts between various counterterrorism regimes.

67 Besson, 'Sovereignty, International Law and Democracy', 160.

68 David Bonner, *Executive Measures, Terrorism and National Security: Have the Rules of the Game Changed?* (Ashgate Publishing, Ltd., 2007) ix.

69 Ibid.

PART 3

Terrorism Sanctions – Conflicts of Sovereignty

CHAPTER 9

Terrorism Sanctions – A Multilayered System

Resolutions emanating from the UN Security Council under Chapter 7 of the Charter are binding on all UN Member States under Article 25 of the UN Charter, yet they are not binding on regional organisations unless expressly stated. In parallel, as shown in Part 2 of this book, regional organisations have adopted counterterrorism measures for their own Member States. Thus, there could be an issue if obligations imposed on States by the UN Security Council clash with obligations imposed on them by regional organisations. This is the case, in particular, with the terrorism sanctions regimes that have been created by the UN, the EU, and Member States. There are a number of conflicts of norms issues raised by international and regional counterterrorism, but the case of terrorist sanctions, especially in the EU, prompts many sovereignty questions.

In situations where norms conflict, the UN Charter declares that the UN obligations will prevail.[1] In the context of terrorism, courts have traditionally supported the principle that legal obligations from the UN and the Security Council, in particular, override other obligations.[2] However, as described in this section, a variety of courts have challenged this traditional conflict resolution in relation to regional organisations, and have introduced the protection of human rights into the core of sanctions regimes. Beyond the conflict of norms that it raises, this case law represents a shift in the traditional relationship between various organisations and questions the concept of State sovereignty. Chapters 10 to 12 offer an analysis of the conflicts of sovereignty. Chapter 10 forms an analysis of the case law dealing with the conflict of obligations and includes the most relevant cases in this area. The focus in this chapter is on cases from the EU and the Council of Europe. The Chapter also includes cases from the UK, as they illustrate how one Member State that belongs to regional organisations as well as the UN has dealt with various and

1 Article 30 of the Vienna Convention on the Law of Treaties quotes and confirms the status of Article 103. See Richard H. Lauwaars, 'The Interrelationship between United Nations Law and the Law of Other International Organizations' (1983) 82 *Michigan Law Review*, 1604, 1606.

2 It has been argued that the political support for the UN is so strong that 'even States that are not Members of the UN nor parties to the Vienna Convention must accept the primacy of the Charter over an older treaty:' Henry G. Schermers, *International Institutional Law* (2nd ed., Sythoff, 1980) §1402. This statement is less relevant today, considering how few non-UN Member States there are.

 | DOI 10.1163/9789004299580_011

possibly conflicting obligations. Chapter 11 includes an analysis of the consequences of this case law on the obligations imposed by the UN and the EU and the evolution of the regimes that ultimately shows the impact of regional organisations on sovereignty. The concluding chapter of this book, Chapter 12, addresses the deeper issue of State sovereignty, which was raised by the terrorist sanctions case law.

1 United Nations Sanctions Regimes

UN sanctions regimes have evolved over the years, targeting States at first, then becoming smart sanctions targeting individuals and groups in order to minimise the impact on the civilian population. In the context of counterterrorism, two sanctions regimes currently exist that do not target States, namely the 1267 sanction regime and the 1373 sanctions regime.

The first terrorism sanctions regime, originally known as the 1267 sanctions regime, was created by Resolution 1267, as previously detailed.[3] Resolution 1267 requires that Member States adopt the following measures:

> Deny permission for any aircraft to take off from or land in their territory if it is owned, leased or operated by or on behalf of the Taliban... Freeze funds and other financial resources, including funds derived or generated from property owned or controlled directly or indirectly by the Taliban, or by any undertaking owned or controlled by the Taliban...and ensure that neither they nor any other funds or financial resources so designated are made available, by their nationals or by any persons within their territory, to or for the benefit of the Taliban.[4]

In addition, Member States were asked to 'bring proceedings'[5] and 'impose appropriate penalties'[6] against those who were included in the list of individuals

3 UN SC Resolution 1214, 8 December 1998, which, *inter alia*, demanded: 'the end of the hostilities between the Taliban and other Afghan factions; that the Afghan factions put an end to discrimination against girls and women and other violations of human rights; that the Taliban stop providing sanctuary and training for international terrorists and their organizations, and that all Afghan factions cooperate with efforts to bring indicted terrorists to justice; and that the Taliban, as well as others, halt the cultivation, production and trafficking of drugs.'

4 UN SC Resolution 1267, 15 October 1999, §4.

5 Ibid., §8.

6 Ibid.

and groups targeted by the sanctions and who were located within their jurisdiction. As previously noted, the Security Council also decided to 'establish…a Committee of the Security Council consisting of all the Members of the Council to undertake the following tasks and to report on its work to the Council with its observations and recommendations.'[7] The Committee, now called the 'ISIL (Da'esh) and Al-Qaida Sanctions' following amendments by later resolutions,[8] manages the sanctions and monitors compliance by Member States. The committee will be referred to here as the 'Al-Qaida Sanctions Committee' for simplicity.

One of the Al-Qaida Sanctions Committee's main functions is to designate which individuals are targeted by the sanctions.[9] To do so, the Committee created a list of targets of the sanctions,[10] currently consisting of 243 individuals and seventy-four entities that are regularly updated.[11] Any Member State may submit a name to the Al-Qaida Sanctions Committee that will be added to the list by consensus. Although the 1267 sanctions regime originally had no process for delisting,[12] after a general review of the list was requested in 2008[13] and was conducted by 2010,[14] some delisting decisions were made. These changes, and others, will be detailed later.

The 1267 sanctions regime was later extended to include an arm and military embargo[15] and approved the freezing of Osama Bin Laden's assets and of Al-Qaida as an organisation.[16] These new measures were to remain in force for a period of twelve months,[17] but they have been subsequently renewed on a regular basis.[18] To date, the 1267 sanctions regime still constitutes the basis for

7 Ibid., §6.
8 UN SC Res 1333, 19 December 2000 and Res. 2253, 18 December 2015.
9 UN SC un sc Res 1267 (1999) §6.
10 UN SC Resolution 1390 (2002) §2.
11 List available at https://www.un.org/sc/suborg/en/sanctions/1267/aq_sanctions_list (last accessed 15.12.2015).
12 The term 'delisting' doesn't appear until UN Resolution 1617 (2005) §5. Section 2 of Chapter 11 details the development of a delisting procedure, which was created at a later stage.
13 UN SC Resolution 1822 (2008) §22.
14 S/2010/497, Report on the review described in Paragraph 25 of Resolution 1822 (2008) submitted pursuant to Paragraph 30 of Resolution 1904 (2009) by the Monitoring Team established pursuant to Resolution 1526 (2004) and extended by Resolution 1904 (2009).
15 UN SC Resolution 1333 (2000) §5.
16 UN SC Resolution 1333, §8(c).
17 Ibid., §23.
18 Ibid., §1; Res 1455 (2003) §1 and 2; Res 1526 (2004) §3; Res 1733 (2007) §33; Res 1904 (2009) §47 and Res 1989 (2011) §59.

counterterrorism sanctions and is regularly expanded to address new threats. For instance, in 2001 the Taliban were forced out of Afghanistan and in 2002 the Security Council passed Resolution 1390 that ordered States to freeze assets with respect to Osama bin Laden, members of the Al-Qaida organisation and the Taliban and other individuals, groups, undertakings and entities associated with them, as referred to in the list created by Resolutions 1267 (1999) and 1333 (2000).[19] As well, Resolution 2178 mentioned the 1267 sanctions regime,[20] which served to strengthen the longevity of this regime and Resolution 2253 updated the mandate and name of the regime. It should also be noted that the 1267 sanctions regime was divided into two regimes in 2011, but throughout the rest of the analysis in this book, it will be referred to by its original name, after the initial Resolution of the regime.[21]

As part of Resolution 1373 examined previously, the Security Council requested States to

> (c) Freeze without delay funds and other financial assets or economic resources of persons who commit, or attempt to commit, terrorist acts or participate in or facilitate the commission of terrorist acts; of entities owned or controlled directly or indirectly by such persons; and of persons and entities acting on behalf of, or at the direction of such persons and entities, including funds derived or generated from property owned or controlled directly or indirectly by such persons and associated persons and entities;
>
> (d) Prohibit their nationals or any persons and entities within their territories from making any funds, financial assets or economic resources or financial or other related services available, directly or indirectly, for the benefit of persons who commit or attempt to commit or facilitate or participate in the commission of terrorist acts, of entities owned or

---

19 UN SC Res 1390 (2002) §2(a).

20 UN SC Res 2178, §9, 20, 21, 23 and 26.

21 In 2011, the Security Council divided the 1267 sanctions regime so that it 'was split up into two separate regimes, one targeting the Taliban as a nationalist movement (the 1988 sanctions regime) and the other targeting al-Qaeda as a global actor (the 1989 al-Qaeda sanctions regime)': see Larissa Van den Herik and Nico J. Schrijver, 'Introduction: the Fragmented International Legal Response to Terrorism' in *Counter-Terrorism Strategies in a Fragmented International Legal Order, Meeting the Challenges* (Cambridge University Press, 2015), 16.

> controlled, directly or indirectly, by such persons and of persons and entities acting on behalf of or at the direction of such persons.[22]

Unlike the 1267 sanctions regime, Resolution 1373 does not provide a specific list of individuals or groups to which these obligations apply. Instead, it is left to Member States to decide whose assets should be frozen and what the definition of terrorism should be in their own jurisdiction. In other words, Resolution 1373 keeps the onus on Member States themselves to decide on the targets of the sanctions.

The CTC is in charge of the implementation of Resolution 1373, in general, and of assisting States in cooperating with each other. Its mandate is, therefore, different than that of the Al Qaida Sanctions Committee that oversees the implementation of sanctions against specific targets. For the purposes of this book, the regime resulting from Resolution 1373 will be referred to as the '1373 sanctions regime'.

Resolution 1373, like Resolution 1267, did not originally call on Member States to comply with human rights obligations, nor did it mention the need for a review procedure of the assets freezing process. Although Resolution 1373's scope is extremely wide, as discussed in the previous section on the role of the Security Council, it still relies on implementation by States for its actual practical enforcement. In that respect, Resolution 1267 is a lot more radical than Resolution 1373, because it imposes specific targets to States. It is noteworthy that Resolution 2178 refers to both the 1267 and the 1373 sanctions regimes, thereby conflating them both and their respective legal issues.

2 European Union Sanction Regimes

In contrast to the OAS, AU, and the Council of Europe that, as regional organisations, have not developed targeted sanction regimes, the EU has developed its own counterterrorism sanctions regime. This is the situation even though Member States of other organisations have, in the context of their own obligations under the UN resolution, adopted sanctions regimes.[23] For this reason, the focus in this chapter will be on the EU.

---

22 UN SC Resolution 1373, 28 September 2001.

23 For instance, the United States has its own sanctions regime (see the website of the US Treasury: http://www.treasury.gov/resource-center/sanctions/Programs/Pages/terror.aspx –

While the EU is not required to implement UN obligations because it is not a Member State of the UN, Declaration 13 to the Lisbon Treaty states that 'the European Union and its Member States will remain bound by the provisions of the Charter of the United Nations and, in particular, by the primary responsibility of the Security Council and of its Members for the maintenance of international peace and security'.[24] Moreover, under Article 5 TFEU, the EU is responsible for ensuring the coordination of economic policies of the organisation and is, therefore, required to define the broad direction and guidelines to be followed by Member States.[25] In practice, the EU made a choice to transpose the Security Council sanctions regimes into its legal order and stated that it is 'committed to the systematic implementation of sanctions decided on by the UN Security Council.'[26] As a result, the EU has adopted sanctions that are the direct application of UN sanctions that were imposed through the Al-Qaida Sanctions Committee resulting from the 1267 sanctions regime. It also created sanctions on the basis of Security Council Resolution 1373. In the context of the latter, the identification of terrorist suspects to be listed is now at the discretion of the EU.

The EU also kept the 1267 and 1373 regimes separate, but there are common elements to both: the methods for creating and developing these regimes are similar and their implementation takes place through Common Positions. Common Positions are implemented through EU Regulations, in effect giving them legal effect in all Member States. It follows that amendments to the UN lists are not automatically incorporated into EU law, but, instead, need to be enforced through European measures. In reality, however, the Commission of the EU has 'faithfully copied every single amendment of the UN lists of terrorist suspects'[27] and has amended EU legislation after some changes at the UN level.[28]

---

last accessed 16.12.2015), but that is under its obligations created by Security Council Resolution 1373 and not because the OAS created its own regime of terrorist sanctions.

24 'Declaration Concerning the Common Foreign and Security Policy', Consolidated version of the Treaty on European Union, OJ C 326, 26.10.2012, 13–390.

25 Article 5(2), Consolidated version of the Treaty on the Functioning of the European Union, OJ C 326, 26.10.2012, 47–390.

26 European Parliament Resolution, 'The Evaluation of EU Sanctions as Part of the EU's Actions and Policies in the Area of Human Rights' (2008/2031 (INI), September 4, 2008) para. F.

27 Christina Eckes, *EU Counter-Terrorist Policies and Fundamental Rights – The Case of Individual Sanctions* (Oxford University Press, 2009) Oxford Studies in European Law, 45.

28 Common Position 2001/771/CFSP, Preamble §6 amends Common Position 96/746/CFSP to reflect changes brought by Resolution 1333 of the UN; with CP 2002/402/CFSP, the Council

The EU reproduced the first sanctions regimes, based on Resolution 1267 and later resolutions, by directly copying the lists of terrorist suspects from the UN resolutions. The first instruments, both implementing Resolution 1267 of the Security Council, were the Common Position 1999/727/CFSP and Regulation (EC) No 337/2000. A series of Common Positions and Regulations were then consecutively adopted that implemented the various resolutions taken by Security Council following Resolution 1267.[29] These were later amended by way of Common Position 2011/487/CFSP[30] and Regulation (EC) 881/2002[31] that currently contain the main obligations for Member States.

Regulation (EC) 881/2002 requests that 'all funds and economic resources belonging to, or owned or held by, a natural or legal person, group or entity designated by the Sanctions Committee and listed in Annex I shall be frozen.'[32] It also prohibits 'technical advice, assistance and or training' to these people.[33] In practice, therefore, it refers States to the list of individuals and groups to be targeted and leaves no discretion as to who is included in the list, copying the UN 1267 list. The list is then updated following changes to the 1267 list.[34]

There is no mention in the Common Position or Regulation (EC) 881/2002 of any procedure about the delisting of individuals and groups. This echoes

---

states that the 'European Union restrictive measures adopted pursuant to UNSCR and 1333(2000) should be adjusted in accordance with UNSCR 1390(2002)', CP, Preamble, §7.

29 CP 96/746/CFSP; CP 2001/154/CFSPP and EC Regulations 337/2000; 467/2001. On 26 March 2013, Commission Regulation (EU) No 290/2013 amended for the 190th time Council Regulation (EC) No 881/2002 in order to reflect the changes brought by the UN to the 1267 listing.

30 Council Decision 2011/487/CFSP of 1 August 2011 amending Common Position 2002/402/CFSP concerning restrictive measures against Usama bin Laden, members of the al-Qaida organisation and the Taliban and other individuals, groups, undertakings and entities associated with them, OJ L 199, 2.8.2011, 73.

31 Council Regulation (EC) No. 881/2002 of 27 May 2002 imposing certain specific restrictive measures directed against certain persons and entities associated with Usama bin Laden, the al-Qaida network and the Taliban, and repealing Council Regulation (EC) No. 467/2001 prohibiting the export of certain goods and services to Afghanistan, strengthening the flight ban and extending the freeze of funds and other financial resources in respect of the Taliban of Afghanistan, OJ L 139, 29.5.2002, 9–22.

32 Council Regulation 881/2002, Article 2(1).

33 Ibid., Article 3.

34 For instance, Commission Implementing Regulation (EU) 2015/1390 amending Council Regulation (EC) 881/2002 added The Army Of Emigrants And Supporters to the EU Al Qaida sanctions list and amended the existing entries for seven people and four entities, in order to implement four recent decisions made by the Al Qaida Sanctions Committee of the UN Security Council.

Security Council Resolution 1267 that also does not include a delisting procedure. Moreover, Regulation (EC) 881/2002 puts aside 'any rights conferred or obligations imposed by any international agreement signed or any contract entered into or any licence or permit granted before the entry into force of this Regulation.'[35] However, as is noted later in the book, this has evolved following case law by various regional courts.[36] This case law led to the European Commission updating its implementation of the 1267 sanctions regime by adopting Regulation (EU) 1286/2009.[37] The main changes brought by this regulation concern human rights and review procedures, which will be analysed in Chapter 11.

Additionally, the EU decided to adopt measures implementing Security Council Resolution 1373[38] and created an independent sanctions regime through Common Position 2001/931/CFSP[39] and Regulation (EC) 2580/2001.[40] The text of Regulation (EC) 2580/2001 states that the Council would draw a list of persons and groups to which the sanctions apply and that:

> Such list shall consist of:
>
> (i) natural persons committing, or attempting to commit, participating in or facilitating the commission of any act of terrorism;
> (ii) legal persons, groups or entities committing, or attempting to commit, participating in or facilitating the commission of any act of terrorism;
> (iii) legal persons, groups or entities owned or controlled by one or more natural or legal persons, groups or entities referred to in points (i) and (ii); or

35 Council Regulation (EC) 881/2002, Article 9.

36 See Chapters 10 and 11 for an analysis of the case law and the resulting changes.

37 Regulation (EU) 1286/2009 passed in December 2009 reforms the listing and delisting procedures following the European case law on sanctions (see §4 of the Regulation).

38 Council Common Position 2001/931/CFSP, Preamble §5 states: 'the European Union should take additional measures in order to implement UNSC Resolution 1373(2001).'

39 Council Common Position of 27 December 2001 on the application of specific measures to combat terrorism, OJ L 344, 28/12/2001 p. 0093–0096.

40 Regulation (EC) 2580/2001 of 27 December 2001 on specific restrictive measures directed against certain persons and entities with a view to combating terrorism, OJ L 344, 28/12/2001 p. 0070–0075 and updated annexes available at http://europa.eu/legislation_summaries/justice_freedom_security/fight_against_terrorism/l24402_en.htm#Amendingacts (last accessed 15.12.2015).

(iv) natural legal persons, groups or entities acting on behalf of or at the direction of one or more natural or legal persons, groups or entities referred to in points (i) and (ii).[41]

According to Regulation (EC) 2580/2001, then, the EU, like Member States of the UN, draws up its own list of terrorist suspects against which sanctions are applied. While this is normal procedure for Member States, the regulation adds a level of specific obligations to EU Member States. While Common Position 2001/931/CFSP provides that the list 'shall be drawn up on the basis of precise information or material in the relevant file which indicates that a decision has been taken by a competent authority in respect of the persons, groups and entities concerned,'[42] in effect, it imposes a European list of terrorist suspects, which EU Member States have to follow, while under Resolution 1373, Member States are supposed to be solely responsible for drawing up their own list.

The independent EU list of individuals and groups targeted by Regulation (EC) 2580/2001 was created, in practice, by Council Decision 2001/927/EC on 27 December 2001. A variety of Council Decisions have amended the list of targets[43] and the list is subject to regular review.[44] The content and scope of obligations, however, remain based on Regulation (EC) 2580/2001,[45] which sets out specific measures to combat terrorism, for example, asset freezing, prohibiting fund provision, prohibiting participation in activities mentioned and requesting the provision of information to authorities about listed individuals and groups. However, Regulation (EC) 2580/2002 is more detailed than both Security Council Resolution 1373 and Regulation (EC) 881/2002 implementing the 1267 UN regime and, in particular, it includes possible exceptions to asset freezing for 'essential human needs of a natural person.'[46]

41 Article 3, Regulation (EC) 2580/2001 of 27 December 2001 on specific restrictive measures directed against certain persons and entities with a view to combating terrorism.

42 Common Position 2001/931/CFSP, Article 1(4).

43 There is more than twenty Council Decisions amending the list: see a list on the website of the UK Treasury: https://www.gov.uk/government/publications/current-list-of-designated-persons-terrorism-and-terrorist-financing#eu (last accessed 16.12.2015).

44 Common Position 2001/931/CFSP, Article 1(6).

45 The current list is available at http://eeas.europa.eu/cfsp/sanctions/consol-list_en.htm (last accessed 16.12.2015).

46 Regulation (EC) 2580/2002, Article 5(1): examples include 'payments for foodstuffs, medicines, the rent or mortgage for the family residence and fees and charges concerning medical treatment of members of that family.'

The consequence of this EU sanctions regimes list is that Member States that belong to both the UN and the EU now face two specific sets of lists of individuals to target. Whereas the UN Resolution 1373 left it to Member States to draw their own sanctions lists, the EU has created a sanctions list that is binding on its Member States. Most Member States' national sanctions regimes reflect this duality, as discussed in the next section. On the other hand, non-EU States, who will also have two terrorist sanctions regimes, will have one list that strictly applies the 1267 list and a completely independent list that they drew themselves.

3 European Union Member States' National Sanctions Regimes

EU Member States have adopted domestic measures necessary to implement the various existing sanctions regimes into their own legal order. Following both the UN and the EU sanctions, Member States usually differentiate between these two types of regimes at the national level. Below are a few examples of national sanctions regimes.

France implements sanctions from both the UN and the EU through its Monetary and Financial Code.[47] However, it distinguishes between the UN sanctions, which States have to transpose, EU sanctions, which are directly applicable in France and national sanctions,[48] which the Finance Minister can adopt independently for 'the defense of national interests.'[49] In this context, France also differentiates between '*terroristes liés au réseau Al Qaida*'[50] and '*autres organisations terroristes*',[51] following the UN model.[52] The national measures are '*arrêtés*', which are executive measures taken in the application of an existing law contained in the Monetary and Financial Code in this particular

47 Article L151-2, Article L562-1 and Article L562-2 of the Code monétaire et financier (Financial Code).

48 'Sanctions financières internationales', text available in French at http://www.tresor.economie.gouv.fr/sanctions-financieres-internationales (last accessed 16.12.2015).

49 Article L151-2 Code monétaire et financier.

50 'Terrorists linked to Al-Qaeda', under an order signed 18 January 2011 and a decree from December 2009, applying various Articles of the Code Monétaire et Financier.

51 'Other terrorist organisations', under an order from January 2012, applying various Articles of the Code.

52 For a full list of financial sanctions imposed by the French government, see the right tab, on http://www.tresor.economie.gouv.fr/sanctions-financieres-internationales (last accessed 16.12.2015).

instance.[53] A legal challenge can be brought before the administrative tribunals in France against the *arrêtés*[54] and before the European courts for European measures.[55]

In comparison, Italy has created a specific Committee for Financial Security within the Treasury Department[56] that is authorised to freeze assets of individuals or organisations associated with terrorist organisations. Moreover, 'the Committee monitors the implementation of EU regulations in this area, supervises the application of the sanctions adopted by the UN Security Council and approves the proposals for the inclusion of individuals or entities into the list of the Sanctions Committee against Al Qaeda and the Taliban.'[57]

In Germany, some information on financial sanctions can be found through its federal bank, the Deutsche Bundesbank, which lists its sanctions regimes that include both Al-Qaida and terrorism in general.[58] For each regime, a list is available through the Deutsche Bundesbank containing the EU measures adopted.[59] Germany also has a national sanctions list, the Bundesanzeiger Verlag, developed by the Federal Gazette.[60] The data for this list contains information from 'the persons and organisations published in the "Official Journal of the European Union", corresponding orders from the German Federal Ministry of Economics and Labour, which are published in the "Bundesanzeiger", various US lists, which have been integrated in the Sanctions List since 2004… the Japanese, Australian, Canadian, Swiss as well as UK.'[61]

In the case of Ireland, both the UN and the EU regimes are listed under the heading 'Terrorist Groups,' and are then classified as 'Osama bin Laden, the Al-Qaida network and the Taliban,' or as 'Counter Terrorism.'[62] The Irish

53 The arrêtés are adopted in application of articles L151-2, L562-1 or L562-2 of the Financial and Monetary Code.

54 Article R411 Code de Justice Administrative.

55 Article 263 TFEU.

56 Law No 431/2001, Decree Law 396/2001, 12 October 2001.

57 'Fight against Terrorism', Italian Minister of Foreign Affairs, see http://www.esteri.it/MAE/EN/Politica_Estera/Temi_Globali/Lotta_Terrorismo/ (last accessed 16.12.2015).

58 Sanktionregimes, see http://www.bundesbank.de/Navigation/DE/Service/Finanzsanktionen/Sanktionsregimes/sanktionsregimes.html (information in German only – last accessed 16.12.2015).

59 Ibid.

60 Information available at http://217.17.30.74/SubDl/index.jsp?user=SLamtsblatt&pass=SLamtsblatt&path=ReadMe-Vorlage1en.pdf (last accessed 15.12.2015).

61 Ibid.

62 See 'Financial Sanctions' on the website of the Minister of Finance: http://www.finance.gov.ie/publications/legislation/financial-sanctions (16.12.2015).

Central Bank is the 'Competent Authority responsible for the administration and enforcement of the EU Sanctions against the Financing of Terrorism and Oppressive Regimes (EU Financial Sanctions) in Ireland.'[63] Ireland acknowledges the UN sanctions, but notes that 'in accordance with EU law, Ireland adheres to the list of sanctioned individuals and entities prescribed by the EU.'[64]

Finally, the UK sanctions regime also echoes the dual system of UN sanctions. In this context, the first instruments creating such regimes were Orders in Council, which are UK government executive decisions made under powers given in a parent act,[65] in this case, the 1946 United Nations Act that authorises the UK government to take such orders as 'are necessary and expedient' as to give effect to UN Security Council Resolutions.[66] These Orders in Council were passed without any parliamentary scrutiny,[67] but following case law, a review is now possible. Further information is included in Chapter 10, Section 2.

Common to these national regimes are the multiple sanctions regimes of both the UN and the EU. Further, it is clear that States use data from other States in order to create their domestic lists in addition to the EU and UN lists.[68] This demonstrates a 'circular interaction' between the EU and States and the UN.[69] Security Council Resolution 2253 actually encourages this cooperation between actors and regimes in their listing and delisting procedures.[70] These multilayered systems also show cooperation between executive branches of States, sharing, and often copying, data on terrorist groups and individuals. As

63 Central Bank of Ireland, 'Introduction to International Financial Sanctions', http://www.centralbank.ie/regulation/processes/Intfs/Pages/default1.aspx (last accessed 16.12.2015).

64 Ibid.

65 'Brief Guide: Delegated Legislation', House of Commons, available at http://www.parliament.uk/about/how/laws/delegated/ (last accessed 16.12.2015).

66 United Nations Act 1946, 15 April 1946.

67 Alison MacDonald, 'Case Comment: *HM Treasury v Ahmed* [2010] UKSC 2', (text available at http://ukscblog.com/case-comment-hm-treasury-v-ahmed-2010-uksc-2 (last accessed 16.12.2015)). For Joe Stevens, this 'lack of Parliamentary debate is typical': Joe Stevens, 'UN Targeted Terrorist Sanctions and the Rule of Law: The UK's Response' (2012) 3 *Journal of Terrorism Research*, 5.

68 See Germany's reference to foreign data, note 60.

69 Christina Eckes, 'EU Counter-Terrorist Sanctions: The Questionable Success Story of Criminal Law in Disguise', *Dirty Assets: Emerging Issues in the Regulation of Crimimal and Terrorist Assets* (Ashgate Publishing, 2014) 327.

70 Resolution 2253, Article 33 states that it '*Encourages* designating States to inform the Monitoring Team whether a national court or other legal authority has reviewed a listed party's case and whether any judicial proceedings have begun, and to include any other relevant information when submitting the standard form for listing.'

well, this shows a desire by all actors involved in counterterrorism to act against the financing of terrorism in a comprehensive and consultative manner. As a result, the EU and Member States chose not to go beyond the obligations set out in the Security Council resolutions and did not include human rights in their sanctions regimes. In the case of any challenge, one would face the argument that States and the EU were simply following their obligations that stemmed from the Security Council. This 'strict' application of existing regimes means that the original lack of human rights safeguards and judicial review at the UN and EU levels were reflected at the national level.

4 Human Rights in Sanctions Regimes

It is important to remember that the sanctions created by Security Council Resolution 1267 and others constitute what was deemed smart sanctions and were considered a better alternative to previous sanctions against a State. While none of these sanctions regimes included human rights safeguards, they demonstrated a 'qualitative change in the UN's sanctions policy.'[71] The protection of human rights was not considered essential, as sanctions against individuals and groups accused of terrorism were deemed necessary in order to deal with the phenomenon.[72] Resolution 1267 only states that human rights are those being violated by the Taliban.[73] In the meeting leading to the adoption of Resolution 1267, there were discussions about the potential humanitarian harm raised by the proposed sanctions. In that context, the United States stated that:

> It is important to remember that these sanctions are limited and that they are targeted very specifically to limit the resources of the Taliban authorities. These sanctions in no way harm the people of Afghanistan, and we will work with the sanctions review Committee to implement them in a way that does not hinder the provision of humanitarian assistance to the Afghan people.[74]

---

71 Helen Keller and A. Fischer, 'The UN Anti-terror Sanctions Regime under Pressure' (2009) 9 *Human Rights Law Review*, 257.

72 International Commission of Jurists, Eminent Jurists Panel on Terrorism, Counter-Terrorism and Human Rights, 'Assessing Damages, Urging Action' 2008, 113.

73 UN SC Resolution 1267, Preamble.

74 UN Security Council 4051st Meeting, 15 October 1999, S/PV.4051, page 3 (document available at http://repository.un.org/bitstream/handle/11176/36711/S_PV.4051-EN.pdf?sequence=3&isAllowed=y (last accessed 16.12.2015)).

However, the Malaysian delegation expressed concerns at 'the effects and impact of the draft resolution on the ordinary, innocent people of Afghanistan.' It called for an assessment of the humanitarian impact of the sanctions.[75] Yet, this was not included in the final draft of the resolution. As well, human rights were not even discussed in the meeting that led to the adoption of Resolution 1373;[76] there was no mention of possible human rights violations regarding the targets of the sanctions despite the sanctions directly targeting specific individuals.

However, as noted earlier regarding the Security Council, there is a clear evolution towards including human rights within the UN security measures adopted to address terrorism. In fact, 'even though the States consider that the use of targeted sanctions is essential in order to combat effectively the financing of terrorism, many of them have expressed their concerns regarding the lack of protection of human rights'[77] with more and more individuals bringing claims against their listing before national and regional courts.[78] In practice, in the first half of the year 2000, a number of States stopped submitting names to the UN sanctions list because 'they were concerned about the lack of effective provisions to protect due process rights.'[79] A 2007 report by the UN 1267 Sanctions Committee itself echoed the concern of some States regarding the fairness of the process.[80] Additionally, a 2008 report to the European Parliament on the effectiveness of European terrorist sanctions explained that:

75 Ibid.

76 UN Security Council 4385th Meeting, 28 September 2001, S/PV.4385, available at https://www.ilsa.org/jessup/jessup08/basicmats/rsc1373.pdf (last accessed 16.12.2015).

77 Juan Santos Vara, 'The Consequences of Kadi: Where the Divergence of Opinion between EU and International Lawyers Lies?' (2011) 17 *European Law Journal*, 252–274, 253.

78 The *Kadi* and *OMPI* cases will be analysed in detail in Chapter 10. However, cases also include: Case C-266/05 P, *Jose Maria Sison v Council* [2007] ECR I-01233, Human Rights Committee (HRC) Communication No. 1472/2006; *Nabil Sayadi and Patricia Vinck v Belgium* (29 December 2008) Case T-338/02; and *Segi and Others v Council* [2004] ECR. For an analysis of these cases, see Sullivan and Hayes, 'Blacklisted: Targeted sanctions, preemptive security and fundamental rights', ECCHR-Report, December 2010 Part 4.

79 Monika Heupel, 'With Power Comes Responsibility: Human Rights Protection in United Nations Sanctions Policy' (2012) *European Journal of International Relations*, 15.

80 Seventh Report of the Analytical Support and Sanctions Monitoring Team appointed pursuant toSecurity Council Resolutions 1617 (2005) and 1735 (2006) concerning Al-Qaida and the Taliban and Associated Individuals and Entities (UN Doc S/2007/677) §8, 10 and 26.

> The present UN blacklisting sanctions violate EU human rights standards, and the European Court of Justice has made this clear. Thus the EU/EC implementation of these systems is very problematic. The EU's own sanctions systems also give rise to human rights problems.[81]

Finally, in 2009, a report on Al-Qaida sanctions showed that only very few States regularly submit names to the list.[82]

An added issue with the sanctions lists was the original lack of a delisting procedure. At the time of establishing its own sanctions regime, the EU did not include a delisting procedure and it did not recognize a right to compensation for potential victims of mistaken or wrongful inclusions.[83] However, it put the EU Council in charge of 'establish[ing], *review*[*ing*] *and amend*[*ing*]' the list.[84] Moreover, the EU's Common Position of 27 December 2001 includes a provision for review at 'regular intervals and at least once every six months.'[85] After a number of legal challenges, recent UN resolutions have created delisting procedures[86] and also require regular updating of sanctions lists in order to remove people that are 'reported or confirmed to have ceased to exist'.[87]

In fact, the controversial issue of the Security Council acting as a legislator identified the need to balance its 'quasi-judicial functions'.[88] The fact that terrorist sanctions are usually adopted, at each level, by the executive branch, raises a number of legal issues, including that of review.

Therefore, because of the lack of human rights protection and procedural safeguards, legal challenges against these regimes have multiplied. Individuals

---

81 Iain Cameron, 'Respecting Human Rights and Fundamental Freedoms and EU/UN Sanctions: State of Play' (European Parliament, Policy Department External Policies, October 2008) ii.

82 Of course, it cannot be proven that the reason for this non-submission is due to human rights concerns. But see D. Cortright (2009) 'Patterns of Implementation: Do Listing Practices Impede Compliance with UN Sanctions? A Critical Assessment,' Policy Brief SSRP 0912-01, Fourth Freedom Forum and the Kroc Institute for International Peace Studies, University of Notre Dame.

83 Jessica Almqvist, 'A Human Right Critique of European Judicial Review: Counter-Terrorism Sanctions' (2008) 57 *International and Comparative Law Quarterly* 303, 307.

84 Regulation (EC) 2580/2002, Article 3 [author's emphasis].

85 Council Common Position of 27.12.2001 on the application of specific measures to combat terrorism, 2001/931/CFSP, Article 1(6).

86 See Chapter 11.

87 Resolution 2253, §80(c).

88 Giessbach II Seminar on Combating the Financing of Terrorism, 'Combating the Financing of Terrorism While Protecting Human Rights: A Dilemma?' (Office for Democratic Institutions and Human Rights, 2008) 3.

and groups included on the assets freezing lists have brought cases before various jurisdictions, arguing that their human rights had been violated as a result of their listing. In response, States have justified their actions on the basis of their obligations to obey Security Council resolutions, as well as the necessity to act against terrorism financing. The next chapters examine case law on terrorist sanctions and their impact both on State sovereignty and the relationship between security and human rights.

CHAPTER 10

Conflict of Sovereignties – A Case Law Study

In international law, there is a 'presumption against normative conflicts' and courts are therefore generally 'expect[ed]...to exhaust the limits of interpretation in order to avoid a conflict'.[1] To this end, courts display a tendency to strive for consistent interpretation. But when consistent interpretation is not possible and where UN binding obligations are involved, courts have traditionally given precedence to the binding obligations, according to Article 103 of the UN Charter. One early example of this deference to the executive in the context of counterterrorism is the *Lockerbie* case where the ICJ, albeit at the stage of provisional measures, gave precedence to a UN Security Council Resolution over a UN Convention, even though the resolution had been adopted after the start of the proceedings.[2] However, in a series of cases, regional courts have developed a jurisprudence that does not entirely follow this principle. In particular, these cases illustrate how courts have dealt with conflicts of obligations in counterterrorism and over time, this case law has had a significant impact on the sanctions regimes. As there have been too many cases to analyse in detail, the focus here will be on some of the major cases for each jurisdiction and each sanction regime. The analysis of these decisions will be divided by legal order, however, some of the cases cross these levels. This reflects that the increasing role of the judiciary in international counterterrorism runs across various legal orders. The focus in this analysis will be on European courts because they show the conflict between various legal regimes the best. Finally, the UK will be taken as a specific case because it is a member both of the EU and the UN, as well as the Council of Europe, thereby providing an example of conflict resolution in terrorist sanctions.

1 Report of the Study Group of the International Law Commission on Fragmentation of International Law (No 16) UN Doc. A/CN.4/L.628 (2002) §37–38.

2 International Court of Justice, Question of Interpretation and Application of the 1971 Montreal Convention arising from the Aerial Incident at Lockerbie, Order-Request for the Indication of Provisional Measures (*Libyan Arab Jamahiriya v United Kingdom*) 14 April 1992, §39.

 | DOI 10.1163/9789004299580_012

1 EU Case Law

1.1 *1373 Regime – The* OMPI *Case*

The *OMPI* case[3] is one of the earliest cases to deal with sanctions regimes. It deals with the consequences of the 1373 sanctions regime on EU human rights standards and therefore, with a regime which is based on UN Resolution 1373 but with leeway in terms of the details and targets for the EU.

In June 2002, the People's Mujahadeen Of Iran (OMPI),[4] an Iranian armed opposition movement in exile, was placed on the EU terrorist list independently set up by the EU Common Position 2001/931/CFSP.[5] OMPI filed a claim against the listing in July 2002 with the Court of First Instance (CFI) of the EU (now called the General Court). In 2006, the CFI held that:

> The contested decision does not contain a sufficient statement of reasons and ... it was adopted in the course of a procedure during which the applicants right to a fair hearing was not observed.[6]

As this was contrary to Article 253 EC,[7] the CFI annulled the decision listing the organisation. In response, the Council of the EU adopted subsequent Decisions that listed OMPI again, but accompanied them this time with statements of reasons.[8] In response, OMPI brought another challenge to the EU courts

3 Case T-228/02 *Organisation des Modjahedines du peuple d'Iran v Council* [2006] ECR II-0000l.

4 The name of the case follows the French appellation of the group and this name will be used in this book too.

5 It had already been placed on the U.S Treasury Department's Office of Foreign Asset Control (OFAC) list since 1997.

6 *Organisation des Modjahedines du peuple d'Iran v Council* [2006], §173.

7 Ibid., §138–141. The Article says 'Regulations, directives and decisions adopted jointly by the European Parliament and the Council, and such acts adopted by the Council or the Commission, shall state the reasons on which they are based and shall refer to any proposals or opinions which were required to be obtained pursuant to this Treaty.' Now art. 296 TFEU.

8 Decisions 2006/379/EC of 29 May 2006 and Decision 2007/445/EC. 'In the statement of reasons enclosed with the letter, the Council pointed out, inter alia, that a decision had been taken with respect to the applicant by a competent authority within the meaning of Article 1(4) of Council Common Position 2001/931/CFSP of 27 December 2001 on the application of specific measures to combat terrorism (OJ 2001 L 344, p. 93) namely, the order of the Secretary of State for the Home Department ('the Home Secretary') of the United Kingdom of Great Britain and Northern Ireland of 28 March 2001proscribing the applicant as an organisation concerned in terrorism, under the Terrorism Act 2000 ('the Home Secretary's order'). After noting that that decision, which under the abovementioned law was subject to review, was

because it claimed that the statements of reasons did not provide any evidence of the facts it presented. In 2008, the CFI stated that the statement of reasons provided with Decision 2007/445/EC of 28 June 2007 was 'obviously insufficient to provide legal justification for continuing to freeze the applicant's funds'[9] and annulled the Decision.[10] The Council then listed OMPI again,[11] despite the national delisting of OMPI by a UK Order dated June 2008,[12] and OMPI appealed again. In its judgment, the CFI held that the Council had failed again to provide OMPI with the necessary information regarding its listing.[13] More precisely, it held that it was impossible 'in the absence of more accurate information, to verify the truthfulness and relevance of the allegation made in the statement of reasons.'[14] Finally, the CFI held that European courts needed to be able to provide a 'strict judicial review, which is independent and impartial'[15] and that this review was 'essential because it constitutes the only safeguard ensuring that a fair balance is struck between the need to combat international terrorism and the protection of fundamental rights.'[16] Following these judgments, OMPI was finally deleted from the EU list in January 2009.[17] Yet, France appealed the 2008 CFI decision, considering that the organisation should still be included in the list.[18] The ECJ rejected the appeal[19] and held that it is:

---

still in force, the Council held that the reasons for including the applicant in the list at issue still applied,' Case T-256/07, *People's Mojahedin Org. of Iran v Council of the European Union* [PMOI II], 2008 WL 4657820 (Oct. 23, 2008) §6.

9 Case T-256/07, *People's Mojahedin Org. of Iran v Council of the European Union* [PMOI II], 2008 WL 4657820 (Oct. 23, 2008) §177.

10 Ibid., §189.

11 Council Decision 2008/583/EC of 15 July 2008.

12 Case T-284/08 *PMOI v Council* of 4 December 2008, §6.

13 Ibid, §56.

14 Ibid., §66.

15 Ibid., §75.

16 Ibid.

17 Common Position 2009/67/CFSP and Council Decision 2009/62/EC, both dated 26 January 2009, remove OMPI from the EU List: see Decision §5.

18 'On 19 March 2007 and 13 November 2007, the Paris anti-terrorist prosecutor's office brought supplementary charges against alleged members of the PMOI. These proceedings were prompted by the need to enquire into further elements arising from the investigations conducted between 2001 and 2007. They particularly focused on the charges of 'laundering the direct or indirect proceeds of fraud offences against particularly vulnerable persons and organised fraud' having a link with a terrorist undertaking as provided for under French law by Act No 2003/706 of 2 August 2003', Case C-27/09 P *French Republic v People's Mojahedin Organization of Iran* [2011] ECR, §10.

19 Case C- 27/09 P *French Republic v People's Mojahedin Organization of Iran* [2011] ECR.

> Fundamental and essential to the rights of defence that the Council must, before taking any decision to maintain a person on its asset-freezing list, notify that person of the incriminating evidence against it and give it the opportunity to make representations.[20]

The main criticism emerging throughout these cases was the lack of reasons and information given to the individuals that are included in the lists, even once the Council had started drafting statements of reasons. Over the years, the court refined its requirement for the statement of reasons and a series of listing measures, appeals and judgments have led the European court to clarify their exact requirement for listing procedures. The current rules for that statement are included in the next chapter.

The cases included in this case law, then, have made an important contribution regarding the need for information to be given to any person or group listed. However, it must be noted that for those cases that concerned the Resolution 1373 regime, the EU did not have detailed obligations emanating from the UN, hence, it may not have been covered by the primacy of the UN Charter under Article 103. Consequently, there was much more room for the EU to incorporate human rights into their own regime. While Member States themselves could, and should, have included human rights in their own regimes, in the case of the 1373 regime in particular, they also had to implement the specific list of the EU and its obligations, which did not include the necessary safeguards. The subsequent case law has aimed to remedy this loss and has made a number of changes to the EU regimes, as will be discussed later. The *OMPI* case law represents checks and balances that exist in a legal order with a separation of branches, as is possible within the EU: measures adopted by the executive branch can be reviewed by its judiciary, as was the case here. Furthermore, the decision has an impact on domestic measures, as the EU regulation must be implemented by States.

With regards to the 1267 regime, the situation was different, because the EU and Member States did not have a similar leeway to act as they were bound by the specific details of the UN List. Therefore, in this case, any claims brought by listed individuals and organisations would have amounted to a criticism of the UN regime itself.

1.2 *1267 Regime – The* Kadi *Case*

The *Kadi* case concerned the 1267 sanctions regime and its application by the EU. In October 2001, Yassin Abdullah Kadi, a Saudi resident, and Ahmed Yusuf

20 Ibid., §64.

Ali, both employees of the Al Barakaat International Foundation established in Sweden, were placed on the US assets freezing list as 'specially designated global terrorists' along with the Al Barakaat International Foundation itself.[21] Days later, they were added to the UN 1267 Sanctions Committee list and were consequently put on the EU list based on Regulation (EC) 881/2002.[22]

Mr Kadi and the Al Barakaat International Foundation filed an appeal with the CFI arguing that the EU Regulation should be annulled because it infringed their fundamental rights, meaning the right to be heard, the right to respect for property, and the right to effective judicial review.[23] In parallel, Ahmed Yusuf filed a claim, alleging 'that the contested regulation [breached his] fundamental rights.'[24] In 2005, the CFI held that, for both of these cases, it could not review the legality of the EU's Regulation (EC) 881/2002, because doing so would mean reviewing the legality of the Security Council's decisions and that, in turn, it would 'be incompatible with the undertakings of the Member States under the Charter of the United Nations, especially Articles 25, 48 and 103 thereof, and also with Article 27 of the Vienna Convention on the Law of Treaties.'[25] It stated it would also be contrary to the principle that 'Community's powers and, therefore, those of the Court of First Instance, must be exercised in compliance with international law.'[26] The CFI, in effect, applied the traditional principle of conflict resolution, confirming the precedence of UN obligations over other obligations.[27] The CFI held, however, that the EU judicial system was able to review the legality of Regulation (EC) 881/2002 in light of *jus cogens*, because even the UN could not derogate from these rights.[28] The CFI itself

21 The US Department of State and the Department of the Treasury both compile lists of individuals and groups to be sanctioned. The Foreign Terrorist Organisations list is compiled by the Department of State whereas the Specially Designated Nationals List, under which Mr Kadi and the Al Barakaat International Foundation were listed, is compiled by the Department of Treasury (List available at http://www.State.gov/j/ct/rls/other/des/123085.htm (last accessed 16.12.2015)).

22 See Commission Regulation 2062/2001/EC of 19 October 2001.

23 Case T-315/01 *Kadi v Council* [2005] ECR II-3649, §233.

24 Case T-306/01 *Yusuf v Council* [2005] ECR II-3533, §78.

25 *Yusuf v Council* [2005], §273 and *Kadi v Council* [2005], §222.

26 *Yusuf v Council* [2005], §274 and *Kadi v Council* [2005], §223.

27 Antonios Tzanakopoulos, 'Collective Security and Human Rights' in *Hierarchy in International Law: The Place of Human Rights* (Oxford University Press, 2012) 51.

28 Article 53 of the 1969 Vienna Convention on the Law of the Treaties defines *jus cogens* as peremptory norms of general international law that are accepted and, as a whole, as norms from which no derogation is permitted. However, in fact, the concept of *jus cogens* is far from clear. See Takis Tridimas and Jose Gutierrez-Fons, 'EU Law, International Law,

defined *jus cogens* as 'a body of higher rules of public international law binding on all subjects of international law, including the bodies of the United Nations, and from which no derogation is possible.'[29] In the case in point, the CFI held that no *jus cogens* was violated and that the sanctions did not 'submit those persons to inhuman or degrading treatment'[30] and that 'so far as respect for the right to property must be regarded as forming part of the mandatory rules of general international law, it is only an arbitrary deprivation of that right that might, in any case, be regarded as contrary to *jus cogens*.'[31] Therefore the CFI rejected the claims.

On 24 August 2006, the UN Security Council Committee removed Ahmed Yusuf Ali from its list, although no reasons were given for the delisting.[32] Yet, Mr Kadi remained on the list and therefore appealed to the ECJ. In its landmark 2008 case, the ECJ overruled the judgment of the CFI and annulled Regulation (EC) 881/2002, because it found a breach of fundamental rights of the EU.[33] The ECJ held that fundamental rights are an integral part of the general principles of the EU law[34] and that the lawfulness of EU acts depends on their respect for human rights, despite the general obligation on the EU to respect international law. The ECJ stressed that the decision concerned the EC regulation and not the Security Council's resolution 'as such',[35] and it specifically recalled that it did not have jurisdiction to review decisions from the UN body.[36] In effect, the ECJ accepted that the success of sanctions lies partly on an element of surprise,[37] but it held that after sanctions are imposed on suspects, the authorities should then provide them with information and reasons for their listing.[38] For these reasons, the ECJ annulled the regulation

and Economic Sanctions Against Terrorism: The Judiciary in Distress?' (2008) 32 *Fordham International Law Journal*, 660.

29 *Kadi v Council* [2005], §226.

30 *Kadi v Council* [2005], §240.

31 *Kadi v Council* [2005], §242.

32 SC/8815, 'Security Council Committee removes one individual from consolidated list; approves change of information regarding five individuals in al-Qaida section' (Press release).

33 Joined Cases C-402/05 P & C-415/05 P, *Kadi & Al Barakaat v Council of the European Union and EC Commission*, 3 C.M.L.R. 41 (2008).

34 Ibid., §283.

35 Ibid., §286.

36 Ibid., §283.

37 Ibid., §340.

38 Ibid., §346.

for Kadi and the Al Barakaat International Foundation on procedural grounds and gave the Council three months to remedy the problem.[39]

The ECJ's main view was that, since the UN regime did not provide an adequate legal mechanism to protect individuals against sanctions, the Court could not refrain from exercising its jurisdiction. For the ECJ, the consequences of this perspective are that 'neither EC Member States nor EC institutions can avoid a review of the conformity of their acts with the basic constitutional charter, the EC Treaty'[40] and that includes acts that were intended to give effect to Security Council resolutions.[41] The ECJ did not pronounce itself on whether the Council of the EU had rightly listed the claimants, but rather, whether the listing was done legally and whether the rule of law had been respected. It is noteworthy that in the case of Stichting Al-Aqsa, an organisation from the Netherlands,[42] the ECJ reinstated its listing on the EU Terrorism List, because it held that due to the fact that the Netherlands had repealed its ministerial regulation on the listing of Al-Aqsa for procedural reasons only, the EU Council's listing was still valid as it was based on valid evidence.[43] In Case T-400/10 *Hamas v Council*, the General Court annulled the listing of the terrorist wing of the Hamas by the EU,[44] but the press release stressed that 'those annulments, on fundamental procedural grounds, do not imply any substantive assessment of the question of the classification of Hamas as a terrorist group within the meaning of the Common Position.'[45]

Kadi is one of the most important cases in the development of the protection of human rights in the sanctions regime and it continues to have an impact on

39 Ibid., §380(3).

40 Mariani, 'The Implementation of UN Security Council Resolutions Imposing Economic Sanctions in the EU/EC Legal System: Interpillar Issues and Judicial Review' (Bocconi Legal Studies Research Paper No. 1354568, March 2009) 19.

41 Payandeh Mehrdad and Heiko Sauer, 'European Union: UN Sanctions and EU Fundamental Rights' (2009) 7 *International Journal of Constitutional Law*, 306, 310.

42 Joined Cases C-539/10 P and C-550/10 P: *Stichting Al-Aqsa v Council* and *Netherlands v Stichting Al-Aqsa*, Court of Justice of the European Union, 15 November 2012.

43 Ibid., §88–90.

44 Case T-400/10, *Hamas v Council of the European Union and European Commission* (intervening), Judgment, 17th December 2014, Court of Justice of the European Union, (2nd Chamber).

45 Press release available at http://curia.europa.eu/jcms/upload/docs/application/pdf/2014-12/cp140178en.pdf (last accessed 15.12.2015).

both the jurisprudence and the legal regimes of both the UN and the EU.[46] In practice, though, reactions from States varied. The UK, as a party to the *Kadi* decision, had 'ask[ed] the Court as a matter of principle to decline all jurisdiction to undertake such indirect review of the lawfulness of those resolutions which, as rules of international law binding on the Member States of the Community, are mandatory for the Court as they are for all the Community institutions.'[47] That was also their stand in the 2007 *Al-Jedda* case, which will be discussed in Section 2 of this chapter. In France, the Vice-Président of the Conseil d'État considered that in the *Kadi* case, the EU acted as a 'factor of balance between globalized law and European legal cultures'[48] and an information report drafted during a session of the French Sénat 'saluted' the *Kadi* decision.[49]

Thus the *Kadi* decision is definitely a landmark decision and it is clear that the ECJ should be praised for considering human rights a core part of international counterterrorism.[50] The higher level of protection that is now offered to human rights standards must be welcomed, as this is something that was largely lacking in the original UN system. *Kadi* also puts both the 1267 and 1373 sanctions regimes at the same level with regards to the necessity to protect human rights and procedural safeguards. Yet, despite the positive reactions to the *Kadi* decision, there was some criticism. The main criticism expressed against this case was that it created, in effect, two different standards of obligations for States that belong both to the UN and to the EU. This was because, although Member States are meant to follow their obligations under Security Council's resolutions, they also have to respect their obligations under European law.[51] The *Kadi* case has created complex legal questions that have serious consequences on issues of sovereignty. These must be considered and will be addressed in Chapter 12.

---

46 De Burca, 'The EU, the European Court of Justice and the International Legal Order after *Kadi*' (2010) 51 *Harvard International Law Journal*, 1; Inge Govaere, 'The importance of International Developments in the case-law of the European Court of Justice: *Kadi* and the autonomy of the EC legal order' (College of Europe Research Paper No. 2009).

47 *Kadi & Al Barakaat v Council of the European Union and EC Commission*, §217.

48 Jean-Marc Sauvé, 'L'Europe dans la globalisation du droit', Statement at the inaugural congress of the European Law Institute, 1 June 2011.

49 'The EU and Human Rights', information report n°246, annexed to Ordinary Session of the Sénat 2008–2009. Author's translation.

50 See Payandeh Mehrdad, and Heiko Sauer, 'European Union: UN Sanctions and EU Fundamental Rights' (2009) 7 *International Journal of Constitutional Law*, 306, 312.

51 De Burca, 'The EU, the European Court of Justice and the International Legal Order after Kadi.'

1.3 Kadi II *and Beyond*

Despite the ECJ judgment in *Kadi*, the European Commission included Kadi and the Al Barakaat International Foundation on another listing after providing them with a statement of reasons.[52] An action was then filed with the General Court on 30 January 2009 against the renewed listing. In June 2010, the UN Security Council finally delisted the Al Barakaat International Foundation after a review conducted according to Security Council Resolution 1822 (2008).[53] The organisation therefore withdrew its EU action for annulment. However, Mr Kadi's name remained on both the UN and the EU lists and, as a result, he proceeded with his claim.

On 30 September 2010, the General Court delivered its decision in what became known as *Kadi II*.[54] In this case, the General Court started by noting that 'certain doubts may have been voiced in legal circles as to whether the judgment of the Court of Justice in Kadi is wholly consistent with.... international law and ... the EC and EU Treaties'[55] and stressed that 'it acknowledges that those criticisms are not entirely without foundation.'[56] In particular, the General Court held that a review by the European Courts of a EU regulation implementing a Security Council resolution 'is liable to encroach on the Security Council's prerogatives,'[57] echoing the traditional deference to the UN of the previous CFI decision on *Kadi* and the legal issues that *Kadi* created.

On the other hand, the General Court added that 'the appellate principle itself and the hierarchical judicial structure which is its corollary generally advise against the General Court revisiting points of law which have been decided by the Court of Justice.'[58] Therefore, it concluded that it could not go against the ECJ's decision and had to follow the ECJ's judgment, albeit, as one

52 Commission Regulation 1190/2008/EC of 28 November 2008. The statement of reason provided to Mr Kadi was provided originally to the French government by the UN Sanctions Committee. The French government then passed it on to the EU. See online updates of Trevor Hartley, *The Foundations of European Union Law* (7th ed., Oxford University Press, 2010) available at http://global.oup.com/uk/orc/law/eu/hartley7e/resources/updates/ (last accessed 16.12.2015). The statement of reason is also included in Case T-85/09 *Kadi v Commission* [2010] OJ C317, §49 and focuses on Mr Kadi's involvement with the Muwafaq Foundation. It did not, however, provide any evidence of this.

53 SC/10549 21 February 2012.

54 Case T-85/09 *Kadi v Commission* [2010] OJ C317.

55 Ibid., §115.

56 Ibid., §121.

57 Ibid., §114.

58 Ibid., §121.

commentator noted, doing so 'grudgingly.'[59] Consequently, the General Court considered that the review system of the sanctions regime of the Security Council was not satisfactory and 'so long as the re-examination procedure operated by the Sanctions Committee clearly fails to offer guarantees of effective judicial protection,'[60] the General Court had to exercise the principle of full review decided by the ECJ in *Kadi*.[61] In that context, the General Court noted that the Commission had not granted the applicant access to evidence against him[62] and he, therefore, did not have any way to challenge the decision to list him. The General Court concluded that the regulation adopted on 28 November 2008 maintaining the freeze of Mr Kadi's assets was unlawful and should, for that reason, be annulled.[63]

The Commission, however, appealed the judgment with the claims that:

> The standard of judicial review adopted by the General Court is legally erroneous because the Court of Justice has not settled the precise standard of judicial review applicable to this case and because the particular standard of judicial review adopted by the General Court cannot be required from the EU.[64]

On 5 October 2012, the UN delisted Mr Kadi, after a 'comprehensive report provided to the Committee by the Ombudsperson.'[65] The EU followed suit on 11 October 2012.[66] Yet, the case was still decided by the ECJ on principle and it detailed the level of review that the ECJ considers necessary in terrorist sanctions.[67]

---

59 Tim Stahlberg, 'Case T-85/09, *Kadi II*', quoted in Lisa Ginsborg and Martin Scheinin, *Judicial Powers, Due Process and Evidence in the Security Council 1267 Terrorist Sanctions Regime: The Kadi II Conundrum* (European University Institute, 2011) 7.

60 Case T-85/09 *Kadi v Commission* [2010] OJ C317, §127.

61 Ibid., §126.

62 Ibid., §173.

63 Case T-85/09 *Kadi v Commission* [2010] OJ C317, §29.

64 Ibid., 'Pleas in law and arguments.'

65 Statement by Ambassador Wittig, Permanent Representative of Germany to the United Nations, Chair of the Al-Qaida Sanctions Committee, accompanying Document SC/10785, 5 October 2012.

66 Commission Implementing Regulation (EU) No 933/2012 of 11 October 2012 amending for the 180th time Council Regulation (EC) No 881/2002 imposing certain specific restrictive measures directed against certain persons and entities associated with the Al-Qaida network, *Official Journal* L278, 12/10/2012, P. 001–0012, available at http://eur-lex.europa.eu/legal-content/EN/TXT/?uri=CELEX:32012R0933 (last accessed 16.12.2015).

67 A separate case by the ECJ confirmed that a delisted person still had an interest in bringing proceedings for annulment of his or her original listing: Case C-239/12 P – *Abdulrahim/Council and Commission*, ECJ 28 May 2013.

The Grand Chamber of the ECJ delivered its decision on the *Kadi II* appeal on 18 July 2013.[68] In the decision, the Grand Chamber upheld the decision of the General Court and dismissed the Commission's appeal. As well, it overturned some of the General Court's reasoning on the scope of judicial review and it confirmed that it would continue to review EU listings implementing strict Security Council obligations as long as the Security Council did not offer sufficient protection of fundamental rights. This meant, in effect, that the ECJ did not consider the Ombudsperson to be a sufficient remedy.[69] Moreover, The ECJ rejected the recommendation made by Advocate-General Bot that the Court should carry out a limited review in cases arising from UN counter-terrorist sanctions.[70] Indeed, it held that European courts would conduct substantive reviews of listings and it detailed the nature and content of these reviews.[71]

Of note, too, is a recent decision by the ECJ on Iran sanctions that held, as was held in the *Kadi* case, that the standard of review for the actions of a State targeted by sanctions had to be the same as for terrorist sanctions and that this review was to be 'complete'.[72]

The EU case law has shed light on the many levels that are involved in sanctions regimes. It is important to also examine UK case law on terrorist sanctions, because it provides an example of the conflict of obligations that transcend levels of jurisdiction. States are under an obligation to freeze assets under EU regulations as well as under UN resolutions, but have also developed their own sets of national obligations. This has resulted in national legal challenges stemming from the UK sanctions regimes, as will be discussed below.

---

68 *Commission v Kadi*, Joined cases C-584/10 P, C-593/10 P and C-595/10 P, Court of Justice of the European Union (Grand Chamber), July 18, 2013.

69 *Commission v Kadi* (2013) §95 and 96.

70 Opinion of Advocate General Bot, delivered on 19 March 2013, Joined Cases C-584/10 P, C-593/10 P and C-595/10 P *European Commission Council of the European Union United Kingdom of Great Britain and Northern Ireland v Yassin Abdullah Kadi*, available at http://curia.europa.eu/juris/document/document.jsf?text=&docid=135223&pageIndex=0&doclang=en&mode=lst&dir=&occ=first&part=1&cid=914112 (last accessed 16.12.2015).

71 Kadi (2013) §134.

72 T-392/11 *Iran Transfo v Council of the European Union*, 16 May 2013, Working document from the ECJ, available (in French only) at http://curia.europa.eu/juris/document/document.jsf?text=&docid=137431&pageIndex=0&doclang=FR&mode=lst&dir=&occ=first&part=1&cid=2985946 (last accessed 16.12.2015).

2 UK Case Law

The UK adopted measures to implement both the UN and the EU regimes. The first UK order in Council implementing Security Council Resolution 1267 was the Afghanistan (United Nations Sanctions) Order 1999 (SI 1999/3133), which provided for the prohibition of the provision of funds to the Taliban[73] and listed the penalties for the obligations mentioned.[74]

Further orders in 2002[75] and 2006[76] reflected the changes made by the Security Council to the 1267 sanctions regime. In particular, the 2006 Order specified the list of people to which the order applied, and thereby echoed the broadening of the 1267 sanctions regime to Al-Qaida in general.[77] The list included

> (a) Osama bin Laden, (b) any person designated by the Sanctions Committee, and (c) any person identified in a direction, is a designated person. (2) In this Part 'direction' (other than in articles 4(2)(d) and 5(3)(c)) means a direction given by the Treasury under article 4(1).[78]

The 2006 Order also provided the UK Treasury with the power to designate further individuals where it had 'reasonable grounds for suspecting that the person' might belong to the list provided.[79] It then listed the prohibitions of the order as assets freezing[80] and provision of funds,[81] as well as exceptions to these prohibitions.[82] The list of obligations contained in the order did not include a right for the individual listed to review.

The Terrorism (United Nations Measures) Order 2001 (SI 2001/3365) was adopted to implement the 1373 sanctions regime. Due to the fact that the UN does not have a specific list under Resolution 1373, the UK order prohibited the provision of funds[83] to and required the freezing of assets[84] of

73 The Afghanistan (United Nations Sanctions) Order 2001 (SI 2001/396), Article 4.
74 Ibid., Article 8.
75 The Afghanistan (United Nations Sanctions) Order 2001 (SI 2001/396), Article 8.
76 The Al-Qaida & Taliban (United Nations Measures) Order 2006 (SI 2006/2952).
77 Ibid., Article 3.
78 Ibid., Article 3.
79 Ibid., Article 4.
80 Ibid., Article 7.
81 Ibid., Article 8.
82 Ibid., Articles 9 and 11.
83 The Terrorism (United Nations Measures) Order 2001 (SI 2001/3365), Article 3.
84 Ibid., Article 4.

> (a) a person who commits, attempts to commit, facilitates or participates in the commission of acts of terrorism, (b) a person controlled or owned directly or indirectly by a person in (a), or (c) a person acting on behalf, or at the direction, of a person in (a).[85]

The original order was then amended to reflect the fact that the EU had created its own list applying UN Resolution 1373, therefore the above-mentioned list now includes '(d) a person on the list (of natural and legal persons, groups and entities) in Article 1 of the Council Decision [2002/974/EC].'[86] While the UK can still add its own individuals and groups to the list, it has to apply the EU's list too, which act as a minimum. Additional orders were adopted as well, reflecting changes that the EU made to its independent terrorist list.[87]

Like in many other cases, the sanctions regimes led to a number of challenges in the UK against their legality, which are analysed here. Between 2006 and 2007, A, K, and M had restrictions applied under the Terrorism Order 2001, while G was told that he was a designated person under the Al-Qaida Order. All of them started proceedings in the UK in order to have their designations set aside. In April 2008, the High Court declared both orders to be *ultra vires*.[88] In *A, K, M, Q & G v HM Treasury*, the English High Court accepted that the Al-Qaida Order in itself was legal. However, it also stressed that individuals that were subject to the order should be allowed the possibility of a judicial review.[89] Additionally, the High Court found that the UK government could not simply implement the UN Security Council resolutions directly, but instead, had to go to Parliament first to get them authorized.[90] For this reason, the High Court declared that the two orders were not lawful and needed to be quashed.[91]

---

85 Ibid., Articles 3 and 4.

86 Ibid., Article 3.

87 The Terrorism (United Nations Measures) Order 2009 (SI 2009/1747); the Terrorism (United Nations Measures) Order 2006 (SI 2006/2657); the Terrorism (United Nations Measures) Order 2001 (Amendment) Regulations 2005 (SI 2005/1525); the Terrorism (United Nations Measures) Order 2001 (Amendment) Regulations 2004 (SI 2004/2309); the Terrorism (United Nations Measures) Order 2001 (Amendment No 3) Regulations 2003 (SI 2003/2430); the Terrorism (United Nations Measures) Order 2001 (Amendment No 2) Regulations 2003 (SI 2003/2209); and the Terrorism (United Nations Measures) Order 2001 (Amendment) Regulations 2003 (SI 2003/1297).

88 *A, K, M, Q & G v HM Treasury*, Court of Appeal – Administrative Court, 24 April 2008, [2008] EWHC 869 (Admin), [2008] 3 All ER 361.

89 Ibid., §18.

90 *A, K, M, Q & G v HM Treasury*, Court of Appeal – Administrative Court, 24 April 2008, [2008] EWHC 869 (Admin), [2008] 3 All ER 361, §38.

91 Ibid., §49.

In 2005, Mr Hay was notified that he had automatically been designated under the Al-Qaida Order as a result of a 1267 Committee designation and that since the UK had not been the designating State, there was, therefore, no possible review. The High Court in *Hay v HM Treasury*[92] held that this 'amounted to the designated person being deprived of its access to a court, something that the sovereign Parliament did not permit in the United Nations Act 1946.'[93] It held that it was still open to the UK government to comply with its international obligations and to freeze the assets of Hay, but only if the Parliament passed legislation which allowed the government to remove the right of access to a court.[94] Therefore the High Court annulled the Al-Qaida Order for being *ultra vires*.

Both *A, K, M, Q & G v HM Treasury* and *Hay v HM Treasury* were merged on appeal in the *Ahmed* case,[95] where the UK Supreme Court, which replaced the House of Lords, accepted, in its first case, the submissions of the claimants' lawyers that the two Orders in Council[96] were 'ultra vires, among other things because those affected were not permitted to see – and hence unable to challenge – the evidence supporting that suspicion, violating their right to a fair hearing.'[97]

The *Ahmed* case confirmed the High Court's approach in *Hay*.[98] Lord Hope did state that 'Convention rights fall into a category of obligations under an international agreement over which obligations under the [UN] Charter must prevail.'[99] However, the Court concluded that the order left designated individuals without any effective judicial remedy and that 'there [was] nothing in

92 *Hay v HM Treasury* [2009] EWHC 1677 (Admin) (10 July 2009).

93 Antonios Tzanakopoulos, 'Stepping Up the (Dualist?) Resistance: The English High Court Quashes Domestic Measures Implementing UN Sanctions', *EJIL Talk*, 9 October 2009.

94 *Hay v HM Treasury*, §46.

95 *HM Treasury v Mohammed Jabar Ahmed and ors* (FC); *HM Treasury v Mohammed al-Ghabra* (FC); and *R* (*on the application of Hani El Sayed Sabaei Youssef*) *v HM Treasury* [2010] UKSC 2.

96 UK Al-Qaida and Taliban (United Nations Measures) Order 2006 (SI 2006/2952) and Terrorism (United Nations Measures) Order 2006 (SI 2006/2657).

97 Francesca Galli, 'The freezing of terrorists' assets: preventive purpose with a punitive effect' in F. Galli and A. Weyembergh (eds.), *Do labels still matter ? Blurring boundaries between administrative and criminal law. The influence of the EU* (Bruxelles: Editions de l'Université de Bruxelles, 2014), 61.

98 *Hay v HM Treasury* [2009] EWHC 1677 (Admin) (10 July 2009).

99 *HM Treasury v Mohammed Jabar Ahmed and ors* (FC); *HM Treasury v Mohammed al-Ghabra* (FC); and *R* (*on the application of Hani El Sayed Sabaei Youssef*) *v HM Treasury* [2010] UKSC 2, §74.

the listing or de-listing procedure that recognises the principles of natural justice or that provides for basic procedural fairness.'[100] Therefore, it quashed, in part, the Al Qaida Order of 2006, because it removed the right of access to an effective remedy.[101]

In practice, the Al-Qaida Order was revoked and in April 2010, the Al Qaida and Taliban (Asset-Freezing) Regulations 2010 were adopted, which made provisions for the enforcement of Regulation (EC) No 881/2002, (which itself implements the Security Council 1267 regime).[102] These regulations were eventually replaced by the Al-Qaida (Asset-Freezing) Regulations 2011.[103] Contrary to the previous orders, this regulation bases its 'designated persons' on the list of the EU regulation,[104] rather than the UN sanctions list, and it contains a similar list of obligations and prohibitions to that of the EU.[105] These regulations also amend the Counter-Terrorism Act 2008 'so that an application to the High Court to set aside any decision of the Treasury under these Regulations is subject to the procedure set out in that Act and in Part 79 of the Civil Procedure Rules,'[106] thereby allowing for a judicial review of the decisions to list individuals.[107]

The Supreme Court also quashed the Terrorism Order as being *ultra vires* because it introduced a 'reasonable suspicion' test, which was not included in Resolution 1373 and, therefore, went beyond what the UK government was allowed to do under the 1946 United Nations Act.[108] Following the judicial challenge of the *Ahmed* case, the Terrorism Order was consequently replaced by the Terrorist Asset-Freezing (Temporary Provisions) Act 2010, which was eventually replaced by the Terrorist Asset-Freezing Act 2010 (TAFA 2010). The latter act is more detailed than the previous orders, and was adopted by Parliament. It still gives power to the Treasury to freeze assets of groups and

---

100 Ibid., §80.

101 Ibid., §81–82.

102 The Al-Qaida and Taliban (Asset-Freezing) Regulations 2010 (SI 2010/1197), Preamble and Interpretation.

103 The Al-Qaida (Asset-Freezing) Regulations 2011 (SI 2011/2742).

104 Ibid., Interpretation, 2.

105 Asset freezing (Articles 3–8), information provisions (Schedule 1).

106 Explanatory notes to the Al-Qaida (Asset-Freezing) Regulations 2011 (SI 2011/2742).

107 See Part 79 at http://www.justice.gov.uk/courts/procedure-rules/civil/rules/part79#IDAKFSBB (last accessed 16.12.2015).

108 *Her Majesty's Treasury v Mohammed Jabar Ahmed and others*; *Her Majesty's Treasury v Mohammed al-Ghabra;* and *R (on the application of Hani El Sayed Sabaei Youssef) v Her Majesty's Treasury*, [2010] UKSC 2, United Kingdom: Supreme Court, 27 January 2010, §61.

individuals thought to be involved in terrorism,[109] and it also includes the EU list. The main changes of the regime are the safeguards that are now included within the act. In particular, the individual listed 'may appeal' against his or her listing.[110] Moreover, Article 31 of the act provides for an independent review of the 'operation' of the act by way of appointment of an independent reviewer who is requested to conduct an initial review and then compile yearly reviews.[111]

On the other hand, in *R (on the application of Youssef) v Secretary of State for Foreign and Commonwealth Affairs*, Hani Youssef had challenged the UK government's decision to list him in accordance with UN Resolution 1267 on the basis, among others, that 'the designation was sought on the basis of the claimant's Egyptian conviction, which was itself based on evidence obtained by torture, and in those circumstances the UK was legally obliged to maintain its hold on the listing.'[112] The High Court held that, while it 'would be very reluctant to accede to the argument that it would have been acceptable for the Foreign Secretary to have relied on evidence which he had reason to suppose was obtained by torture in agreeing to an indefinite freeze on the claimant's assets,'[113] it did 'not believe that it would be right for the court to dictate to the Foreign Secretary that he must instruct other member states as to what might be a permissible basis for the designation, and must prevent a designation (for which in his view the criteria were satisfied) unless and until he was satisfied that they were all proceeding on a basis which he considered to be proper.'[114] The court, therefore, rejected Mr Youssef's claim.[115]

In June 2013, the UK Supreme Court quashed an order made against Bank Mellat because of its alleged connection to the Iranian nuclear weapons programme, arguing, among other matters, that it was 'unlawful for want of prior notice to them or any procedure enabling them to be heard in advance of the order being made.'[116] The decision follows a similar decision made at the EU level.[117] The Court also stressed that 'with a measure such as this one, targeted

109 Part 1, Terrorist Asset-Freezing Act, 2010.

110 Articles 26–28, Terrorist Asset-Freezing Act 2010.

111 The reviews are available on the website of the independent reviewer: see https://terrorismlegislationreviewer.independent.gov.uk/ (last accessed 16.12.2015).

112 *R (on the application of Youssef) v Secretary of State for Foreign & Commonwealth Affairs* [2012] EWHC 2091 (Admin)', p., EWHC (Admin.).

113 Ibid., §89.

114 Ibid., §90.

115 Ibid., §100.

116 *Bank Mellat v Her Majesty's Treasury (No. 2)* [2013] UKSC 39 (19 June 2013) §49.

117 In January 2013, the EU General Court held that the EU had failed to provide sufficient evidence of the bank's links to Iran's nuclear efforts (see Case T-496/10 *Bank Mellat v.*

against "designated persons", it is not possible to say that procedural fairness is sufficiently guaranteed by Parliamentary scrutiny or to suppose that Parliament in enacting the Counter-Terrorism Act ever thought it was.'[118] A separate judgment also raised specific issues of evidence.[119] Yet, for the purpose of this study, it confirms that national courts consider that principles of fairness need to be applied to sanctions regimes and consider themselves as able to control this fairness.

These cases show the attempts of the judicial branch to ensure the executive measures adopted to address terrorism do not violate fundamental freedoms and procedural fairness. Other cases have further contributed to the defining of the relationship between the UN and its Member States when it comes to security and human rights. In *Al-Jedda v Secretary of State for Defence*,[120] the UK House of Lords decided the case based on the regular conflict resolution of Article 103 of the UN Charter. This case did not focus on sanctions regimes, but it gives an idea of the UK's position vis-à-vis its obligations towards the UN. In September 2004, Mr Al-Jedda, an Iraqi and British citizen, was arrested in Baghdad, without charge, on suspicion of involvement in terrorism and was detained by British troops in Basra until 2007. In a case before the English courts, he complained that his continuing preventive detention breached his right to liberty, but he lost in first instance and on appeal.[121] At both levels, the courts held that the UK's obligations under the UN Security Council resolutions authorising the role of the multinational force in Iraq prevailed over the provisions of both the ECHR and the Human Rights Act.[122] In 2008, the House of Lords held that:

> In the event of a conflict between the obligations of the Members of the United Nations under the present Charter and their obligations under any other international agreement, their obligations under the present Charter shall prevail.[123]

Council, 29 January 2013). An appeal by the EU Council is currently pending and, in the meantime, Bank Mellat remains on the EU list.

118 *Bank Mellat v Her Majesty's Treasury (No. 2)* [2013] UKSC 39 (19 June 2013) §47.

119 The separate judgment focused on the issue of closed hearing for secret evidence. This issue is too complex to be analysed here.

120 *R (on the application of Al-Jedda) v Secretary of State for Defence, House of Lords* [2007] UKHL 58.

121 Ibid.

122 Ibid., §35 and following.

123 Ibid., §132.

The main argument of the claimant was that Resolution 1546 was '*authorising* the multinational force to take the measures required to fulfil its mandate,'[124] and that this authorisation, therefore, did not constitute an obligation under the meaning of Article 103 of the UN Charter. However, Lord Bingham said that, in the context of a clash between obligations:

> The UK may lawfully, where it is necessary for imperative reasons of security, exercise the power to detain authorised by UNSCR 1546 and successive resolutions, but must ensure that the detainee's rights under Article 5 [of the ECHR] are not infringed to any greater extent than is inherent in such detention.[125]

Here, it is clear that the court followed the line of argument found in the *Lockerbie* case and in the CFI's *Kadi* case. The *Al-Jedda* case reached the ECtHR, whose judgement is analysed in Section 3 of this chapter.

The UK followed the UN and the EU in adopting executive measures to deal with financing sanctions against terrorist suspects and the Taliban. In conflicts before the courts, it mainly gave precedence to UN obligations. However, the UK Supreme Court prompted significant changes to these regimes and measures have now been adopted through more democratic ways that include the possibility of judicial review. Nonetheless, the UK government's tendency to favour its international obligations under the UN has prompted regional courts to address the situation. In this context, the ECtHR, like the ECJ, has made an important contribution to the jurisprudence on human rights within counterterrorism.

3 Council of Europe Case Law

While the Council of Europe did not create a sanctions regime on the model of the EU, it has produced a case law, which has influenced other regimes, that focuses on the protection of human rights stemming from the ECHR. For instance, the *Al-Jedda* case, discussed above, ended before the ECtHR[126] and it looked at legal clarity of UN resolutions and held that:

---

124 Security Council Resolution 1546 (2004): the situation between Iraq and Kuwait.

125 *R (on the application of Al-Jedda) v Secretary of State for Defence, House of Lords* [2007] UKHL 58, §39.

126 *Al-Jedda v UK* – 27021/08 [2011] ECHR 1092.

> There must be a presumption that the Security Council does not intend to impose any obligation on Member States to breach fundamental principles of human rights.[127]

The ECtHR said that the protection of human rights is an 'important role' of the UN and that, therefore, if the Security Council intended Member States to act in conflict with their human rights obligations, it should be 'expected to use clear and explicit language' to that effect.[128] In conclusion, the ECtHR held that the UK was responsible for violating Article 5(1) of the ECHR dealing with unlawful detention, because the State had jurisdiction over the facts and because it was not under a specific obligation by the UN to detain people preventively and without any review. In *Al-Jedda*, therefore, the ECtHR avoided a norm conflict through the interpretation of a UN Security resolution.

Another case arose, however, where this kind of interpretation was not possible.[129] In October 2000, the Swiss Federal Council adopted an order implementing UN Resolution 1267.[130] This order provided for the freezing of assets and financial resources of those concerned and it prohibited the provision of funds or financial resources to them and restricted their entry into or transit through Switzerland. Following a freezing of assets by UN authorities, Mr Nada, an Italian man living in the Italian enclave of Campione situated in Switzerland, was placed on the UN Sanctions Committee list. His name was later added by the Swiss authorities to the list of people of concern based on the anti-Taliban order.[131] As a result, Mr Nada was prohibited from leaving the Italian enclave. In 2002, Mr Nada requested that his name and the names of the organisations associated with him be deleted from the list, claiming that the travel ban violated his rights to liberty and security under Article 5 and his rights to private and family life under Article 8 of the ECHR. In November 2007, the Swiss Federal Court dismissed the case and held that

---

127 Ibid., §102.

128 In that respect, Judge Poalelungi dissented from the majority and, in a similar argument to the House of Lords, said that such decision 'would seriously undermine the effectiveness of the UN's role in securing world peace'(see *Al-Jedda v UK* – 27021/08 [2011] ECHR 1092, Dissenting Opinion, §4).

129 Special Rapporteur on the promotion and protection of human rights and fundamental freedoms while countering terrorism: 'Promotion and protection of human rights and fundamental freedoms while countering terrorism' (UN General Assembly, Sixty-Seventh Session 26 September 2012) para. 17.

130 This order is now the Ordinance on Measures Against Persons and Organisations with Ties to Usama Bin Laden, the Al-Qaida Group or the Taliban (CC 946.203).

131 See 'the facts', '*Nada v Switzerland* – 10593/08 – HEJUD [2012] ECHR 1691', p., ECHR (2012).

> Switzerland had acted in accordance with its international obligations. It nevertheless requested the Swiss authorities to ascertain whether it was possible, having regard to their international obligations, to waive the measure barring Mr Nada from entering the country.[132]

Here, the Federal Court followed the same reasoning as did the CFI in *Kadi* and the UK House of Lords in *Al-Jedda* and gave precedence to UN obligations.

However, Mr Nada filed a complaint with the ECtHR.[133] In March 2010, the Swiss government informed the Security Council that it has been instructed by the Swiss Parliament to disobey the Security Council and cancel targeted sanctions against specific individuals on the basis of Swiss guarantees of human rights.[134] The Chairman of the 1267 Committee responded to this letter by reiterating Member States' obligations under Article 103 of the Charter.[135] Meanwhile, on 23 September 2009, Nada was removed from the UN Consolidated List, and in October 2009, the Taliban ordinance was amended accordingly.[136]

On 12 September 2012, the ECtHR still held in favour of Mr Nada. In *Nada v Switzerland*, the Court started by saying that it could not apply the same reasoning as was used in the *Al-Jedda* case, as Resolution 1390 clearly made travelling a prohibition.[137] However, it then said that 'Switzerland enjoyed some latitude, which was admittedly limited but nevertheless real, in implementing the relevant binding resolutions of the UN Security Council.'[138] In the case in point, the Court considered that the applicant's situation should have been taken into account by the Swiss government.[139] Moreover with regard to the claim for effective remedy, the Court expressly mentioned the *Kadi* case before the ECJ and the need for review. It held that 'the applicant did not have any effective means of obtaining the removal of his name from the list annexed to the Taliban Ordinance and therefore no remedy in respect of the Convention violations that he alleged.'[140] The Court concluded that

132 'Principal Facts', ECHR, Press Release issued by the Registrar of the Court no. 769 20.10.2010.

133 See 'the facts', '*Nada v Switzerland* – 10593/08 – HEJUD [2012] ECHR 1691.'

134 Ibid., §63.

135 'Committee on Legal Affairs and Human Rights Information note: Compatibility of UN Security Council and EU [terrorist] Black Lists with European Convention on Human Rights requirements,' AS/Jur/Inf (2010) 05, 7 December 2010, 8.

136 '*Nada v Switzerland* – 10593/08 – HEJUD [2012] ECHR 1691', §62.

137 Ibid., §172.

138 Ibid., §180.

139 Ibid., §196.

140 '*Nada v Switzerland*', §212.

Switzerland had interfered with Mr Nada's rights,[141] and it ordered Switzerland to pay Mr Nada the sum of €30,000.[142]

A more recent case in the sanctions saga – albeit not terrorist sanctions – is the *Al-Dulimi and Montana Management Inc v Switzerland* case, decided by the ECtHR in December 2013[143] and currently before the Grand Chamber of the ECtHR.[144] Switzerland, acting under UN Security Council Resolution 1483 that froze the assets of those connected with the government of Iraq, has frozen the assets of an Iraqi national alleged to have been the finance manager for the Iraqi secret services under the regime of Saddam Hussein.[145] Al-Dulimi first challenged this freezing before the Swiss courts, but was rejected under the argument that Switzerland was obligated to implement the UN resolution.[146] In its 2013 judgment, the ECtHR held that Switzerland had violated Article 6 of the ECtHR (due process), in particular, because there was a lack of forum to challenge this listing and also because the UN system did not provide for sufficient protection.[147]

In both *Al-Jedda* and *Nada*, the ECtHR made an effort of interpretation in order to avoid a norm conflict. In *Al-Jedda*, it specifically chose to read human rights into a resolution by the Security Council, thereby refusing the State's argument that it was following specific obligations. On the other hand, in *Nada*, it stated that Switzerland had some leeway in the manner in which it implemented UN resolutions, although this approach was criticised, including by the concurring judges, as being unconvincing.[148] Just as the ECtHR had distinguished its legal reasoning in *Al-Jedda* and *Nada*, in *Al-Dulimi* the Court held that the obligations stemming from the UN resolution did not leave any leeway to Switzerland[149] and it, therefore, had to apply its 'equivalent protection doctrine' developed in the 2005 *Bosphorus* case.[150]

141 Ibid., Decision, §4.

142 Ibid., Decision, §7.

143 *Al-Dulimi & Montana Management Inc. v Switzerland* [2013] ECHR 1173.

144 Grand Chamber hearing: *Al-Dulimi and Montana Management Inc. v. Switzerland* (no. 5809/08).

145 UNSC Res 1483 (22 May 2003) UN Doc S/Res/1483.

146 The Swiss Federal Tribunal rejected the complaints in three cases: BGE 2A.783/2006, BGE 2A.784/2006 and BGE 2A.785/2006 on 23 January 2008.

147 *Al-Dulimi* 2013, §134 and §136–140.

148 *Nada v Switzerland* (Joint Concurring Opinion of Judges Bratza, Nicolau and Yudkivska) §1, 3 and 5.

149 Ibid., §117–121.

150 *Bosphorus Hava Yollari Turizm ve Ticaret Anonim Sirketi v Ireland* [2005] 42 EHRR 1.

This doctrine is similar to the argument used in the 2008 *Kadi* case and the German *Solange* case.[151]

Going back to the initial conflict between human rights and security, the ECtHR seems to try to avoid norm conflicts and rather, it tries to integrate human rights as an inherent part of counterterrorism. It does so by placing a power of latitude in the hands of Member States. This, of course, raises questions of responsibility, where States could be responsible for ensuring the protection of human rights in parallel to other international obligations. This issue is too complex to fully address here, but it will be referred to briefly in the next two chapters.

The case law analysed here represents the various ways in which regional courts deal with conflicts of obligations. In other words, where deference was traditionally given to UN obligations in application of Article 103 of the UN Charter, the recent jurisprudence on terrorist sanctions has shown a desire to qualify this deference, in particular, when it is regarding the protection of human rights. All decisions have stressed the importance of safeguards in the context of counterterrorism. These decisions fit in with the general evolution towards a better protection of human rights and have had a significant impact on international counterterrorism.

151 *Solange I* [1974] 2 CMLR 540. In this case, the German court held they were still reserving the right to measure Community acts against the benchmark of their own constitutional guarantees, although they have suspended this competence 'so long' as the European Council acts provide for equivalent protection of human rights.

CHAPTER 11

The Impact of Case Law on the EU and UN Sanctions Regimes

Changes have been made to the various sanctions regimes over time, which almost certainly resulted from the extensive EU and ECtHR case law, rather than from being prompted by the Security Council itself. In this respect, courts have had a significant impact on the sovereignty of States, as well as their representatives at the international level.

1 European Union Measures

After the first *OMPI* case, the EU Council established a new procedure for notification of individuals who were listed. Currently, the EU provides an explanatory note to listed individuals on how to apply for 'humanitarian exemption,' obtain a list of reasons, and request a reconsideration of the listing procedure through a Notice published by the Council.[1] Central to this reform was the creation of an EU 'Working Party on implementation of Common Position 2001/931/CFSP on the application of specific measures to combat terrorism.'[2] Since 2002, the Common Position is reviewed by the EU every six months, using a review mechanism that was established with its adoption. Under this system, the Council must provide a statement of reasons to the persons listed, which must include the specific terrorist acts allegedly committed, information on the competent national authority making the decision,[3] and the type of decision made. The Council Secretariat is in charge of drafting this statement of reasons on the basis of consultations with EU Member States. The statements of reasons are examined by the Working Party created by CP 2001/931/CFSP before being adopted by Council.[4]

Furthermore, as a result of the 2008 *Kadi* case, the European Commission proposed amendments to Regulation (EC) 881/2002 itself in April 2009. This

---

1 Notice for the attention of the persons, groups, and entities on the list provided for in Article 2(3) of Council Regulation (EC) No 2580/2001 on specific restrictive measures directed against certain persons and entities with a view to combating terrorism (2007/C 144/01).

2 EU Council doc.10826/1/07.

3 See Article 1(4) CP 2001/931/CFSP.

4 Eriksson, 'In Search of a Due Process – Listing and Delisting Practices of the European Union', 33.

 | DOI 10.1163/9789004299580_013

then led to the introduction by EU Regulation 1286/2009 of procedural and due process reforms to the implementation of the UN 1267 regime in the EU. The 2009 regulation actually refers to the *Kadi* case as the basis for the need to amend Regulation (EC) 881/2002 in order 'to provide for a listing procedure ensuring that the fundamental rights of the defence and in particular the right to be heard are respected.'[5] With Regulation 1286/2009, the EU does not simply copy the UN regime without applying its own procedural safeguards. Instead, after the EU Commission is notified of a new UN 1267 listing and has been sent the corresponding 'statement of reasons' by the UN Sanctions Committee, it needs to send the statement 'without delay' to the individual or entity listed in Annex I[6] and invite them to express their views on the listing decision. As well, under this regulation, the Commission must take into account the views of those on the list, and where comments are submitted, must review its decision in light of those comments.[7] The Commission must then communicate the result of its review to the individual or entity concerned and to the Committee experts. The Commission may also conduct another review if a request is made based on substantial new evidence. This review may lead to the subsequent removal of an individual or entity from Annex I.[8]

Furthermore, the Lisbon Treaty of the EU, which contains an express provision empowering the EU to take 'restrictive measures against natural or legal persons and groups or non-State entities'[9] also includes a provision stating that the ECJ has jurisdiction to review 'the legality of decisions providing for restrictive measures against natural or legal persons' adopted on the basis of the EU's common and foreign security policy.[10] Thus this jurisdiction that was first developed by the Court in *Kadi* was recognised *a posteriori* by the EU in the Lisbon Treaty.[11] The changes adopted at the EU level have repercussions at the domestic level, as States have to implement EU measures on terrorist sanctions. However, even though States must also implement their UN obligations, the Lisbon Treaty only focuses on the review of EU measures and does not address the review of UN measures or how to solve a conflict of norms. This

5 Council Regulation (EU) No 1286/2009, Preamble §4.
6 Council Regulation (EU) No 1286/2009, Article 9.
7 Ibid.
8 Ibid.
9 Article 215 (2) TFEU.
10 Article 275 TFEU: this is one of the exceptions under which the Court has jurisdiction with respect to the provisions relating to the common foreign and security policy.
11 The importance of due process and legal control were also recognised in a Declaration attached to the Treaty: Declaration 25 on Article75 and 275 on the TFEU.

still leaves room for an issue as to whether UN treaty obligations prevail over other international obligations, such as human rights.

2 United Nations Measures

As noted previously, the Security Council itself has acknowledged the need to incorporate human rights within its mandate and has included them in the Preamble to each of its resolutions in the 1267/1989 sanctions regime. In the July 2012 review of its National Global Counter-Terrorism Strategy, 'the General Assembly again called upon all United Nations entities involved in supporting counterterrorism efforts to continue to facilitate the promotion and protection of human rights, due process and the rule of law.'[12]

In practice, changes occurred slowly. In 2006, the Security Council created the 'Focal Point', a contact mechanism within the Security Council Secretariat that coordinates all delisting requests.[13] This delisting procedure was created in order to receive delisting requests from anyone affected by the UN sanctions. The requests are forwarded by the Secretariat to the State of the designated person or organisation and those on the list can then follow a few steps if the State refuses to delist them.[14] Nonetheless, the State requesting the listing still has the last word,[15] thus while the Security Council stressed that it was 'committed to ensuring that fair and clear procedures exist for placing individuals and entities on sanctions lists and for removing them, as well as for granting humanitarian exemptions', the Focal Point was criticized for being no more than a 'mailbox'[16] with no authority to review the legality of a listing. Instead, it places the last decision in the hands of States and is dependent on the Secretariat of the Security Council, thereby lacking any independence. Despite this, however, the Focal Point procedure is still in place today.[17]

12 Special Rapporteur on the promotion and protection of human rights and fundamental freedoms while countering terrorism, 'Promotion and protection of human rights and fundamental freedoms while countering terrorism', 18 (see GA Resolution 66/282, para. 9).

13 S/RES/1730 (of 19 December 2006).

14 Ibid., Article 6.

15 Ibid., Article 6(c).

16 Clemens A. Feinäugle, The UN Security Council Al-Qaida and Taliban Sanctions Committee: Emerging Principles of International Institutional Law for the Protection of Individuals?' (2008) 11 *German Law Journal*, 9, 1530.

17 See the website of the Focal Point at http://www.un.org/sc/committees/dfp.shtml (last accessed 16.12.2015).

To remedy criticisms raised by the Focal Point procedure and '*taking note* of challenges, both legal and otherwise, to the measures implemented by Member States,'[18] the Security Council, through Resolution 1904, created the Office of the Ombudsperson whose mandate was included in Annex II of Resolution 1904 and was later updated, as can be found in Annex II of Resolution 2253. The Ombudsperson, as is stipulated in Resolution 1904, must have specific expertise in human rights, counterterrorism and sanctions[19] and is charged with assisting the Sanctions Committee with the delisting process.[20] In creating this new position, the Security Council aimed to address the 'shortcomings' of the listing process[21] by creating an office that is 'independent and impartial.'[22] In July 2010, the UN appointed Kimberley Prost, a Canadian judge, to the position of Ombudsperson.[23] On 17 June 2011, the Security Council adopted Resolutions 1988 (2011) and 1989 (2011), which extended the original eighteen-month mandate of the Office of the Ombudsperson and the Monitoring Team for an additional eighteen months.[24] In July 2015, Prost was replaced by Catherine Marchi-Uhel[25] whose mandate has now been extended by Resolution 2253 (2015) for another twenty-four months after December 2017, the end of her current mandate.[26]

The Office of the Ombudsperson is tasked with helping the Al-Qaida Committee gather information and with communicating with the applicant and preparing reports on delisting requests. States and individuals can email requests for delisting to the Ombudsperson who will then process them as follows. The Ombudsperson will begin by gathering information over a four-month period. Next, over a two-month dialogue period, the Ombudsperson will act as an intermediary between the individual who requested the delisting

18 Security Council, Resolution 1904, S/RES/1904 (2009), Preamble.

19 SC Resolution 1904 (2009) §20.

20 SC Resolution 1904 (2009) §20. It must be noted that the Ombudsperson only has a mandate for sanctions under the 1267 Committee, but not for sanctions under Resolution 1373, which are still examined through the Focal Point procedure.

21 UN Security Council 6247th Meeting, 17 December 2009, S/PV.6247.

22 Ibid.

23 James Reinl, 'No-fly list appeals can be filed online', *The National Newspaper*, 16 July 2010, available at http://www.thenational.ae/news/world/no-fly-list-appeals-can-be-filed-online (last accessed 16.12.2015).

24 Joe Stevens, 'No New Weapons for the UN Ombudsperson?' (2011) 2 *Journal of Terrorism Research*, 3.

25 Appointment letter S/2015/534 available at http://www.un.org/ga/search/view_doc.asp?symbol=S/2015/534 (last accessed 15.12.2015).

26 UN Security Council Resolution 2253 (2015) §54.

and the Committee that might have questions[27] and will also prepare a report on the request and state whether or not she or he supports the delisting. Finally, the report will be forwarded to the Committee members for their consideration, and the Ombudsperson will then present the report's recommendations to the Committee.[28]

A number of resolutions amended the scope of the Ombudsperson's mandate and the procedures for delisting. For instance, Resolutions 1988 (2011) addressed two major shortcomings of Resolution 1904 (2009). Originally the Ombudsperson did not have a formal power to make recommendations. In practice she took advantage of her reports to express her recommendations and therefore, Resolution 1989 gives the Ombudsperson a mandate to make consequential recommendations regarding processed delisting requests.[29] Moreover, under Resolution 1904, decisions for delisting used to be decided by consensus, but with Resolution 1988:

> A delisting recommendation by the Ombudsperson now takes effect automatically 60 days after the Committee completes its consideration of the comprehensive report, unless the Committee decides otherwise by consensus. If there is no consensus, any member of the Committee may refer the delisting request to the Security Council (the 'trigger mechanism' procedure).[30]

In December 2012, the Security Council adopted Resolutions 2082 (2012) and 2083 (2012), which updated the sanctions regimes and the role of the Ombudsperson. Resolution 2083 (2012), concerning Al-Qaida, did not make the Ombudsperson's mandate permanent, but, instead, extended it for thirty months dating from the resolution.[31] It focuses on the need to provide information for any listing, including any that are confidential.[32] As well, it states that, in exceptional circumstances, the Ombudsperson can request a lift of a travel ban in order to allow a listed person to meet with her.[33] These proposed changes have been implemented, in practice, by the new Guidelines adopted

27 SC Resolution 1904 (2009) Annex II, §5 and 6.

28 Ibid., §7 and 8.

29 Ibid., §21.

30 See SC Resolution 1989 (2011) §23.

31 Security Council Resolution 2083, 17 December 2012, §19.

32 Ibid., §11, 13 and 15 provide information of national court proceedings; 16 provides information sharing between States; and 23.

33 Ibid., §36.

by the Sanctions Committee in April 2013.[34] These changes are welcome, even if they are only 'small steps towards more transparency and fairness.'[35]

It is important to note that the Ombudsperson is an independent person although his or her decisions are not binding. The Ombudsperson has some 'distinguished advantages' relative to other dispute resolution mechanisms, because his or her resolution mechanism is 'quite quick, informal and more easily accessible than for example a court.'[36] However, the Ombudsperson is not a court and has no judicial power. It must be noted that the current Ombudsperson herself 'has made it clear that it is not her function to consider whether the original listing was justified, but whether continued listing remains justified in current circumstances.'[37]

In *Ahmed*,[38] the UK Supreme Court had 'rejected this introduction of an Ombudsperson as a radical step towards creating a regime that would deserve its deference.'[39] While it welcomed the move, the Court still considered that the 1267 sanctions regime does not offer any access to effective judicial remedies.[40] This was echoed in *Kadi II* where the General Court held that 'the Security Council has still not deemed it appropriate to establish an independent and impartial body responsible for hearing and determining, as regards matters of law and fact, actions against individual decisions taken by the Sanctions Committee.'[41] In September 2012, Ben Emmerson, the UN Special Rapporteur on the promotion and protection of human rights and fundamental

---

34 'Security Council 1267/1989 Committee Revises Its Guidelines', SC/10979, 17 April 2013, available at http://www.un.org/press/en/2013/sc10979.doc.htm (last accessed 16.12.2015).

35 Kristen Boon, 'Small Steps Towards More Transparency and Fairness in the Al Qaida Sanctions Regime', *Opinion Juris* December 18, 2013, available at http://opiniojuris.org/2012/12/18/small-steps-new-resolution-contains-some-improvements-on-transparency-and-fairness-in-the-al-qaida-sanctions-regime/(last accessed 16.12.2015).

36 Adele J. Kirschner, 'Security Council Resolution 1904 (2009): A Significant Step in the Evolution of Al-Qaida and Taliban Sanctions Regime?' (2010) 70 Zeitschrift für ausländisches öffentliches Recht und Völkerrecht, 3, 597.

37 General Assembly, Sixty-seventh session, Agenda item 69 (b), 'Promotion and protection of human rights and fundamental freedoms while countering terrorism', 26 September 2012, §54.

38 *HM Treasury v Mohammed Jabar Ahmed and ors* (FC); *HM Treasury v Mohammed al-Ghabra* (FC); and *R* (*on the application of Hani El Sayed Sabaei Youssef*) *v HM Treasury* [2010] UKSC 2.

39 Antonios Tzanakopoulos, 'The UK Supreme Court Quashed Domestic Measures Implementing UN Sanctions', *EJIL Talk*, February 23, 2010.

40 Ahmed, § 78, 80, 239.

41 Case T-85/09, *Yasin Abdullah Kadi v European Commission*, General Court of the European Union, 30 September 2010, §128.

freedoms while countering terrorism, published a report on the sanctions regimes of the UN. He concluded that 'the mandate of the Ombudsperson still does not meet the structural due process requirement of objective independence from the Committee.'[42] He also 'endors[ed] the recommendation of the High Commissioner for Human Rights that the Security Council must now explore "every avenue of possibility for establishing an independent quasi-judicial procedure for review of listing and delisting decisions."'[43] It is also interesting to note that, in his opinion for the *Kadi* appeal by the ECJ, the Advocate General considered that the 'improvements in the procedure before the Sanctions Committee,'[44] including those relating to the Ombudsperson, were sufficient and allowed for a limited review by the ECJ. However, the ECJ held, in its 2013 *Kadi* decision, that the Office of the Ombudsperson 'does not offer any guarantee of judicial protection'.[45]

In practice, fifty-nine cases have been examined by the Ombudsperson since the beginning of her mandate. Eight requests are currently being considered for decision either by the Office of the Ombudsperson or by the Sanctions Committee.[46] More than forty-five cases have led to delisting, including, between December 2011 and February 2012, the Al Barakaat Foundation and various organisations linked to it[47] and in October 2012, Mr Kadi's delisting. Only a handful of requests were denied. In his report, Ben Emmerson acknowledged that these results 'tend[] to suggest that the Ombudsperson process has been effective in those cases that have so far been processed.'[48] Yet, serious concerns must be raised here, because while delisting is a positive outcome, the fact that so many groups and individuals have been delisted as soon as a review was available through the Ombudsperson, potentially means that most of them should not have been listed in the first place.

---

42 Ibid., §35.

43 Ibid.

44 Opinion of Advocate General Bot, delivered on 19 March 2013, Joined Cases C-584/10 P, C-593/10 P and C-595/10 P: *European Commission Council of the European Union, United Kingdom of Great Britain and Northern Ireland v Yassin Abdullah Kadi*, §81.

45 *Kadi* 2013, §95.

46 See the list of cases at http://www.un.org/en/sc/ombudsperson/status.shtml (last accessed 15.12.2015).

47 UNSC Press Release SC 10549, http://www.un.org/News/Press/docs/2012/sc10549.doc.htm (last accessed 16.12.2015).

48 GA, 67th, 26 September 2012, A/67/396, Report of the Special Rapporteur on the Promotion and protection of human rights and fundamental freedoms while countering terrorism, Ben Emmerson, §30.

It must also be noted that the improvements brought by the creation of the Ombudsperson are to be welcomed, but they are strictly limited to the 1267 sanctions regime and do not extend to other regimes. The lack of connection to a State makes the 1267 sanctions regime a special case and individuals and groups targeted by other sanctions regimes can still apply to the Focal Point for delisting, and can bring cases before national and international courts. It is not clear whether an expansion of the Ombudsperson's mandate to other regimes would be possible.

One must wonder, as well, whether or not there is a risk that the Sanctions Committee or the Security Council, in general, would get complacent if the ECJ considered that the Office of the Ombudsperson allowed a sufficient remedy. As was pointed out above, the improvements brought about by the creation of the Office of the Ombudsperson came from outside the UN. Therefore, the possibility must be raised that if the Security Council is not challenged on its human rights record, would it actually feel the need to improve it?

Besides the changes that resulted from the creation of the Office of the Ombudsperson, a second significant change in counterterrorism happened with the adoption of Resolution 2178 that included, as noted above, reference to human rights protection *within* operative paragraphs of the resolution.[49] This is crucial because it means that human rights protection now becomes part and parcel of the obligation to fight terrorism, in tandem with the specific obligations of the resolution. The requirement, by the Security Council, to abide by human rights obligations means that States' human rights obligations should, in theory, obtain the same binding nature as any counterterrorism obligation. As a result, States are prompted to include human rights protection into their counterterrorism measures.

The various obligations resulting from terrorism sanctions have led to conflicts between counterterrorism norms, especially for those States that have to implement these conflicting obligations. These conflicts have given way to an extensive jurisprudence, both at the national and regional level. Notably, the *Kadi* case changed the traditional way courts have looked at the conflict between UN obligations and other obligations, in particular regarding human rights. This case has had a significant impact on the nature of the sanctions regimes, such that improvements were made at all levels and there was a move towards a more democratic way to create and review the listing and delisting processes. At the same time, *Kadi* raised many issues about the conflicts of sovereignty, which will be further discussed in Chapter 12.

---

49 See Chapter 2, Section 2.

CHAPTER 12

Conflicts

The *Kadi* case has shown the conflict between norms that are created by various sources of international law. These different sources belong to different legal orders that then may conflict with each other. This conflict of legal orders often leads to loss of clarity in the distribution of competences where the traditional hierarchy of legal orders is questioned. Within these legal orders, the executive has been particularly active in acting against terrorism, while the judiciary has traditionally had a secondary role, although this has recently changed with the case law on sanctions. Here, the possibility must be raised of the occurrence of a conflict of branches, where the balance of powers in existence in a national legal order is not present at the international level.

1 Conflict of Sovereign Legal Orders

The sanctions regimes that were analysed in this book represent situations where 'strictly binding ("sovereign" or "governmental") decisions [are] made at various levels of governance (international, regional, domestic).'[1] Similar regimes of counterterrorism measures are adopted by various institutions of various legal orders and are all legally binding on Member States. Competences in this area are shared by different actors, as is stated by Christina Eckes:

> The different norms governing individual sanctions do not stand in a straightforwardly hierarchical relation towards each other but require relating by the force of legal reasoning, either on the basis of a technical legalistic argument or on the basis of substantive considerations. It is certain that the implications of how these norms relate go far beyond the individual case: it determines which of the two legal spheres has the last word.[2]

This conflict raises concerns about the traditional question of State sovereignty in the face of the actions of international institutions. On the one hand, this

1 Antonios Tzanakopoulos, '*Kadi II*: The 1267 Sanctions Regime (Back) Before the General Court of the EU', *EJIL Talk* November 16, 2010.

2 Christina Eckes, 'Protecting Supremacy from External Influences: A Precondition for a European Constitutional Legal Order?' (2012) 18 *European Law Journal* 230, 14.

 | DOI 10.1163/9789004299580_014

'multilevel fighting against terrorism…suggests that all these levels cooperate for the ultimate objective of fighting international crime and maintaining international peace and security.'[3] Indeed, it is clear from this analysis that the sanctions regimes from all the various legal orders were strikingly similar, at least at the origin. The EU and Member States directly copied the content of Security Council resolutions into their own legal regimes. Moreover, Member States and organisations shared intelligence, which led to individuals being listed.[4] An international response to terrorism needs the coordination of various systems, thus the duplication of the UN lists and obligations by the EU ensures consistency and contributes to the creation of a tight counterterrorism framework without regulatory gaps. It also means that States replicate their domestic agenda at the international level, creating a 'circular interaction' that seems to reinforce State sovereignty, as is described in Chapter 9, Section 3.

At the same time, this strict implementation means that problematic issues, such as the lack of human rights, are also strictly implemented. The many cases in which individuals' rights were violated by the sanctions regimes are proof of this coordinated response when it lacks safeguards. In practice, differences began to appear between the various legal orders and it has been seen that some Member States became more reluctant to suggest names for the listing.[5] Some of the intelligence was rejected by courts for not being sufficient[6]

3 Giulia Gargantini, 'European cooperation in counter-terrorism and the case of individual sanctions' (2011) 3 *Perspectives on Federalism*, 162.

4 For instance, in the case of the OMPI listings, the first EU listing of the organisation had been based on 'an order proscribing PMOI in the United Kingdom', while the second was based on 'two pieces of information supplied by the French Government: the first, relating to the opening in 2001 of a judicial investigation by the anti-terrorist prosecutor's office of the Tribunal de Grande Instance of Paris and the second, relating to two supplementary charges in 2007 against alleged members of PMOI:' Court of Justice of the European Union, Press Release No 137/11, Luxembourg, 21 December 2011, Judgment in Case C-27/09 P, *French Republic v People's Mojahedin Organization of Iran*. In other cases, investigations by one State have led to the deletion of an individual in another State or organisation. In the case of Mr Nada, the Swiss Federal Prosecutor's Office confirmed that the police investigation 'in respect of his client had not produced any indications or evidence to show that he had ties with persons or organisations associated with Osama bin Laden, al-Qaeda or the Taliban' and sent a letter to the Security Council Sanctions Committee in this respect. Consequently, Mr Nada was delisted from the UN Sanctions 1267 list: '*Nada v Switzerland* – 10593/08 – HEJUD [2012] ECHR 1691', §61 and 62.

5 See Section 4 of Chapter 9.

6 See for instance, Case T-284/08 *PMOI v Council* of 4 December 2008, §66, where the CFI held that is it not possible, 'in the absence of more accurate information, to verify the truthfulness

and as well, because some of the intelligence is classified, States may, therefore, be reluctant to share it.

Through their case law, regional organisations have brought human rights to the core of the sanctions regime. This has led, not only to a conflict of obligations, but more deeply, to the questioning of the relationship between the various actors involved in the sanctions regimes. Indeed, it can be argued that the ECJ *Kadi* judgment challenges the UN sanctions regime because the EU, and therefore its Member States, now must incorporate UN sanctions lists and 'at the same time make sure that the listing actions at the UN follow adequate procedures that meet the standards that the European courts require.'[7] From a general perspective, this may compromise compliance with international obligations because although regional courts have increased the due process profile of sanctions regimes, they have also, in effect, created a standard that is different from that of the UN and this might 'threaten to place States in breach of their Chapter 7 obligations.'[8] Member States that belong to both the UN and the EU face the complex problem of trying to accommodate two different sets of sanctions regimes, while always trying to deal with security within their own territory, as expressed by Resolution 1373.

The participation of States in international institutions is complicated, as well, by the new dynamics created by the case law, as stated:

> Should other countries or regional groups also decide that the application of Security Council decisions is dependent on their compatibility with national or regional values, and in particular their own view on human rights issues, this could endanger the authority of the Security Council in the maintenance of international peace and security.[9]

In effect, the European courts have focused on the European legal order only, instead of also integrating international human rights into their argument. In *Kadi*, the EU only referred to its own human rights standards and *jus cogens*, but did not refer to the obligations of States as regards human rights derived

---

and relevance of the allegation made in the statement of reasons'. The statement of reason was provided by the Council based on a French investigation.

7 Eriksson, 'In Search of a Due Process – Listing and Delisting Practices of the European Union', 23.

8 Kent Roach, *The 9/11 Effect – Comparative Counter-Terrorism* (Cambridge University Press, 2011) 37.

9 Juan Santos Vara, 'The Consequences of *Kadi*: Where the Divergence of Opinion between EU and International Lawyers Lies?' (2011) 17 *European Law Journal*, 252, 265.

from international law. To do so would have strengthened the EU's argument because it would have inscribed European human rights into the more general questions of the place of human rights in the international norms.[10] Therefore, the ECJ was criticised for not trying to fit its argument into a more general question of international law. In particular, it must be stressed that the ECJ 'did not pay sufficient attention to the source of the violation; it did not allow any leeway to the Security Council'[11] even though the Security Council is one of the main actors in counterterrorism. It must be also stressed that the EU itself, through its Council, had faithfully followed the lead of the UN's organ in its original Positions and Regulations, without adding any human rights protection. In that respect, the judgment has been called 'euro-centric rather than internationalist.'[12]

Over the years, the EU has built its own constitutional order by reference to its Member States through the principles of primacy and subsidiarity. It has been generally considered that EU law was directly applicable into national systems, based on monism.[13] For example, in the *Kadi* case, the ECJ even stated the existence of a 'basic constitutional charter, the EC Treaty.'[14] Member States themselves have defined the place of European and international law within their own legal order.[15] Yet, in the *Kadi* case, it is noteworthy that the ECJ has treated

10 Ibid.

11 Chatham House International Law Discussion Group, 'UN and EU Sanctions: Human Rights and the Fight against Terrorism – The *Kadi* case', 22 January 2009.

12 Tridimas and Gutiérrez-Fons, 'EU Law, International Law and Economic Sanctions against Terrorism: The Judiciary in Distress?' 701.

13 Lando Kirchmair, 'The "Janus Face" of the Court of Justice of the European Union: A Theoretical Appraisal of the EU Legal Order's Relationship with International and Member State Law' (2012) 4 *Göettingen Journal of International Law*, 677, 679.

14 Joined Cases C-402/05 P and C-415/05 P *Yassin Abdullah Kadi and Al Barakaat International Foundation v Council of the European Union and Commission of the European Communities*, 3 September 2008.

15 See the German constitutional court's *Solange* cases where they were still reserving the right to measure Community acts against the benchmark of their own constitutional guarantees, although they have suspended this competence 'so long' as the European Council acts provide for equivalent protection of human rights. In Poland, the Constitutional Tribunal ruled that while EU law may override national statutes, it does not override the Constitution. In case of a conflict between EU law and the Constitution, Poland can make a sovereign decision as to how this conflict should be resolved: Verdict of the Constitutional Tribunal of Poland of 11 May 2005; K 18/04. In *Administration des Douanes v Société Cafés Jacques Vabre and J Weigel et Compagnie SÀRL*, the French Conseil D'Etat changed its previous position to accept EU law primacy. New member States have expressly stated EU law primacy in their Constitution, for instance Art. 2 of the

international norms as external norms emanating from 'distinct legal orders.'[16] In response to the legal issues the *Kadi* case has raised, a number of authors have therefore advocated for a pluralist approach, which allows for reconciliation of the various legal orders.[17]

At the same time, it was noted that EU sanctions precisely copy those of the UN and their regimes are completely similar. The ECJ's case law, therefore, contributes to the 'fragmentation in the implementation of sanctions,'[18] in that States now face different requirements for the similar sanctions regimes of the various orders. This dual approach runs the risk of making the sanctions regimes, originally coherent, ineffective.

Moreover, it raises issues of responsibility, which can only briefly be referred to here: violations of EU human rights are attributable to a State if the State designates individuals or groups without the necessary safeguards. However, States also have to implement obligations imposed by the UN. As discussed above, the ECtHR in two cases stressed that States have leeway in the way they implement terrorist sanctions[19] and this puts the onus on States to follow their human rights obligations while addressing the terrorist threat. On the other hand, the EU held in *Kadi II* that a European judicial review would be necessary as long as the UN did not include the necessary safeguards in its regime and States are therefore caught between the two requirements.[20] The ECtHR *Al-Dulimi* case is similar to the *Kadi* case in that respect and both seem to aim for confrontation with the Security Council. For Erika de Wet, States are thereby 'forced to disobey either a decision of the CJEU or a UNSC resolution, which will trigger state responsibility under either the one or the other regime.'[21]

Constitutional Act of the Republic of Lithuania on Membership of the Republic of Lithuania in the European Union, Art. 7(2) of the Slovak Constitution and Art. 3a of the Slovenian Constitution.

16 See *Kadi* 2008, §285 *et seq.*, 326–327.

17 For a discussion on the *Kadi* case and pluralism, see, among others, Samantha Besson, 'European Legal Pluralism after Kadi' (2009) 5 *European Constitutional Law Review*, 237; Gráinne de Búrca and JHH Weiler, *The Worlds of European Constitutionalism* (Cambridge University Press, 2011); and Nico Krisch, *Beyond Constitutionalism: The Pluralist Structure of Postnational Law* (OUP Oxford, 2010).

18 Misa Zgonec-Rozej, 'Kafka, Sisyphus, and Bin Laden: Challenging the Al-Qaida and Taliban Sanctions Regime Rights' (2011) 8 *Essex Human Rights Review*, 97.

19 *Nada* case, §180.

20 Case T-85/09 *Yassin Abdullah Kadi v European Commission*, §128.

21 Erica de Wet, 'From Kadi to Nada: Judicial Techniques Favoring Human Rights Over United Nations Security Council Sanctions', *Chinese Journal of International Law*, 12 (2013): 14.

The result of this variety of decisions and methods of interpretation of conflicts confuses legal categories and presents a juxtaposition of independent legal orders. Yet, it is also clear that these conflicts might lead to a positive change, in that the mechanisms that emerge from this case law might 'fill the vacuum that was created in the place where the [State] is no longer accountable and the international organization operates de facto.'[22] Indeed, in many of the national cases, States have argued that it is their obligation to follow the Security Council Resolutions,[23] even if that means violating some human rights standards. With *Kadi*, the ECJ excludes 'more clearly than previously that Member States can use the UN as a forum to circumvent EU law.'[24] Additionally, the inclusion of human rights within Resolution 2178 should reinforce this. For Marko Milanovic, 'this at least will serve to blunt overly extravagant arguments relying on the primacy clause in Article 103 of the UN Charter.'[25]

At this point, a caveat to this analysis must be stressed, as it focused on the sanctions regimes of States that are UN, EU, and Council of Europe Members. The EU and the Council of Europe are strong legal systems, which have had a major impact on the legislation taken in the context of sanctions regimes. However, there are many States that do not belong to the EU or the Council of Europe and, therefore, the individuals and groups that are listed by these non-Member States do not have access to the aforementioned regional courts. Hence, they do not have the possibility of challenging their listing, except by going through the procedure of the Ombudsperson, with all the shortcomings that it presents and the fact that it only applies to the 1267 regime. Moreover, national courts are often unable, or unwilling, to review the executive of their State. This creates an inequality for individuals and groups that are listed in certain States and it makes it all the more important that the sanctions regimes themselves, in particular those of the UN, be fair and respect human rights to start with, as most regimes implement those of the UN.

In this respect, the European case law has brought some positive changes to the UN regime itself, as shown in the previous Chapter. The reference to human rights within the text itself of Resolution 2178 has the potential to remedy this

22 Shelly Danosh, 'The *Kadi* Case: the International Position of the European Union after the Ruling' (Working Paper, European Forum at the Hebrew University, 2009) 42.

23 See *R (on the application of Al-Jedda)* (FC) *v Secretary of State for Defence*, [2007] UKHL 58, United Kingdom: House of Lords (Judicial Committee), 12 December 2007, §34.

24 Eckes, 'Protecting Supremacy from External Influences: A Precondition for a European Constitutional Legal Order?' 245.

25 Milanovic, 'UN Security Council Adopts Resolution 2178 on Foreign Terrorist Fighters', EJIL:Talk, 2014.

discrepancy and allow consistency between States, especially those who do not belong to regional organisations but demand the protection of human rights and fundamental freedoms in their fight against terrorism. It also means that national courts are more likely to be able to argue that they can hold the State responsible for violations of human rights. In effect, it makes human rights protection a part of this duty to fight terrorism, instead of an obstacle to it. There has not yet been case law related to Resolution 2178, but the inclusion of human rights within the document does not mean that there will not be any in the future. Indeed, the reference to human rights as part of States' obligations in counterterrorism does not mean there is 'equivalent protection' in the UN system. The case law will focus, instead, on the balance between various obligations imposed by the UN. The checks and balances necessary for counterterrorism will be expanded on in the next section.

In summary, then, the above analysis of the UK presented an example of the conflict of legal orders for a State that is both a Member of the UN and a permanent Member of the Security Council, as well as a Member of the EU and the Council of Europe. In the context of terrorist sanctions, the UK has shown conflict between its internal branches, as the sanctions regimes were originally purely executive measures. Thanks to a significant amount of case law, though, the regimes have become more ready to consider human rights issues with regards to counterterrorism measures. It should be noted, however, that recent cases continue to show certain deference by the courts to the UK government through its UN obligations[26] and to the needs for security in its territory. For this reason, the conflict of branches must be analysed.

2 Conflict of Branches or Traditional Separation of Powers?

The status of the terrorist sanctions has created a debate among both the literature and the bodies in charge of creating and reviewing them. The status and nature of the sanctions are important because they determine the application of a legal regime, as well as 'what standard of proof should be required for listing and delisting decisions, and whether sanctions under the regime should

26 In the pending *Al-Dulimi* case, the UK Advocate General has argued that a Security Council Resolution should 'trump the European Convention of Human Rights when a country is expected to comply with both': see News Release 'Attorney General appears before European Court of Human Rights', UK government website, 10 December 2014, available at https://www.gov.uk/government/news/attorney-general-appears-before-european-court-of-human-rights (last accessed 16.12.2015).

last indefinitely or be time-limited.'[27] Moreover, the issue of the nature of the power adopting these measures and, therefore, the legality of such measures, is raised in the debate, especially in the case of terrorist sanctions where the source of intelligence for the listing is usually classified.

The measures included in the UN resolutions are said to be preventative[28] rather than criminal measures. The Monitoring Team of the 1267 Sanctions Committee stated, in this respect, that 'after all, the sanctions do not impose a criminal punishment or procedure, such as detention, arrest or extradition, but instead apply administrative measures such as freezing assets, prohibiting international travel and precluding arms sales'[29] and Resolution 2253 reiterated that sanctions are 'preventative in nature and are not reliant upon criminal standards set out under national law'.[30] For Eckes, EU sanctions, therefore, constitute 'an exception to the criminal justice model that the EU has adopted in the counterterrorism context.'[31]

Yet, because of their impact, some have deemed sanctions as 'inevitably punitive.'[32] A number of scholars and UN Special Rapporteurs have pointed out that the effects of sanctions listing are serious enough to qualify as the determination of a criminal charge.[33] Due to the 'profound impact that long-term

27 *Her Majesty's Treasury (Respondent) v Mohammed Jabar Ahmed and others* (FC) (Appellants) [2010] UKSC 2, [2010] 2 AC 534, para. 58, referred to in General Assembly, 'Promotion and protection of human rights and fundamental freedoms while countering terrorism', 55.

28 Mirroring the language of earlier resolutions, preliminary Paragraph 10 of Resolution 1904, adopted in December 2009, reads: 'Reiterating that the measures referred to in Paragraph 1 of this resolution are preventative in nature and are not reliant upon criminal standards set out under national law.'

29 UN Doc. S/2005/572 (2005), at paras. 39–44, in particular para. 39: 'The List is not a criminal list. Rather it contains the names of those who have engaged in or supported al-Qaeda or Taliban terrorism in some tangible way, regardless of whether any authority has formally charged them with a criminal offence.'

30 UN Security Council Resolution 2253 (2015), §44.

31 Eckes, *EU Counter-Terrorist Policies and Fundamental Rights – The Case of Individual Sanctions*, 69.

32 Zgonec-Rozej, 'Kafka, Sisyphus, and Bin Laden: Challenging the Al-Qaida and Taliban Sanctions Regime Rights', 76.

33 See, for example, Protection of Human Rights and Fundamental Freedoms while Countering Terrorism, UN Doc. A/61/267, (2006), at para. 35; Andrea Bianchi, 'Security Council's Anti-terror Resolutions and their Implementation by Member States', (2006) 4 *Journal of International Criminal Justice*, 1044, at 1066; and Erika de Wet and A. Nollekeamper, 'Review of Security Council Decisions by National Courts', (2002), 45 *German Yearbook of International Law*, 166, 177.

freezing of assets has on an individual's life,' some have argued that sanctions 'should in fact be characterized as being a criminal law measure.'[34] The Advocate General, however, held in his opinion of the *Kadi* case that sanctions do not 'constitute criminal sanctions' but, rather, are temporary preventive measures.[35] This was confirmed in the 2013 *Kadi* case,[36] however, significantly, the Court stated that this did not prevent a negative effect on the individual targeted, who should, therefore, benefit from the possibility of obtaining a review of the measures.[37]

The nature of sanctions is directly linked to the authority in charge of adopting them. In this respect, it is traditionally the executive authorities within a State that adopt sanctions, as opposed to Parliament through criminal legislation. These measures also usually do not include a possibility for judicial review. This is explained both by the nature of terrorism, considered a security threat to a State, but also by the need to act behind the scenes with intelligence that is not available to the general public. In parallel, there has been 'the transfer of power from institutions subject to strong accountability mechanisms, to those that are much less accountable.'[38] In this area, the 'greatest beneficiary has been the UN Security Council,'[39] because it has increased its binding power through its resolutions, but, as previously described, international law generally favours the executive branch of States. This increasing power has led to criticism that the Security Council, a purely executive organ, is 'legislating' in the area of counterterrorism.[40] Moreover, 'the regular reporting to the Security Council as required by the [Al-Qaida] Committee Guidelines amounts to nothing more than self-reporting, given that the composition of the Sanctions Committee is the mirror image of the composition of the Security Council.'[41] There have also been criticisms about the composition of the

34 Larissa Van den Herik, 'The Security Council's Targeted Sanctions Regimes: In Need of Better Protection of the Individual' (2007) 20 *Leiden Journal of International Law*, 797, 806.

35 Opinion of Advocate General Bot, §68.

36 *Commission v. Kadi*, 18 July 2013, §130.

37 Ibid., 132.

38 Cian C. Murphy, EU Counterterrorism & the Rule of Law in a Post-'War on Terror' World, in Scheinin, Martin, ed., 'European and United States Counter-Terrorism Policies, the Rule of Law and Human Rights', (EUI RSCAS PP March 2011), 11.

39 Scheinin, ibid.

40 See Chapter 4.

41 Erika de Wet, 'Holding International Institutions Accountable: The Complementary Role of Non-Judicial Oversight Mechanisms and Judicial Review' (2008) 9 *German Law Journal*, 11, 1996.

CTC,[42] made up of Security Council Members. In other words, there can be no impartial reporting possible by the CTC as long as the same individuals are in charge of listing terrorist suspects and reviewing the legality of the listing procedure. The creation of the Focal Point did not improve things, as this procedure still happens through the context of the Secretariat of the Security Council. Even the introduction of the Ombudsperson only changes the situation in a limited way, as it only concerns one type of regime and follows a complex procedure. These criticisms echo those expressed against the Security Council acting as a legislator, in that the concentration of powers in the hands of one organ, especially the executive one, is problematic.

In practice, and at each level, the executive has been favoured in creating sanctions against terrorist suspects, because 'conducting foreign policy is – both within the EU and at the national level – first and foremost a task of the executive.'[43] Therefore, it has been said that the 'listing procedure is an example of triple executive dominance,'[44] for the following reasons: the listing process is initiated by States without procedural control and discussions of the listing happen in an inter-governmental forum, and ultimately, the Security Council, as the executive of the UN, remains the organ in charge of the process. In the EU, most counterterrorism measures gave powers to the Security Council and were adopted 'through processes, which sidelined the European Parliament.'[45] The lack of democratic control is 'particularly striking with respect to the autonomous EU blacklist.'[46] Indeed, most decisions in the context of the listing regime have been taken in the framework of the EU Council, where States are represented by government officials exercising delegated powers on their collective behalf. A report on the listing regime describes the procedure that was used, known as the 'written procedure', which is usually 'reserved for uncontroversial measures':[47]

---

42 See Chapter 4.

43 Eckes, 'Protecting Supremacy from External Influences: A Precondition for a European Constitutional Legal Order?' 232.

44 C.H. Powell, 'Terrorism and the Separation of Powers in the National and International Spheres' (2005) 18 *South African Journal of Criminal Justice*, 151.

45 Cian C. Murphy, *EU Counterterrorism & the Rule of Law in a Post-'War on Terror' World*, in Scheinin, 'European and United States Counter-Terrorism Policies, the Rule of Law and Human Rights', 12.

46 Sullivan and Hayes, 'Blacklisted: Targeted sanctions, preemptive security and fundamental rights', 11.

47 Ibid., 12.

> In 2001, following preliminary discussions in the Council, the legislative measures establishing the EU blacklist together with the initial list of banned organizations was simply faxed around the foreign ministries of the then 15 Member States on the day after Christmas. The regime became European law on the following day (27 December 2001).[48]

At the national level, a number of States, in reports to the Security Council, explicitly declared that 'they have found a way to [freeze assets in accordance with Resolution 1373] directly without an intervening decision of a domestic body to confirm the order'.[49] France, for instance, has reported that requests to freeze assets of terrorist suspects are handled in an 'automatic' fashion.[50] Names of persons and groups whose assets should be frozen pass directly from the Sanctions Committee to French banks, without a separate order from the French government. Other States have stated that there is no need for internal law 'in order for these treaties to produce a direct effect in our system'[51] and if there is internal action, it is by way of the executive branch, 'bypassing both courts and parliament.'[52] As well, in the UK, measures to freeze assets of terrorist suspects were originally taken as orders that did not involve the Parliament at all. This has now changed following the *Ahmed* case by the UK Supreme Court.

As in other areas, case law has aimed to change this trend of unfettered executive power. In the *Rehman* case, the House of Lords noted that 'it is for

48 Ibid., 11.

49 Scheppele, The International Standardization of National Security Law' (2010) 4 *Journal of National Security Law and Policy*, 437, 446.

50 Second supplementary report submitted by France to the Counter-terrorism Committee pursuant to Security Council resolution 1373 (2001), U.N. Doc. S/2003/270 Annex (3 March 2003), at 8, available at http://www.un.org/en/sc/ctc/resources/1373.html ('France,' then 'S/2003/270' hyperlink – last accessed 16.12.2015).

51 Permanent Representative of Spain to the United Nations, Letter dated 30 May 2003 addressed to the Chairman of the Security Council Committee established pursuant to resolution 1373 (2001) concerning counterterrorism, U.N. Doc S/2003/628 Annex (June 9, 2003), available at http://www.un.org/en/sc/ctc/resources/1373.html ('Spain,' then 'S/2003/628' hyperlink – last accessed 16.12.2015).

52 Second supplementary report to the National Report on the Activities of the Republic of Bulgaria to Counteract Terrorism in implementation of Resolution 1373 (2001) of the UN Security Council on measures that the UN Member States need to take in the fight against terrorism, U.N. Doc. S/2003/632 Enclosure (May 30, 2003), at 3, available at http://www.un.org/en/sc/ctc/resources/1373.html ('Bulgaria,' then 'S/2003/632' hyperlink) (last accessed 16.12.2015).

the executive to decide what is in the interests of national security.'[53] However, in 2005, in *A v Secretary of State*, Lord Bingham held that 'the function of independent judges charged to interpret and apply the law is universally recognised as a cardinal feature of the modern democratic State.'[54] Lord Phillips observed in the *Ahmed* case again that:

> It is particularly appropriate that these should be the first appeals to be heard in the Supreme Court of the United Kingdom, for they concern the separation of powers.[55]

The judgment was an 'emphatic reminder to the executive that, if it wants to interfere with fundamental rights, it must do so openly and through the Parliamentary process.'[56] Indeed, while the case in point concerns human rights of terrorist suspects, a deeper issue is whether the right to impose sanctions regime belongs to the right authority and whether the authority includes enough safeguards for human rights. The importance of judicial review was stressed in this context as follows:

> In the absence of judicial oversight of the listing and delisting process, there is always a significant risk that the sanctions regime may be used for politically motivated designations.[57]

Judicial redress is 'not the only option for sound review, but there must be a body or a person with some level of independence and impartiality that can substantively review petitions for delisting.'[58] In that respect, the creation of the Ombudsperson Office has certainly improved the system and has advantages that judicial review does not possess. For example, the Ombudsperson mechanism does not have the constraint of deference to the executive branch and is also a much quicker process.[59] However, it is not a review mechanism for the listing process and, instead, only provides a delisting framework. Moreover, this framework only applies to the 1267 sanctions regime and, in

---

53 *Rehman* [2002] 1 All ER 123.

54 *A v Secretary of State for the Home Department* [2005] 2 WLR 87.

55 *Ahmed*, §85.

56 MacDonald 'Case Comment: *HM Treasury v Ahmed* [2010] UKSC 2'.

57 Misa Zgonec-Rozej, 'Kafka, Sisyphus, and Bin Laden: Challenging the Al-Qaida and Taliban Sanctions Regime Rights', 84.

58 Van den Herik 'The Security Council's Targeted Sanctions Regimes: In Need of Better Protection of the Individual', 807.

59 It is important to note that it took ten years for Mr Kadi to be delisted, whereas the Ombudsperson mechanism can take only a few months.

general, does not question the ability of the executive to take sanctions. Indeed, the sanctions regimes still 'remain intergovernmental and [are] based on secret intelligence often forcing those who claim to be wrongly listed to seek indirect domestic remedies.'[60] On the other hand, it seems that Resolution 2178 holds the potential for a fairer system at the onset, although it is clear that its application will still depend on the will of Member States.

The significance of *Kadi*, then, is that it represents a general evolution towards better human rights protection, but is nonetheless mitigated by the legal questions it raised and is limited to the European continent. This case questions the traditional relationship between various legal orders and goes beyond the relationship between an international organisation and its Member States, which questions State sovereignty, as it calls into question the relationship between international organisations themselves. As well, the traditional prevalence of UN measures was altered by the ECJ case law.

The consequence of the aforementioned conflicts is a questioning of the traditional hierarchy in international law where counterterrorism is usually the prerogative of the executive and some basic safeguards are possibly set aside. In the case of terrorism sanctions, while the executive branch across the various international actors is in charge of acting against terrorism, in order to protect peace and security, the judiciary has taken upon itself to ensure a balance of power thereby making sure human rights and procedural safeguards are protected. Terrorism sanctions used to show how the traditional separation of power of States had come under threat because of the increasing role of the executive in counterterrorism and suffered from the lack of a review mechanism at the international level.

With the current case law, courts are aiming to ensure that human rights play a crucial role in the terrorism sanctions regimes. By focusing on European rights however, courts may have sacrificed legal clarity because they have differentiated between legal orders. If human rights are not fully integrated within the sanctions regimes themselves, States still have the opportunity to take executive decisions even if they later have to answer to the courts:

> The ECJ's ruling in *Kadi* is an attempt to stop the executive from hollowing-out the rule of law from above, but the struggle between the courts and the executive to find the right balance in the fight against terrorism will go on.[61]

60 Roach, *The 9/11 Effect – Comparative Counter-Terrorism*, 15.

61 Deirdre Curtin and Christina Eckes, 'Kadi Case: Mapping the Boundaries between the Executive and the Judiciary in Europe, The' (2008) 5 *International Organizations Law Review*, 365, 369.

While other courts have preferred using traditional ways of interpretation to avoid norm conflicts, the ECJ has attempted to address the issue in a new way. The awareness of human rights in terrorism sanctions raised by the ECJ case law is to be welcomed, especially in view of the changes adopted by the UN Security Council as a consequence. The legal uncertainty that the *Kadi* case has created must be weighed against the positive advances that are being made in human rights protection.

In terms of sovereignty, the European case law has reinforced the idea that sovereignty should include the protection of human rights and, more generally, the existence of obligations as well as powers for States. The transfer of competences to international organisations, even when it applies to security issues, do not allow the suspension of human rights and States still bear the primary responsibility in ensuring that this is the case.

Conclusions

'The notion of an obligatory international institution runs directly counter to the common assumption that States jealously guard their sovereignty and that the international arena is characterised by anarchy.'[1] While this statement was definitely true before the Second World War, this idea does not apply today in the same way: relationships between States have changed and the desire to maintain some stability means that 'paradoxically, while States jealously guard their sovereignty they are also enthusiastic about forming regional groupings that have the potential to diminish their sovereignty.'[2] These are the sovereignty-bargains that States decide to strike in order to ensure the safety of their population.

The terrorist attacks of September 11, 2001 brought terrorism to the international stage. It raised many legal questions, both on the nature of terrorism itself and the responses to the phenomenon. This book has analysed these legal questions in the context of State sovereignty and examined international counterterrorism in its relation with States. As well, a variety of responses to the phenomenon by the UN and four regional organisations have been detailed and the book has taken a descriptive approach to the question of transfer of competences and enforcement of measures. The purpose of this book lied in both comprehending the rationale for international actions in regard to terrorism and the consequences on international law and State sovereignty.

Many international law analyses consider the concept of State sovereignty obsolete or in need of reform. It is obvious that the concept has evolved, can be challenged, and definitely does not represent absolutism anymore, although it is frequently used by States in order to impose some domestic measures or question territorial challenges. Yet, in the case of counterterrorism, it remains extremely relevant for the following two reasons. Firstly, terrorism concerns national security and States consider that they have the primary duty to protect their citizens. In practice, this is a considerable obstacle to true global counterterrorism. Secondly, the absence of an international definition of terrorism further questions the possibility of an international counterterrorism regime and it keeps the primary responsibility on States.

1 Darren Hawkins and Carolyn M Shaw, 'The OAS and Legalizing Norms of Democracy', *Promoting Democracy in the Americas* (JHU Press, 2007) 23.

2 Kripa Sridharan, 'Regional Organisations and Conflict Management: Comparing ASEAN and SAARC' (Crisis States Research Center, Working Paper 33, March 2008) 1.

 | DOI 10.1163/9789004299580_015

More specifically, the existence of challenges to State sovereignty points to some conflicts, used as the basis for the analysis in this book, that underpin the concept. Firstly, the existence of international organisations clearly raises a conflict between legal orders that is not limited to terrorism issues. This is notably because of the binding nature of measures adopted by the Security Council and the independent legal order of the EU. Secondly, the emergence of an international order has generally favoured the executive branch even more so because most international organisations do not have strong judicial branches. This is particularly flagrant in counterterrorism where, more than anywhere else, issues of security necessarily lead to an emphasis on executive measures and courts have usually deferred to the executive. Finally, the conflict between security and human rights, which in itself should be considered as a balance of values, has instead taken a particular importance after September 11, 2001 due to the increase in measures that were adopted that did not conform to human rights standards and the lack of review mechanisms. These conflicts formed the backdrop of this analysis, which focuses on the competences that were transferred to international organisations, their actual implementation and the means of review of these measures.

Traditionally, terrorism questions governments and their ability to provide a safe environment for their citizens. As a result, counterterrorism usually takes the shape of national measures adopted in order to restore this safety. The threat to national security means that the legal area of counterterrorism strikes at the core of the sovereignty of a State. As a result, most international responses to terrorism consisted of bi-lateral agreements or inter-governmental treaties, which States could choose to ratify but not implement, and the bulk of the intelligence-sharing and judicial cooperation took place between specific States to address specific threats.

Nonetheless, this was all challenged by the attacks of September 11, 2001 that demonstrated that the existing response to terrorism was insufficient. The nature of the events of September 11, 2001 not only led to the update or adoption of national measures against terrorism, but also to a change in the nature of international measures. Resolutions 1373 and 2178 address terrorism *per se* and require States to criminalise it in their national legal order even though their wide scope and increasingly detailed measures have led to criticism about the role of the Security Council. Yet, these resolutions create a binding framework for addressing terrorism, which applies to all States whether or not they are targeted by terrorism and/or have the capacities or the political will to address it. The fact that they leave discretion to States to define terrorism and implement the various measures, however, might be problematic for the rule of law and for the protection of human rights and fundamental freedoms, as

States are left free to adopt measures against what they consider terrorism to be. In terms of sovereignty, though, the impact is limited. States have not transferred their competences on terrorism to the Security Council, but, rather, have transferred the competence to frame its scope. As well, as even the Security Council has not defined terrorism, the regime allows States to provide an international basis for their own domestic agenda.

Most regional organisations also follow a State consent-based approach to terrorism, which, therefore, relies on implementation and enforcement and allows States discretion in practice. The analysis of their expanding counterterrorism regimes shows the continual limits of inter-governmental measures. The cultural and historical similarities do lead to better implementation than in some other international regimes, but their lack of binding powers prove the strength of discourses based on sovereignty.

The EU has developed a counterterrorism regime that is very advanced and, more generally, its stance of the primacy of its legal order has prompted many studies on its impact on sovereignty. Some of the EU's counterterrorism measures are binding and require reporting from Member States, but these also leave discretion to States as to the way they implement the framework. This has led to a number of States simply arguing that their domestic measures are already compliant, and it reinforces the idea that States use international organisations as platforms for their counterterrorism agendas.

What is evident from this analysis is the focus of counterterrorist regimes, at least immediately post-September 11, 2001, on executive measures. In other words, the nature of the terrorist threats has led to a number of emergency measures that took place without the balance of a judicial review or parliamentary oversight. Terrorism sanctions are an example of this type of measure adopted by the executive branch of a legal order. The sanction regimes of the UN and the EU, as well as their domestic implementation, show the increasing cooperation, in a horizontal way, between the executive bodies of States and international organisations. Executive measures are the preferred way for counterterrorism for reasons of speed, secrecy and separation of powers. Moreover, the concerted way in which States and international organisations adopt these measures enables a consistency that it offers against the evolving threat of international terrorism. Many experts therefore welcome the efforts of the Security Council to close gaps in counterterrorism.

Yet, the case of terrorist sanctions is also a testimony to the judiciary's more recent attempt to protect human rights in the context of counterterrorism. In this respect, the main difference between regional organisations and the UN is that most of the former include a judicial system within their mandate. This has been crucial in the context of counterterrorism, in particular, in order to balance human rights concerns with security needs. The various organisations have set some human rights standards for addressing terrorism within their counterterrorism regimes, but have also made a significant impact through their courts' case law. This role has become fundamental especially given the targeting of individuals, rather than States, by the sanctions regimes.

Thus, the absence of an international court with jurisdiction to deal with terrorism means that the international framework inherently lacks the element of control over States and over their own executive. By conducting a judicial review of terrorist cases, the European courts have sought to rectify this, going as far as prompting changes to the sanctions regimes both at the European level and at the UN level. States condemned by the European courts will want to ensure that their UN obligations do not clash with European human rights. In that respect, the biggest impact on State sovereignty has probably been through the increasing role of regional courts because of their focus on human rights obligations. If we consider that State sovereignty includes obligations for States, and that means they have a responsibility to protect the human rights of their citizens, the European case law on terrorist sanctions is aiming to bring the checks and balances, which are usually found at the domestic level, to international counterterrorism.

The existence of so many varied, and sometimes conflicting, regimes leads to legal uncertainty. This legal uncertainty, coupled with the lack of an international definition of terrorism, means that the framework remains national because it is the States themselves who define the phenomenon. The more recent case law on human rights in counterterrorism is slowly redefining the balance of power between the executive and the judiciary and regional courts are increasingly intervening in security matters.

The framework of State sovereignty allows these changes to be brought to light. It shows that international organisations, far from being a challenge to State sovereignty, have contributed to States' security agenda. On the other hand, it proves that the concept of sovereignty as a responsibility is making its way outside of the State through regional courts. This is all the more significant because of the risk of abuse linked to security measures. As has been shown throughout the book, State sovereignty is still highly relevant in the context of international counterterrorism, both as the attempts of States to assert their grasp of the security in their jurisdiction but also, for sovereignty considered to include responsibilities towards citizens.

Bibliography

'Global Terrorism, Task Forces on Strengthening Multilateral Security Capacity' (International Peace Institute, Blue Papers, No 4, 2009).

Abass, Ademola, *Regional Organisations and the Development of Collective Security: Beyond Chapter VIII of the UN Charter* (Hart Publishing, 2004).

Abramowitz, David, 'President, the Congress, and Use of Force: Legal and Political Considerations in Authorizing Use of Force against International Terrorism' (2002) 43 *Harvard International Law Journal* 71.

Akande, Dapo, 'The International Court of Justice and the Security Council: Is there Room for Judicial Control of Decisions of the Political Organs of the United Nations?' (1997) 46 *International & Comparative Law Quarterly* 309.

Akande, Dapo and Marko Milanovic, The Constructive Ambiguity of the Security Council's ISIS Resolution, EJIL:Talk, 21 November 2015.

Almqvist, Jessica, 'A Human Right Critique of European Judicial Review: Counter-Terrorism Sanctions' (2008) 57 *International and Comparative Law Quarterly* 303.

Alvarez, José E., 'Judging the Security Council' (1996) 90 *The American Journal of International Law* 1.

Alvarez, José, E., 'The UN's "War" on Terrorism' (2003) 31 *International Journal of Legal Information* 238.

Alvarez, José, E., *International Organizations as Law-Makers* (Oxford University Press, 2006).

Ambos, Kai and Anina Timmermann, 'Terrorism and Customary International Law', *Research Handbook on International Law and Terrorism* (Edward Elgar Publishing Limited, 2014).

Arnold, Roberta, *The ICC as a New Instrument for Repressing Terrorism* (Transnational Publishers, 2004).

Benvenisti, Eyal, 'The US and the Use of Force: Double-Edged Hegemony and the Management of Global Emergencies' (2004) 15 *European Journal of International Law* 677.

Benvenisti, Eyal, 'Sovereigns as Trustees of Humanity: On the Accountability of States to Foreign Stakeholders' (2013) 107 *American Journal of International Law* 295.

Benwell, Richard and Oonagh Gay, "The Separation of Powers" (Parliament and Constitution Centre, 15 August 2011).

Besson, Samantha, 'European Legal Pluralism after Kadi' (2009) 5 European Constitutional Law Review 237.

Besson, Samantha, 'Sovereignty, International Law and Democracy' (2011) 22 *European Journal of International Law* 373.

Bianchi, Andrea, ed., *Enforcing International Law Norms Against Terrorism* (Hart Publishing, 2004).

Bianchi, Andrea, 'Assessing the Effectiveness of the UN Security Council's Anti-terrorism Measures: The Quest for Legitimacy and Cohesion' (2006) 17 *European Journal of International Law* 881.

Bianchi, Andrea and Alexis Keller (eds.), *Counterterrorism: Democracy's Challenge* (Hart Publishing, 2008).

Biersteker, Thomas J., and Cynthia Weber, *State Sovereignty As Social Construct* (Cambridge University Press, 1996).

Bonner, David, *MeasuresExecutive, Terrorism and National Security: Have the Rules of the Game Changed?* (Ashgate Publishing, Ltd., 2007).

Boon, Kristen, 'Sanctions On the Upswing by Regional Bodies in Africa' (Opinio Juris, 16 January 2013a).

Boon, Kristen, 'Small Steps Towards More Transparency and Fairness in the Al Qaida Sanctions Regime' (Opinio Juris, 18 December 2013b).

Bossong, Raphael, *The Evolution of EU Counter-Terrorism: European Security Policy After 9/11* (Routledge, 2012).

Boulden, Jane, and Thomas G. Weiss, eds., *Terrorism and the UN: Before and After September 11* (Indiana University Press, 2004).

Byers, Michael, 'Terrorism, the Use of Force and International Law after 11 September' (2002) 16 *International Relations* 155.

Cameron, Iain, 'Respecting Human Rights and Fundamental Freedoms and EU/UN Sanctions: State of Play' (European Parliament, Policy Department External Policies, October 2008).

Caron, David D., 'The Legitimacy of the Collective Authority of the Security Council' (1993) 87 *American Journal of International Law* 552–588.

Cassese, Antonio, 'Terrorism is Also Disrupting Some Crucial Legal Categories of International Law', (2001), 12 *European Journal of International Law* 5, 993.

Cassese, Antonio, *International Criminal Law* (2nd ed., OUP Oxford, 2008).

Cavallaro, James, and Stephanie Brewer, 'Reevaluating Regional Human Rights Litigation in the Twenty-First Century: The Case of the Inter-American Court' (2008) 102 *American Journal of International Law* 768.

Charney, Jonathan I., 'The Use of Force against Terrorism and International Law' (2001) 95 *American Journal of International Law* 835.

Chatham House International Law Discussion Group, 'UN and EU Sanctions: Human Rights and the Fight against Terrorism – The *Kadi* Case' (22 January 2009).

Chryssochoou, Dimitris N., 'The European Synarchy: New Discourses on Sovereignty' (2009) 1 *Göttingen Journal of International Law* 115.

Cilliers, J. and Kathryn Sturman, eds., "Africa and Terrorism: Joining the Global Campaign" (Monograph Series No 74, ISS 2002).

Comras, Victor, 'Europe's New Anti Terrorism Convention Strong on Substance, Short on Adherents', *Counterterrorism Blog*, 6 June 2007.

Corn, Geoffrey S and others, *The War on Terror and the Laws of War: A Military Perspective* (Oxford University Press, 2015).

Cortright, David, 'A Critical Evaluation of the UN Counter-Terrorism Program: Accomplishments and Challenges' (Transnational Institute, Crime & Globalisation Paper, April 2005a).

Cortright, David, 'Can the United Nations Battle Terrorism Effectively?' *USA Magazine*, January 2005b.

Cortright, David, and George A. Lopez, *Sanctions and the Search for Security: Challenges to the UN Action* (Lynne Rienner, 2002).

Cortright, David, George A. Lopez, Alistair Millar and Linda Gerber, 'An Action Agenda for Enhancing the United Nations Program on Counter-Terrorism' (Fourth Freedom Forum and the Kroc Institute for International Peace Studies, September 2004).

Crawford, James, *The Creation of States in International Law,* (2nd edn., Oxford University Press, USA, 2006).

Criddle, Evan J. and Evan Fox-Decent, 'Human Rights, Emergencies, and the Rule of Law' (2012) 34 *Human Rights Quarterly* 39.

Cryer, Robert and others, *An Introduction to International Criminal Law and Procedure* (Cambridge University Press, 2007).

Curtin, Deirdre, and Christina Eckes, '*Kadi* Case: Mapping the Boundaries between the Executive and the Judiciary in Europe' (2008) 5 *International Organizations Law Review* 365.

Danosh, Shelly, 'The *Kadi* Case: the International Position of the European Union after the Ruling' (Working Paper, European Forum at the Hebrew University, 2009).

Davis, Sean, 'Responding to Foreign Terrorist Fighters: A Risk-Based Playbook for States and the International Community' (Global Center on Cooperative Security 2014), November 2014.

De Burca, Grainne, 'The EU, the European Court of Justice and the International Legal Order after *Kadi*' (2010) 51 *Harvard International Law Journal* 1.

De Búrca, Gráinne and J.H.H. Weiler, *The Worlds of European Constitutionalism* (Cambridge University Press, 2011).

De Wet, Erica, *The Chapter VII Powers of the United Nations Security Council* (Hart Publishing, 2004).

De Wet, Erika, de 'Holding International Institutions Accountable: The Complementary Role of Non-Judicial Oversight Mechanisms and Judicial Review' (2008) 9 *German Law Journal* 11, 1987.

De Wet, Erica, 'From Kadi to Nada: Judicial Techniques Favoring Human Rights Over United Nations Security Council Sanctions', *Chinese Journal of International Law* 12 (2013).

Dicey, Albert V., *Introduction to the Study of the Law of the Constitution* (Liberty Fund Inc, 8th Edition with new Introduction 1982).

Duffy, Helen, *The "War on Terror" and the Framework of International Law* (Cambridge University Press 2005).

Eckes, Christina, *EU Counter-Terrorist Policies and Fundamental Rights–The Case of Individual Sanctions* (Oxford University Press, 2009).

Eckes, Christina, 'Protecting Supremacy from External Influences: A Precondition for a European Constitutional Legal Order?' (2012) 18 *European Law Journal* 230.

Eriksson, Mikael, 'In Search of a Due Process – Listing and Delisting Practices of the European Union' (Department of Peace and Conflict Research, Uppsala University, 2009).

Ewi, Martin and Kwesi Aning, 'Assessing the role of the African Union in preventing and combating terrorism in Africa' (2006) 15 *African Security Review* 32.

Farrall, Jeremy Matam, *United Nations Sanctions and the Rule of Law* (Cambridge University Press, 2007).

Fassbender, Bardo, 'The United Nations Charter as Constitution of the International Community' (1997) 36 *Columbia Journal of Transnational Law* 529.

Fawcett, Louise, 'Regional Governance Architecture and Security Policy' (Dialogue on Globalization Briefing Papers, Friedrich Ebert Stiftung, February 2006).

Feinäugle, Clemens A., 'The UN Security Council Al-Qaeda and Taliban Sanctions Committee: Emerging Principles of International Institutional Law for the Protection of the Individuals' (2008) 9 *German Law Journal* 1513.

Feinberg, Myriam, 'International Counterterrorism–National Security and Human Rights: Conflicts of Norms or Checks and Balances?' (2015) 19 *International Journal of Human Rights* 4.

Fernandez-Sanchez, Pablo Antonio, ed., *International Legal Dimension of Terrorism*, vol. 23 (Martinus Nijhoff Publishers, 2009).

Flynn, E.J., 'The Security Council's Counter-Terrorism Committee and Human Rights' (2007) 7 *Human Rights Law Review* 371.

Ford, Jolyon, *African Counter-Terrorism Legal Frameworks a Decade after 2001* (Institure for Security Studies, 2011).

Fowler, Michael, and Julie Marie Bunck, *Law, Power, and the Sovereign State: The Evolution and Application of the Concept of Sovereignty* (Penn State University Press, 1995).

Franck, Thomas, M., 'Terrorism and the Right of Self-defense' (2001) 95 *American Journal of International Law* 839.

Frank, Jonathan A. 'A Return to Lockerbie and the Montreal Convention in the Wake of the September 11 Terrorist Attacks: Ramifications of Past Security Council and International Court of Justice Action' (2002) 30 *Denver Journal of International Law and Policy* 532.

Frankowski, Pawel, 'Liquid sovereignty in the post-modern world order' (Paper prepared for the Sixth Pan-European Conference Standing Group on International Relations, Torino, September 12–15, 2007).

Galli, Francesca and Weyembergh, Anne, eds., *EU counter-terrorism offences: What impact on national legislation and case-law?* (Editions de l'Université de Bruxelles, 2012).

Ginsborg, Lisa and Martin Scheinin, 'You Can't Always Get What You Want: The *Kadi II* Conundrum and the Security Council 1267 Terrorists Sanctions Regime' (2011a) 8 *Essex Human Rights Review* 7.

Ginsborg, Lisa and Martin Scheinin, *PowersJudicial, Due Process and Evidence in the Security Council 1267 Terrorist Sanctions Regime: The Kadi II Conundrum* (European University Institute, 2011b).

Glazer, Nathan and John Dickey Montgomery, *Sovereignty under Challenge: How Governments Respond* (Transaction Publishers, 2002).

Global Center on Cooperative Security, Human Security Collective and International Centre for Counter-Terrorism–The Hague, 'Addressing the Foreign Terrorist Fighters Phenomenon from a European Union Perspective: UN Security Council Resolution 2178, Legal Issues, and Challenges and Opportunities for EU Foreign Security and Development Policy,' December 2014.

Goldman, Zachary, 'The Foreign Fighter Resolution: Implementing a Holistic Strategy to Defeat ISIL,' *Just Security*, 29 September 2014.

Goold, Benjamin J. and Liora Lazarus, eds., *Security and Human Rights* (Hart Publishing, 2007).

Govaere, Inge, 'The importance of International Developments in the case-law of the European Court of Justice: *Kadi* and the autonomy of the EC legal order' (College of Europe Research Paper No 2009).

Gowlland-Debbas, Vera, *National Implementation of United Nations Sanctions: A Comparative Study* (Brill, 2004).

Greenwood, Christopher, 'International Law and the Pre-emptive Use of Force: Afghanistan, Al-Qaida, and Iraq' (2003) 4 *San Diego International Law Journal* 7.

Griller, Stephan, and Jacques Ziller, *The Lisbon Treaty: EU Constitutionalism without a Constitutional Treaty?* (Springer, 2008).

Gross, Oren and Fionnuala Ní Aoláin, *Law in Times of Crisis: Emergency Powers in Theory and Practice* (Cambridge University Press, 2006).

Guillaume, Gilbert, 'Terrorism and International Law' (2004) 53 *International and Comparative Law Quarterly* 3, 537.

Halberstam, Malvina, 'The Evolution of the United Nations Position on Terrorism: From Exempting National Liberation Movements to Criminalizing Terrorism Wherever and by Whomever Committed' (2003) 41 *Columbia Journal of Transnational Law* 573.

Happold, Matthew, 'Security Council Resolution 1373 and the Constitution of the United Nations' (2003) 16 *Leiden Journal of International Law* 593.

Harper, Keith, 'Does the United Nations Security Council Have the Competence to Act as Court and Legislature' (1994) 27 *New York University Journal of International Law and Politics* 103.

Hawkins, Darren and Carolyn M Shaw, 'The OAS and Legalizing Norms of Democracy', *Promoting Democracy in the Americas* (JHU Press, 2007).

Herik, Larissa Van den, 'The Security Council's Targeted Sanctions Regimes: In Need of Better Protection of the Individual' (2007) 20 *Leiden Journal of International Law* 797.

Heupel, Monika, 'Adapting to Transnational Terrorism: The UN Security Council's Evolving Approach to Terrorism' (2007) 38 *Security Dialogue* 4, 477.

Heupel, Monika, 'With Power Comes Responsibility: Human Rights Protection in United Nations Sanctions Policy' (2012) 6 *European Journal of International Relations*.

High level Panel on Threats, Challenges and Change, 'A More Secure World: Our Shared Responsibility–UN Doc.A/59/565(2004)' (United Nations Document, 2004).

Hoffman, Bruce, *Re-thinking Terrorism in Light of a War on Terrorism* (Rand Corporation, 2001).

Hoffman, Paul, 'Human Rights and Terrorism' (2004) 26 *Human Rights Quarterly* 932.

Hollis, Duncan, 'China invokes UNCLOS in claiming sovereignty over the Diaoyu/ Senkaku Islands', Opinio Juris, 17 December 2012.

Horspool, Margot and Matthew Humphreys, *European Union Law* (6th ed., Oxford University Press, 2010).

Howard-Hassmann, Rhoda E., 'Human Security: Undermining Human Rights?' (2012) 34 *Human Rights Quarterly* 88.

Hurd, Ian, *AnarchyAfter: Legitimacy and Power in the United Nations Security Council* (Princeton University Press, 2007).

International Commission of Jurists, Eminent Jurists Panel on Terrorism, Counter-Terrorism and Human Rights, 'Assessing Damages, Urging Action' 2008.

Jackson, J.H., 'Sovereignty-modern: a New Approach to an Outdated Concept,' (October 2003), 9 *American Journal of International Law* 4, 782.

Joffe, Josef, 'Rethinking the Nation-State: The Many Meanings of Sovereignty' (1999) *78 Foreign Affairs* 122.

Johnstone, Ian, 'Legislation and Adjudication in the UN Security Council: Bringing down the Deliberative Deficit' (2008) 102 *American Journal of International Law* 275.

Keohane, Daniel, 'The EU and Counter-Terrorism' (Centre for European Reform, Working Papers, May 2005).

Keohane, Daniel, 'The Absent Friend: EU Foreign Policy and Counter-Terrorism' (2008) 46 *Journal of Common Market Studies* 125.

Kirchmair, Lando, 'The "Janus Face" of the Court of Justice of the European Union: A Theoretical Appraisal of the EU Legal Order's Relationship with International and Member State Law' (2012) 4 *Goettingen Journal of International Law* 677.

Kirschner, Adele J., 'Security Council Resolution 1904 (2009): A Significant Step in the Evolution of Al-Qaida and Taliban Sanctions Regime?' (2010) 70 *Zeitschrift für ausländisches öffentliches Recht und Völkerrecht* 3.

Klabbers, Jan, *Advanced Introduction to the Law of International Organizations* (Edward Elgar Publishing Limited, 2015).

Konstadinides, Theodore, *Division of Powers in European Union Law: The Delimitation of Internal Competence between the EU and the Member States* (Kluwer Law International, 2009).

Koskenniemi, Martti, 'The Police in the Temple: Order, Justice and the UN: A Dialectal View' (1995) 6 *European Journal of International Law* 325.

Krisch, Nico, Beyond Constitutionalism: The Pluralist Structure of Postnational Law (OUP Oxford, 2010).

Kroc Institute, and SSRP, 'Human Rights and Targeted Sanctions: An Action Agenda for Strengthening Due Process Procedures' (November 2009).

Lagos, Enrique, 'Latin Americas: Views on Contemporary Issues in the Region Preventing, Punishing and Eliminating Terrorism in the Western Hemisphere: A Post 9/11 Inter-American Treaty' (2003) 26 *Fordham International Law Journal* 401.

Lagos, Enrique and Timothy D. Rudy, 'The Third Summit of the Americas and the Thirty-First Session of the OAS General Assembly' (2002) 96 *American Journal of International Law* 173.

Laqueur, Walter, *A History of Terrorism* (Transaction Publishers, 2011).

Lauwaars, Richard H., 'Interrelationship between United Nations Law and the Law of Other International Organizations' (1983) 82 *Michigan Law Review* 1604.

Litfin, Karen T., 'Sovereignty in World Ecopolitics' (November 1997) 41 *Mershon International Studies Review* 2, 176.

Litfin, Karen T., *The Greening of Sovereignty in World Politics* (MIT Press, 1998).

Long, D., *The Anatomy of Terrorism* (NY: Free Press, 1990).

Luck, Edward, C., *UN Security Council: Practice and Promise* (Routledge, 2006).

MacDonald, Alison, 'Case Comment: *HM Treasury v Ahmed* [2010] UKSC 2', (UK Supreme Court Blog, 2 February 2010).

Magliveras, Konstantinos D., 'The Sanctioning System of the African Union: Part Success, Part Failure?' Expert Roundtable on "The African Union: The First Ten Years", Institute of Security Studies, Addis Ababa, Ethiopia, 11–13 October 2011.

Malanczuk, Peter, *Akehurst's Modern Introduction to International Law* (Routledge, 1997).

Manusama, Kenneth, *The United Nations Security Council in the Post-cold War Era* (Martinus Nijhoff Publishers, 2006).

Marschik, Alexander, 'The Security Council as World Legislator? Theory, Practice and Consequences of an Expanding World Power' (Institute for International Law and Justice, Working Paper, 2005).

Max Weber, 1918, Speech *Politik als Beruf* (Politics as a Vocation).

Maxwell, Bruce, *Terrorism: A Documentary History* (1st Revised edition, CQ Press, 2002).

Milanovic, Marko, 'Al-Skeini and Al-Jedda in Strasbourg' (2012) 23 *European Journal of International Law* 121.

Moeckli, Daniel, 'The Emergence of Terrorism as a Distinct Category of International Law' (2008a) 44 *Texas International Law Journal* 2, 157.

Moeckli, Daniel, *Human Rights and Non-discrimination in the 'War on Terror'* (Oxford University Press, 2008b).

Monar, Jörg, 'Common Threat and Common Response? The European Union's Counter-Terrorism Strategy and Its Problems' (2007a) 42 *Government and Opposition* 292.

Monar, Jörg, 'The EU's Approach Post-September 11: Global Terrorism as a Multidimensional Law Enforcement Challenge' (2007b) 2 *Cambridge Review of International Affairs* 267.

Murphy, Cian C., *EU Counter-Terrorism Law: Pre-emption and the Rule of Law* (Hart Publishing, 2012).

Murphy, Sean D, 'Terrorism and the Concept of Armed Attack in Article 51 of the U.N. Charter' (2002) 43 *Harvard International Law Journal* 41.

Murray, Rachel and Debra Long, *The Implementation of the Findings of the African Commission on Human and Peoples' Rights* (Cambridge University Press, 2015).

NATO, 'The Fight against Terrorism: Impact and Implications for the Atlantic Alliance,' NATO Committee Report, 174 PCTR 07 E rev 1, 2007 Annual Session.

Newman, Saul, 'Terror, Sovereignty and Law: On the Politics of Violence' (2004) 5 *German Law Journal* 569.

Ní Aoláin, Fionnuala, 'Europe's Newest Attempts at Anti-terror Regulation Could Shake the Foundations of the EU', *Just Security*, 7 February 2015.

Omotola, J. Shola, 'Assessing Counter-Terrorism Measures in Africa: Implications for Human Rights and National Security' (2008) 2 *Conflict Trends* 41.

Payandeh, Mehrdad and Heiko Sauer, 'European Union: UN Sanctions and EU Fundamental Rights' (2009) 7 *International Journal of Constitutional Law* 306.

Petculescu, Ioana, 'The review of the United Nations Security Council Decisions by the International Court of Justice' (2005) 52 *Netherlands International Law Review* 167.

Phelan, William, 'Does the European Union Strengthen the State? Democracy, Executive Power and International Cooperation' (Centre for European Studies, Working Paper No. 95, 2003).

Pieth, Mark, 'Criminalising the Financing of Terrorism' (2006) 4 *Journal of International Criminal Justice* 1074.

Plantey, Alain, *International Negotiation in the Twenty-First Century* (UT Austin Studies in Foreign and Transnational Law, Routledge, 2007).

Pokalova, Elena, 'Legislative Responses to Terrorism: What Drives States to Adopt New Counterterrorism Legislation?' (2015) 27 *Terrorism and Political Violence* 474.

Poole, Thomas, 'Sovereign Indignities: International Law as Public Law' (2011) 22 *European Journal of International Law* 351.

Portela, Clara, 'Where and Why Does the EU Impose Sanctions?' (2005) 3 *Politique européenne* 17, 83.

Proulx, Vincent-Joël, *TerrorismTransnational and AccountabilityState: A New Theory of Prevention* (Hart Publishing, 2012).

Raustiala, Kal, 'Rethinking the Sovereignty Debate in International Economic Law' (2003) 6 *Journal of International Economic Law* 841.

Reisman, W. Michael, 'The Constitutional Crisis in the United Nations' (1993) 87 *American Journal of International Law* 83.

Reus-Smit, Christian, 'Human Rights and the Social Construction of Sovereignty,' (2001) 27 *Review of International Studies* 519.

Roach, Kent, *The 9/11 Effect – Comparative Counter-Terrorism* (Cambridge University Press, 2011).

Rosand, Eric, 'The Security Council As "Global Legislator": Ultra Vires or Ultra Innovative?' (2004) 28 *Fordham International Law Journal* 542.

Rosand, Eric, Alistair Milar and Jason Ipe, 'The UN Security Council's Counterterrorism Program: What Lies Ahead?' (International Peace Institute, Policy Paper, October 2007).

Rosand, Eric, Alistair Milar, Jason Ipe and Michael Healey, 'The UN Global Counter-Terrorism Strategy and Regional and Subregional Bodies: Strengthening a Critical Partnership' (Center on Global Counterterrorism Cooperation, October 2008).

Salinas de Frias, Ana Maria, Katja LH Samuel and Nigel D White, eds., *Counter-Terrorism: International Law and Practice* (Oxford University Press, 2012).

Sambei, Arvinder, Anton Du Plessis and Martin Polaine, *Counter-Terrorism Law and Practice. An International Handbook* (Oxford University Press, 2009).

Samuel, Katja, *The OIC, the UN, and Counter-Terrorism Law-Making: Conflicting or Cooperative Legal Orders?* (Hart, 2013).

Sands, Philippe and Pierre Klein, *Bowett's Law of International Institutions* (6th ed., Thomson Reuters, 2009).

Sarooshi, Dan, 'The Essentially Contested Nature of the Concept of Sovereignty: Implications for the Exercise by International Organizations of Delegated Powers of Government' (2004) 25 *Michigan Journal of International Law* 1107.

Saul, Ben, 'Reasons for Defining and Criminalizing "Terrorism" in International Law' (2006) 6 *Mexican Yearbook of International Law* 419.

Scheinin, Martin, ed., 'European and United States Counter-Terrorism Policies, the Rule of Law and Human Rights' (EUI RSCAS PP, March 2011).

Scheinin, Martin, 'The Council of Europe's Draft Protocol on Foreign Terrorist Fighters is Fundamentally Flawed' *Just Security*, 18 March 2015.

Scheinman, Lawrence, ed., 'Implementing Resolution 1540: The Role of Regional Organisations' (United Nations Institute for Disarmament Research, 2008).

Scheppele, Kim Lane, 'The International Standardization of National Security Law' (2010) 4 *Journal of National Security Law and Policy* 437.

Schermers Henry G., *International Institutional Law* (2nd ed., Sythoff, 1980).

Schermers, Henry G. and Niels Blokker, *International Institutional Law: Unity within Diversity* (Martinus Nijhoff Publishers, 2003).

Schweigman, David, *The Authority of the Security Council under Chapter VII of the Charter: Legal Limits and the Role of the ICJ* (Kluwer Law International, 2001).

Shany, Yuval, 'No Longer a Weak Department of Power? Reflections on the Emergence of a New International Judiciary' (2009) 20 *European Journal of International Law* 73.

Sinclair, Adriana and Byers, Michael 'When US Scholars Speak of "Sovereignty", What Do They Mean?' (June 2007) 55 *Political Studies* 2.

Sridharan, Kripa, 'Regional Organisations and Conflict Management: Comparing ASEAN and SAARC' (Crisis States Research Center, Working Paper 33, March 2008).

Starski, Paulina, '"Legitimized Self-defense" – Quo Vadis Security Council' EJIL Talk, 10 December 2015.

Steiner, Henry G., Alston, Philip and Goodman, Ryan, *International Human Rights in Context: Law, Politics, Morals*, (Oxford University Press, 3d ed., 2008).

Stevens, Joe, 'No New Weapons for the UN Ombudsperson?' (2011) 2 *Journal of Terrorism Research* 3.

Stevens, Joe, 'UN Targeted Terrorist Sanctions and the Rule of Law: The UK's Response' (2012) 3 *Journal of Terrorism Research*, 5

Sullivan, Gavin and Ben Hayes, 'Blacklisted: Targeted Sanctions, Preemptive Security and Fundamental Rights' ECCHR-Report, December 2010.

Szasz, Paul, C., 'The Security Council Starts Legislating' (2002) 96 *American Journal of International Law* 901.

Talmon, Stefan, 'The Security Council as a World Legislature' (2005) 99 *American Journal of International Law* 175.

Tams, Christian J., 'The Use of Force against Terrorists' (2009) 20 *European Journal of International Law* 359.

Tierney, Stephen and Warbrick, Colin, eds. *Towards an International Legal Community: The Sovereignty of States and the Sovereignty of International Law* (British Institute of International and Comparative Law, 2006).

Tittemore, Brian D., 'Guantanamo Bay and the Precautionary Measures of the Inter-American Commission on Human Rights: A Case for International Oversight in the Struggle against Terrorism' (2006) 6 *Human Rights Law Review* 378.

Tridimas, Takis and José A. Gutiérrez-Fons, 'EU Law, International Law and Economic Sanctions against Terrorism: The Judiciary in Distress?' (2008) 32 *Fordham International Law Journal* 660.

Tridimas, Takis, 'Terrorism and the ECJ: Empowerment and Democracy in the EC Legal Order' (2009) 34 *European Law Review* 103.

Tzanakopoulos, Antonios, 'Stepping Up the (Dualist?) Resistance: The English High Court Quashes Domestic Measures Implementing UN Sanctions', EJIL Talk, 9 October 2009.

Tzanakopoulos, Antonios, 'The UK Supreme Court Quashed Domestic Measures Implementing UN Sanctions', EJIL Talk, 23 February 2010.

Tzanakopoulos, Antonios, *Disobeying the Security Council: Countermeasures against Wrongful Sanctions* (Oxford University Press, 2011).

United Nations Secretary General Office, In Larger Freedom: Towards Development, Security and Human Rights for all, (NY: UN, 2005).

Van den Herik, Larissa and Nico J Schrijver, Counter-Terrorism Strategies in a Fragmented International Legal Order: Meeting the Challenges (Cambridge University Press, 2013).

Vara, Juan Santos, 'The Consequences of *Kadi*: Where the Divergence of Opinion between EU and International Lawyers Lies?' (2011) 17 *European Law Journal* 252.

Verdirame, Guglielmo, *The UN and Human Rights: Who Guards the Guardians?* (Cambridge University Press, 2011).

Verdirame, Guglielmo, 'A Normative Theory of Sovereignty Transfers' (2013) 49 *Stanford Journal of International Law* 371.

Vidmar, Jure and Erica de Wet, eds., *Hierarchy in International Law* (Oxford University Press, 2012).

Wagner, Adam, 'Context is everything – European Court of Human Rights struck out 99% of UK cases in 2012', *UK Human Rights Blog*, 24 January 2013.

Waldron, Jeremy, 'Are Sovereigns Entitled to the Benefit of the International Rule of Law' (2011) 22 *European Journal of International Law* 315.

Walker, Neil, ed., *Sovereignty in Transition* (Hart Publishing, 2003).

Weiler, J.H.H., *The Constitution of Europe: "Do the New Clothes Have an Emperor?" and Other Essays on European Integration* (Cambridge University Press, 1999).

Weiss, Thomas, *Humanitarian Intervention: Ideas in Action* (Cambridge: Polity Press, 2007).

Weiss, Thomas G. and Sam Daws, eds., *The Oxford Handbook on the United Nations* (Oxford University Press, 2008).

White, Nigel D., *The Law of International Organisations* (Manchester University Press, 1996).

Wood, Michael, 'The UN Security Council and International Law', Second Lecture, Hersch Lauterparcht Memorial Lectures, 7 November 2006.

Zgonec-Rozej, Misa, 'Kafka, Sisyphus, and Bin Laden: Challenging the Al-Qaida and Taliban Sanctions Regime Rights' (2011) 8 *Essex Human Rights Review* 8.

Index

www.ingramcontent.com/pod-product-compliance
Lightning Source LLC
Chambersburg PA
CBHW031324230926
51848CB00001B/77
9789004299573